Luminos is the Open Access monograph publishing program
from UC Press. Luminos provides a framework for preserving and
reinvigorating monograph publishing for the future and increases
the reach and visibility of important scholarly work. Titles published
in the UC Press Luminos model are published with the same high
standards for selection, peer review, production, and marketing as
those in our traditional program. www.luminosoa.org

ISLAMIC HUMANITIES

Series Editor: Shahzad Bashir

Publication of this Luminos Open Access Series is made possible by the Islam and the Humanities Project of the Program in Middle East Studies at Brown University.

Forging the Ideal Educated Girl

Forging the Ideal Educated Girl

The Production of Desirable Subjects in Muslim South Asia

———

Shenila Khoja-Moolji

UNIVERSITY OF CALIFORNIA PRESS

University of California Press, one of the most distinguished university presses in the United States, enriches lives around the world by advancing scholarship in the humanities, social sciences, and natural sciences. Its activities are supported by the UC Press Foundation and by philanthropic contributions from individuals and institutions. For more information, visit www.ucpress.edu.

University of California Press
Oakland, California

Suggested citation: Khoja-Moolji, S. *Forging the Ideal Educated Girl: The Production of Desirable Subjects in Muslim South Asia*. Oakland: University of California Press, 2018. DOI: https://doi.org/10.1525/luminos.52

Library of Congress Cataloging-in-Publication Data

Names: Khoja-Moolji, Shenila, author.
Title: Forging the ideal educated girl : the production of desirable subjects in Muslim South Asia / Shenila Khoja-Moolji.
Description: Oakland, California : University of California Press, [2017] | Series: Islamic humanities ; 1 | Includes bibliographical references and index. |
Identifiers: LCCN 2018000776 (print) | LCCN 2018005177 (ebook) | ISBN 9780520970533 () | ISBN 9780520298408 (pbk. : alk. paper)
Subjects: LCSH: Muslim women —Education—South Asia. | Muslim women—South Asia. | Women—South Asia—Social conditions.
Classification: LCC LC2410.5 (ebook) | LCC LC2410.5 .K56 2017 (print) | DDC 370.8422—dc23
LC record available at https://lccn.loc.gov/2018000776

25   24   23   22   21   20   19   18
10   9   8   7   6   5   4   3   2   1

For my beloved MHI

CONTENTS

ILLUSTRATIONS

ACKNOWLEDGMENTS

Even though this piece of writing bears my name, it is a product of the guidance and good wishes of many colleagues, mentors, and friends.

First and foremost, I am thankful to my research participants in Pakistan, my hosts and the staff at the University of Karachi, University of Punjab, Bedil, and Mushfiq Khwaja libraries. They were most generous with their time, knowledge, and resources (including a constant supply of chai and samosas)! During my research trips, I often stay with extended family members, and I am grateful to them for their love and hospitality.

I began writing this book at Columbia University under the rigorous mentorship of Nancy Lesko, Lila Abu-Lughod, and Daniel Friedrich. They have continued to be a constant source of guidance for me. At Columbia, Neferti Tadiar, Monisha Bajaj, Lesley Bartlett, Thomas Hatch, Srikala Naraian, and Hamid Dabashi were also instrumental to my learning. I found amazing colleagues at the University of Pennsylvania's Program on Democracy, Citizenship, and Constitutionalism, and the Alice Paul Center for Research on Women, Gender, and Sexuality. I am particularly grateful to Rogers Smith, Nancy Hirschmann, Kathleen Brown, Jamal J. Elias, Sigal Ben-Porath, Ameena Ghaffar-Kucher, Anne Esacove, Demie Kurz, Matt Roth, and Luz Marin.

My editors at the University of California Press, Reed Malcolm and Cindy Fulton, and their associates, have been most wonderful to work with. Reed, in particular, has been one of the biggest cheerleaders of this book. I first pitched him the idea while I was still a young graduate student attending an anthropology conference—it was my first ever pitch to a university press and he was most generous with his feedback. I am, therefore, delighted that I ended up with UCP. I am also pleased that Brown University's Islamic Humanities grant is making the e-version of this book available for free. My gratitude to Shahzad Bashir for selecting this book to be a part of the series. I also want to thank the editors of the journals, *Discourse: Studies in the Cultural Politics of Education* and *Diaspora, Indigenous, and Minority Education* for giving me the permission to reproduce some materials in the book.

I have so many mentors and colleagues to thank: Hussein Rashid has read my work on extremely short notice with much generosity, and it was upon his urging that I mustered the courage to write for a nonscholarly audience; I first explored Urdu literature at Harvard with Ali Asani, whose encouragement of my early writings set me on this path; Leila Ahmed, who was my advisor at Harvard, encouraged me during my first semester as a master's student to publish my work; Ann Braude and Diane Moore at Harvard introduced me to critical interdisciplinary scholarship on gender, sexuality, religion, and youth studies; Nargis Virani took every opportunity to show her faith in my work; Moon Charania gave valuable feedback during the early stages of writing this book; and Ayesha Khurshid, Celene Ayat Lizzio, and Mary Ann Chacko have provided deep intellectual friendship and are truly sisters I never had. I am also grateful to Reverend Janet Cooper Nelson, who made my time at Brown intellectually fulfilling and has now been my mentor for over a decade.

My friends have been a constant source of joy and my thinking partners. Thank you, Alyssa, Amin, Bessie, Erum, Esther, Hilda, Karishma, Lydia, Natasha, Nausheen, Omar, Raheem, Sameer, Steph, ZBK, and many more. Coffees with you have been most generative for my mind and soul. While I was revising the manuscript, I had a chance to work on a youth development project in Pakistan with the Global Encounters team. The group's commitment to social development reenergized me in ways words cannot describe. I thank them, too, and hope to spend many more summers working with them.

Highest gratitude goes to my family. My parents, Farida and Sikander Ali Khoja, migrated to the United States from Pakistan so that their children could obtain quality education. From a young age, I have seen them dedicate their time, labor, and knowledge to advance the welfare of those who are pushed to the periphery of society. From working in rural villages in Sindh to raising funds for poverty alleviation in Atlanta, my parents' consistent effort to think beyond themselves has served as an inspiration for me. I can only hope to follow in their footsteps. My in-laws have always been generous with their love and support. My father-in-law has read many of my papers with keen interest and I thank him for his critique. And, I could not have survived grad school without the weekly care packages from my mother-in-law. Being Guddu's and Sunny's sister is truly a gift; it is, in fact, the most joyful part of my life. I could not have asked for more kind, *masti-khor,* and giddy brothers. I am delighted to have recently gained two sisters-in-law and *billi,* who have made my world so much brighter.

Finally, there are no words to acknowledge the contribution of my husband, Amyn. He has read every word that I have ever written, has been my constant thought-partner, and has encouraged me to use my scholarly voice to advance the quality of life of my communities, in Pakistan as well as in the United States. His relentless faith in me and my work gives me the energy to keep on moving: *Mowla abad rakhay.*

This book is dedicated to my beloved MHI.

Girls' Education as
a Unifying Discourse

In 2012, Malala Yousafzai, a Pakistani girl then fifteen years old, was shot in the head by a member of Tehrik-e-Taliban (Pakistan), a tribal-political group. Malala's father, Ziauddin, owned and operated a school, where she was also a student. The rise in recent years of a particular segment of Taliban leaders in Swat had made it difficult for him to keep the school running. In order to save their livelihood as well as afford children the chance to attend school, the father and daughter had started speaking up against the mounting extremism in their region. Malala had been writing a blog for BBC Urdu under a pseudonym since 2009, and had participated in two videos produced by the *New York Times* documenting the difficulties of living under the Taliban regime. The father's and daughter's actions were interpreted as besmirching the name of the Taliban and a few members of the group took it upon themselves to silence her.

Although Malala recovered shortly after the shooting, the news of this incident has since received significant attention. Educational development and aid organizations, heads of nation-states, and nongovernmental groups have rallied around Malala to express support not only for her but also for the education of girls more broadly in Pakistan and beyond. Malala was offered an opportunity to meet with Ban Ki Moon, the then United Nations secretary general, and address the United Nations general assembly; she met with President Obama to highlight the importance of education for girls; Gordon Brown, the former prime minister of the United Kingdom and later the United Nations Special Envoy for Global Education, issued a petition entitled "I am Malala" to promote universal access to primary schooling for girls. Malala secured a book contract for her coauthored autobiography, *I Am Malala* (2013), a children's version of which was published in

2014, and a film in 2015. In October 2014, she was awarded the Nobel Peace Prize for her efforts for girls' education. In October 2017, she published an illustrated book, *Malala's Magic Pencil.*

Elsewhere, in April 2014, a militant organization that called itself Boko Haram kidnapped approximately three hundred girls from a boarding school in Chibok, Nigeria. We learned that this fringe group was composed of Muslim men. Analysts and lay people started speculating about the origins of Boko Haram, their links to Somalia, and their intentions. Several journalists translated the organization's name to "western education is a sin." It was believed that these girls were kidnapped because they were in school, which seemed logical enough—as Malala's case had recently demonstrated, Taliban/Muslim militants/Boko Haram were against girls' education.[1] Except for a couple of articles[2] detailing the grievances of Boko Haram related to the legacies of British colonialism in Nigeria, the entanglement of the United States in the persistent poverty in the region, and so on, no additional details about the kidnapping or the group surfaced. In the immediate aftermath of the kidnapping, the conversations focused predominantly around whether or not military intervention by the United States would be a good strategy. However, after some time, the issue was assimilated into calls for girls' education, which became the primary framework through which it was discussed. For instance, in the opening sentences of an opinion piece published in the *New York Times* in May 2014, Nicolas Kristof establishes a direct link between the kidnapping of the Nigerian girls and their education, calling on audiences to assimilate this new event in previously circulating certainties about the subjugation of (Muslim) girls in places like Pakistan and Afghanistan:

> When terrorists in Nigeria organized a secret attack last month, they didn't target an army barracks, a police department or a drone base. No, Boko Haram militants attacked what is even scarier to a fanatic: a girls' school. That's what extremists do. They target educated girls, their worst nightmare. That's why the Pakistani Taliban shot Malala Yousafzai in the head at age 15. That's why the Afghan Taliban throws acid on the faces of girls who dare to seek an education. Why are fanatics so terrified of girls' education? Because there's no force more powerful to transform a society. The greatest threat to extremism isn't drones firing missiles, but girls reading books.[3]

Besides the gross misdirection in his commentary—since Boko Haram had been known to target state and international symbols, such as attacking the United Nations headquarters in Abuja in 2011, and had been involved in several instances of killing and kidnapping boys and men[4]—Kristof draws sturdy connections across distinct events from Nigeria, Pakistan, and Afghanistan, and articulates girls' education as not only the cause of violence but also the solution. Julia Gillard, former Australian prime minister, makes similar linkages: "There have been some truly shocking incidents that have caused us to have tears in our eyes and sharply intake our breath—what happened to Malala, what has happened with the Nigerian schoolgirls—that powerfully remind us that in some part of the world, getting an education is still a very dangerous thing for a girl. . . . It's [education] being targeted because it's powerful."[5]

Likewise, Gordon Brown in his commentary entitled "Girl Power" for *Project Syndicate* begins by discussing the kidnapping of the Nigerian girls and the military support required by the Nigerian government, but quickly moves on to violence against women in countries as diverse as Pakistan, Bangladesh, Morocco, India, Ethiopia, Mozambique, and South Africa, concluding with a clarion call for girls' rights and opportunities:

> The Chibok girls—kidnapped simply because they wanted an education—have become a powerful symbol of this wider struggle for girls' rights. They are not the only symbols. There are also the Indian girls who were recently raped and hanged, the Bangladeshi girls now declaring child-marriage-free zones, the Pakistani girls demanding their right to education, and the African girls—from Ethiopia and Morocco to Mozambique and South Africa—demanding an end to child trafficking and genital mutilation. All of them are now more vociferous in demanding support for a world in which patriarchs no longer determine their rights and opportunities. It is their struggle, and they are increasingly leading it.[6]

In the course of a few sentences, issues as complicated and contextual as rape, child marriage, kidnapping, hanging, trafficking, and genital mutilation are fused together and transformed into concerns to be addressed by the international human rights regime and its advocates, patriarchs such as, such as Gordon Brown himself. The particularized issues and victims are erased to create an abstract, homogenous collective of "girls" who are demanding their rights, specifically education.

There is a systematicity across these narratives. Radically specific forms of violence are assimilated into preestablished maps of meaning,[7] where brown and black girls are articulated as perennial victims of angry black and brown men and backward cultures and traditions. Differences of race, nation, and class are omitted, and a larger-than-life figure of "the girl in crisis" is constructed. If we know one (Malala), we know them all (Nigerian girls). If we design a development intervention for one, we can apply it to all. And, what better intervention is there than formal schooling, which promises deliverance not only from ignorance but also poverty, terrorism, child marriage, and genital mutilation? Education can thus empower girls to fight their own wars by reshaping themselves, asserting their choices, and demanding their rights. A graphic featured in the 2011 Nike Foundation's Girl Effect report and later displayed at the World Bank building in Washington DC and the Department for International Development building in London illustrates this point vividly. In it, a brown or black girl in a school uniform, effecting an almost superheroic gesture, deploys her book as a shield and her pen as a weapon to single-handedly attack a dragon, named "poverty."[8]

Such representations of girls abound in the textual and visual archives of contemporary girls' education and empowerment campaigns: Girl Effect, Girl Up, Girl Rising, G(irls)20 Summit, Because I Am a Girl, Let Girls Learn, Girl Declaration. Education appears as the social practice that can not only save girls, but also miraculously empower them to confront historical and structural issues of gender-based violence, poverty, and terrorism. This almost messianic promise of education is accompanied with a sturdy economic rationalization that educated girls will be able to enter the labor force, pull themselves out of poverty and contribute to the national GDP. Indeed, when asked about the purpose of the Malala Fund, the then CEO, Shiza Shahid, responded: "The Malala Fund . . . believes in a world where every girl is in school, and empowered with the skills to improve her life and be a change-maker in her community."[9] When probed further about why the fund focuses on girls' education, she elaborated: "We believe that girls are the most powerful force of change in the world. If you can invest in a girl between the ages of 10 to 14, before she is married and becomes pregnant, you prevent her from falling into poverty. You would also give her choice—choice over when she gets married, when she has children, and the ability to earn an income."[10]

What we have then is an ideal, empowered, educated girl who is capable of producing radical change at multiple levels—personal, familial, and national. This book attempts to interrogate these sedimented knowledges about "the girl" and her education by unraveling a specific modality of this figure: the Muslim woman/girl.[11]

THE MUSLIM WOMAN/GIRL

Contemporary campaigns about girls' education are not idealistic notions without a historical and geographical place. Edward Said notes that "every idea or system of ideas exists somewhere, it is mixed in with historical circumstances."[12] Looking for the place of ideas directs attention to the "embodied locus of social experience."[13] The recent global rallying around girls' education has been in relation to *specific* populations and nations in the global South, where it is assumed that poverty, terrorism, and gender-based violence are an effect of the lack of girls' access to schooling. Since schooling is viewed as a sign of modernity and progress, lack of access often signals a lack of awareness and a disengagement with modernity. Oftentimes, the composite figure of the Muslim woman/girl emerges as an example par excellence of this backward femininity—she is threatened by religion, tradition, patriarchy, and local customs, is ill-equipped to survive in the modern social order, and is thus unable to fulfill her potential. It is this passive feminine figure that was invoked by Laura Bush in 2001, when as first lady of the United States she cited the plight of the Afghan women as one of the rationales for American military intervention: "The fight against terrorism is also a fight for the rights and dignity of women."[14] Earlier during the Gulf War, the American government and media made extensive use of the maltreatment of women to represent the moral, cultural, and political deficiencies of the Islamic world, warranting the 1991 operation against Iraq.[15]

Most recently, during his election campaign, the current U.S. president, Donald Trump, activated the trope of the oppressed Muslim woman by criticizing Ghazala Khan, the Pakistani-American mother of U.S. Army Captain Humayun Khan, who was killed in 2004 in Iraq. Khan and her husband appeared at the Democratic National Convention, during which he spoke but she was quiet. Trump remarked, "If you look at his wife, she was standing there. She had nothing to say. She probably . . . maybe she wasn't allowed to have anything to say. You tell me."[16] Trump pointed to prevailing knowledge about Muslim women's oppression to add fodder to his prior claims about Islam being alien to American values and his calls for banning Muslims. Khan later said that she was too emotional to speak on stage. Subsequently, President Trump issued an executive order on "Protecting the Nation from Foreign Terrorist Entry into the United States," which also invoked violence against Muslim women to garner support for greater policing and regulation of Muslims in America.[17] The Executive Order commits the Trump administration to publicly make available news about the "number and types of acts of gender-based violence against women, including honor killings, in the United States by foreign nationals." It thus deploys the trope of "honor killings" to cast foreign-born immigrants—primarily from Muslim countries—as suspect.

The discursive trope of the oppressed Muslim woman/girl is quite malleable and can be grafted onto any girl from Muslim-majority countries or the Muslim diaspora. We already know Malala's story. In another instance, in 2016, Nicholas Kristof wrote an article entitled "Meet Sultana, the Taliban's Worst Fear," which tells the story of Sultana, a girl from Afghanistan who under the Taliban-dominated south struggles to acquire an education.[18] Hers is an inspiring example of courage and tenacity. She figured out ways to study at home, creatively using online applications, thus defying the Taliban's injunctions. This is a story of a Muslim girl who, with the support of her family, found creative ways to subvert local configurations of patriarchy in a conflict zone. But that is not how Kristof relates the story. Instead, we learn about the efforts of an American professor, Lawrence M. Krauss, and a student, Emily Robert, who are impressed with Sultana and try to get her admitted to a community college in Iowa. In Kristof's version, it is the withdrawal from her family and country, and movement toward the 'land of the free' and a community college education that is the ultimate achievement of justice for Sultana. He, thus, calls out the U.S. administration for not awarding girls like Sultana an American visa. Earlier, he had documented the struggles of Mukhtar Mai, a Pakistani woman from Merawala who was gang-raped but triumphed against the atrocities by launching a campaign for girls' education and human rights. Her story too—in the way Kristof tells it—confirms the regressive nature of Islam, Muslims, and Pakistanis, and bolsters the human rights agenda.[19]

There is, then, a persistent and almost predictable storyline about the figure of the Muslim woman/girl. Malala, Sultana, and Mukhtar Mai simultaneously represent the oppression of Muslim women and girls and the emancipation from local cultures and traditions that is possible through education. The subject position of the "educated hence empowered girl" has been installed as the ideal toward which all Muslim girls must aspire. What we are left with, then, is a sturdy binary that pits Muslim girls against empowered girls, a binary that is invoked and solidified across multiple discursive fields from development and humanitarian campaigns to literature and news media.

I have been frustrated and challenged by what seems to be an impossible task of interrupting this storyline. Several years ago, I started examining the politics of race, gender, and religion in the deployment of the figure of the girl-in-crisis in girls' education and empowerment campaigns such as Girl Effect, #BringBackOurGirls, and #IamMalala. I was reminded of how this girl resembles her predecessor, the "Moslem woman" or "Musalman woman" who, too, during the eighteenth and nineteenth centuries in colonial India, emerged as a figure to be saved from backward cultural practices of *purdah,* seclusion, early marriage, and religious superstitions. Colonial administrators, Christian missionaries, as well as Muslim social reformers—for different reasons—claimed that education would save/civilize/reform these women. Christian missionaries established schools for girls and initiated *zenana*-visitation programs.[20] The colonial administration established book prizes, encouraging local authors to write books in the vernacular for girls. Muslim reformers wrote didactic texts to educate women and girls, guiding them away from "superstitious" rituals and toward the "correct" practices of Islam.

While the missionaries, colonial officers, and social reformers differed in their conceptualization of the end toward which women and girls were to be educated, as well as what constituted this education—as this book will delineate—what is critical to note is that then, too, Muslim women had emerged as an ideal site for reform. Tied to them was the survival of the future social order; they offered a guarantee for positive futurities. These frames are not much different from how girls are articulated today in the transnational development regime. The former UN secretary general Ban Ki-moon sees girls as an "untapped natural resource" and a "smart investment,"[21] and the UN Foundation's Girl Up campaign positions girls as "bright, talented and full of potential."[22] Investment in girls' education is a key area of advocacy and one of the main issues in global agendas from the Millennium Development Goals to the Sustainable Development Goals.

So, women's and girls' education has been a pregnant discursive space, enticing a broad range of groups to advance their social projects. When ideal girlhood is defined, its "other" too is delineated. We thus find myriad articulations of failed girlhoods in the past as well as the present. This book is an effort to trace such knowledge-making practices. However, given the extensive work already underway on colonial narratives about Muslim women and the current western discourses on Muslim girls (including my own work), in this book I focus on debates *internal* to Muslim societies. I examine discourses on Muslim women's and girls' education across three moments in the history of colonial India and postcolonial Pakistan and track the production of ideal educated girlhoods. I ask: Who is this educated girl? What is she expected to know? Who is authorized to teach her? Where does she learn? Toward what ends? I track the processes, forces, logics, and impulses of educative missions to point to the diverse kinds of citizen-subjects, religious subjects, gendered subjects, and worker-subjects that they produce. Such an effort hopefully will illustrate the historical and contingent production of the ideal girl-subject, and dismantle assumptions about the uniform character of Muslim womanhood and girlhood. Furthermore, it will give the reader a sense of the internal debates and tensions around the construction of Muslim womanhood/girlhood. Centering the narratives of Muslim social reformers or focusing on Pakistan does not mean that I avoid attending to the transnational flows of ideas, capital, and peoples. These narratives, as the book will show, are in fact deeply shaped by transnational contexts.

Specifically, I examine discourses on girls' education at the turn of the twentieth century in colonial British India; the first decades after the political establishment of Pakistan; and the contemporary moment, defined as the turn of the twenty-first century in postcolonial Pakistan. I explore a broad range of texts—novels, political speeches, government documents, periodicals, advertisements, television shows, and first-person narratives—to understand the rationales given for women's and girls' education, the ideal curriculum for girls, as well as the most suitable spaces for this education. This investigation provides insights into the creation of ideal Muslim woman-/girl-subjects, who have specific relationships with themselves, the patriarchal family, Islam, the nation-state, and paid work. Viewing gender and education as discursive projects, then, opens up these categories to an analysis of relations of power, enabling me to elaborate on how the figure of the Muslim girl functioned socially and culturally. It also creates space for an examination of multiple, even contrasting, articulations of this subject. In this way, I illuminate the ways in which education, as a social project, facilitates self- and populational-governance, and gender emerges as a key social construction in and through which these processes unfold. In particular, the book demonstrates how visions of education for girls are variable and historically contingent. They reflect the dominant, and at times competing, conceptions of feminine subjectivity, driven by the material and cultural struggles for power. I read the discourse on girls' education as a site for the construction of not only gender but also class, religion, and nation. By examining the figure of the "educated girl" genealogically, we can understand why Muslim girls and women have occupied the roles that they have, and begin to imagine alternatives for both feminine subjectivity and educational opportunity.

The Making of Gender

My orientation to gender is informed by feminist poststructuralist theories which decenter the humanist Cartesian subject who thinks, represents, and acts.[23] Instead, feminist poststructuralist concerns direct researchers to consider the discursive practices that bring objects and subjects into being, as well as examine the historical conditions that make particular subject positions possible.[24] Foucault describes discursive practices as:

> not purely and simply ways of producing discourse. They are embodied in technical processes, in institutions, in patterns for general behavior, in forms for transmission and diffusion, and in pedagogical forms, which, at once, impose and maintain them. . . . These principles of exclusion and choice, whose presence is manifold, whose effectiveness is embodied in practices, and whose transformations are relatively autonomous, are not based on an agent of knowledge (historical or transcendental) who successively invents them or places them on an ongoing footing; rather, they designate a will to knowledge that is anonymous, polymorphous, susceptible to regular transformations, and determined by the play of identifiable dependencies.[25]

Examining this "will to knowledge" entails attending to the speech acts, institutional policies, and practices that produce gendered subjects and subject positions. It also includes a consideration of the circulation and exercise of power that authorizes particular representational claims as inevitable or dominant. Judith Butler explains, "gender is not always constituted coherently or consistently in different historical contexts, and because gender interacts with racial, class, ethnic, sexual and regional modalities of discursively constituted identities . . . it becomes impossible to separate out 'gender' from the political and cultural intersections in which it is invariably produced and maintained."[26]

Thus, in this book, I explore the multiple articulations of educated girlhoods, paying attention to the dense historical networks within which they take shape. In doing so, the book enacts core feminist commitments to the fluidity of gender formation and sees gender categories as always *in-the-making*.[27] In fact, a key move that I make is to trace the production of categories of gender. I do not take "woman" and "girl" to be self-evident. These categories are socially constructed and their content changes with time. In the archives considered for this book, in some moments the distinction between woman/girl does not hinge on age but on marital status; in other moments, it is securely centered on biological age. Yet, in other cases, the state adamantly refuses a distinction between women and girls, as was the case of the British colonial state.[28] Even these distinctions are not always a given, because social class also has repercussions on who gets marked as a "woman" and who is infantilized into a "girl," and when. Indeed, the point of narration or the speaker's positionality matters too. As I will show in the book, the Pakistani state often infantilizes women through terms such as *bachi* (girl-child), which are used to describe even women over eighteen years old.[29] In doing so, such women are brought securely under the control of the state and the patriarchal family. In the texts considered for this book we encounter Muslim women and girls in myriad forms: *Musalman aurat, sharif bibi, sughar beti, sharif larki, parda-nasheen,* teddy girls, ultramodern, *buri aurat, quam ki bachi, bazari aurat,* empowered girl, and student. The same female can emerge as a woman in one articulation and be marked as a girl in another. My task, then, has been to unpack these circumstances and the politics surrounding them. It is crucial to pay attention to these characteristics and dynamics when considering the making of woman/girl. Muslim womanhood/girlhood thus comes into being as an effect of identity statements, roles, and limitations that are used to describe particular bodies.[30]

This does not mean that we cannot detect dominant representational frames of Muslim women and girls in the archives. Indeed, one of the key arguments that I advance in this book is that over the century, with the expansion of mass schooling, the extension of the juridical powers of the state, as well as the convergence on the figure of the girl in the international development regime,[31] we observe a disaggregation of the composite figure of Muslim woman/girl that was previously dominant. South Asian historian Ruby Lal has observed that while during the early decades of the nineteenth century we can detect a female figure engaged in playful activities who can be read as a "girl," this figure morphs over the course of the century into a compound of girl-child/woman.[32] Girls come to be invoked primarily as future wives and future mothers. The texts that I have surveyed in this book from the turn of the twentieth century show instances where the girl/woman is articulated outside the discursive frames of future wife and future mother as well. What we have then are the beginnings of the emergence of a "Muslim girl" and her distinction from the Muslim woman. By the turn of the twenty-first century, I argue, the Muslim girl crystalizes as a dominant figure in her own right that deserves protection, education, and advocacy. Entities as wide-ranging as representatives of nation-states, multilateral development agencies, philanthropists, human rights activists, and journalists participate in the production of this subject. As an affectively charged figure, she calls forth projects and funds to reform not only her but also her family and her community and, in doing so, legitimizes myriad state and nonstate interventions.

REFORMING WOMEN AND GIRLS: THEN AND NOW

The recent focus on gender in the field of international development emerged during the 1970s and 1980s, when it was argued that women were marginalized in development projects. This awareness was an effect of, and grounded in, broader political and social movements, including women's and civil rights movements in the United States, anticolonial and nationalist struggles in the global South, and geopolitical contestations during the Cold War. Since then, many formal efforts to include women in the development paradigm have taken place under the rubrics of Women in Development, Women and Development, and Gender and Development.[33] During the 1980s and 1990s, however, a consensus arose that not only women but adolescent girls as well could participate in promoting development. Since high fertility rates were negatively correlated with national GDP, it seemed logical that focusing on girls, keeping them in schools, and delaying marriage and childbearing would be a sound policy. This consensus was institutionalized through a range of programs during the 1990s and 2000s that focused specifically on girls. The United Nations, for instance, declared 1991–2001 as the Decade of the Girl Child; the fourth World Conference on Women held in 1995 in Beijing cited "the girl-child" as one of the twelve critical areas of concern; the World Bank founded its Adolescent Girls Initiative in 2007; the UK's Department for International Development launched Girl Hub in 2010; the United Nations marked October 11 as the Day of the Girl Child in 2011; and most recently, in 2015, the White House launched the Let Girls Learn campaign.[34] These efforts have been given additional weight by transnational corporations and foundations such as Wal-Mart, Intel, Procter & Gamble, Nike, Plan International, and NoVo Foundation, which have launched their own campaigns for girls. Journalists, too, have been at the forefront of reinscribing the convergence on the girl with documentary series such as *Girl Rising* (girlrising.com), and popular books, such as *Half the Sky: Turning Oppression into Opportunity for Women Worldwide*, written by Nicolas Kristof and Sheryl WuDunn; and *I Am Malala*, written by Malala Yousafzai and Christina Lamb. The broader focus on gender in development, then, has congealed around the figure of the girl as the "change agent." While other projects aimed at women's development, in particular microcredit, are still considered significant, there has been a marked policy and investment shift toward girls and their access to schooling.[35]

The figure of the girl, then, promises all kinds of societal rewards.[36] However, differently racialized girls offer different types of rewards and are hence policed differently. Unlike their counterparts in the global North, educated girls from the global South, racialized as brown or black, promise not only social harmony but also economic growth, an end to terrorism, and population control. Black girls, for instance, are often viewed as the key to ending the epidemic of HIV/AIDS in African countries; likewise, brown, Muslim girls are popularly touted as ideal for reforming the extremist tendencies in Muslim-majority nations. As noted earlier, these promises are not a new invention; they are the current episode in a long series of productions where brown women's and girls' education is portrayed as the best way to save not only them but also their communities and nations. Indeed, in the context of colonial India, native women's emancipation through education was one of the key discursive tropes that legitimized colonial intervention, paved the way for Christian missionaries to enter the homosocial spaces of the *zenana* (a part of the house reserved for women), as well as provided new opportunities for Indian nationalists to regulate women's bodies and mobility.

A range of actors, from British colonial officers, female teachers, and mission-aries, to Hindu and Muslim social reformers, took up the call for Indian wom-en's education to express their particularized views about ideal femininities and, relatedly, about ideal class relations, and religious and nationalist subjectivities. For instance, during the eighteenth and nineteenth centuries, certainty about the barbarity of Muslims was established through the framing of the Muslim woman as simultaneously victimized and capable of inciting fanaticism in men. In 1871, the bishop of Calcutta wrote that "female education is of the utmost moment in India for religious, social, and even political reasons, there being no more effectual nurses of the fanaticism of the Musalman and of the superstition of the Hindoo than the women of India."[37] Likewise, references to the practices of *purdah,* infan-ticide, widow remarriage, child marriage, and polygamy abound in colonial archives. Texts written by social reformers, such as Helen Barrett Montgomery's *Western Women in Eastern Lands* (1910) and Annie Van Sommer and Samuel Zwemmer's *Our Moslem Sisters* (1907), narrate the oppression of Muslim women. Such texts incited pity from their readers (who were often Protestant Christian women) toward their "moslem sisters," and disgust toward "Moslem law" and the "Muhammadan religion." Women's magazines such as the *Heathen Woman's Friend* (1869), *Englishwoman's Review* (1886), and *Women's Missionary Advocate* (1880), among others, similarly conveyed Indian women's deprivation. These texts reinscribed the racial logics that undergirded colonial adventures. Native women were viewed as biologically inferior, a reasoning that worked well within the social Darwinist ideas popular in late nineteenth-century Britain. The colonial state, too, signaled its superiority in and through laws centering on the female body. These included the Sati Abolition Act (1829), the Widow Remarriage Act (1856), and the Age of Consent Act (1891), among others.

The British colonizers' interest in female education in India began with learn-ing more about the deficits of Indians as well as providing proper education to mixed-race children of British soldiers and those Indians who were closely related to British commerce.[38] Hence, much of the funding for female education was directed by a racial logic. Over time, and with the efforts of the missionaries, native women too were engaged in the educational enterprise. The Charter Act of the East India Company in 1813 provided the requisite permission for missionaries to start experimental girls' schools in North India. American missionary societ-ies, for instance, established day schools—often called "bazaar schools." One of the ways in which girls were lured to these schools was through a daily atten-dance allowance, an incentive that appealed to poor Muslims and Hindus alike. This made such schools popular for poor and lower-caste girls, but unpopular for upper castes and nobility. Both Hindu and Muslim elites did not send their daugh-ters to these schools due to the fear of Christian proselytizing as well as a desire to avoid exposure to lower classes. This prompted the missionaries as well as the colonial administration to rethink their strategies around women's education, and education in the *zenana*s emerged as a viable alternative. Per this policy, missionary women would enter the homosocial spaces of the *zenana* to educate native elite women, and continue to educate Christian converts in orphanages and boarding schools. Significantly, in relation to the *zenana*, the assumption was that in addition to direct teaching, mere contact with missionary women would reform the natives. Thus, during the latter half of the nineteenth century, missionaries lost interest in the enterprise of public girls' schooling since it did not provide access to local elites; instead, they strengthened the *zenana* visitation programs. Observing this trend, historian Tim Allendar notes that while educative efforts in the early nineteenth century were limited to mission schools, by the early twentieth century, female education was politicized and can be viewed as an effort by the raj to support specific forms of feminine subjectivities.[39] Overall, however, there is much more discourse on female education than real funding or infrastructure. Scholars have estimated that by the end of the nineteenth century only 1 to 2 percent of school-age girls were in schools.[40]

The discourse on Indian women's education also created the space for the emergence of an agentic British woman. Historian Jane Haggis notes that the project of empire building offered British women several avenues to secure a public role for themselves and to assert their agency in relation to both British men and the colonized peoples. She traces the link between the struggle of British women to obtain the right to vote at home and their portrayal of themselves as resourceful, enlightened, independent agents vis-à-vis victimized Indian women.[41] Missionaries and other women who chose to travel to India to save their sisters often sought not only to convert Indian women to Christianity but also to introduce Victorian middle-class social mores, aimed at transforming native women into good wives and mothers.[42] This was in contrast to the positions that they sought for themselves—positions of active workers, hoping to leave behind their lives as domesticated wives.[43] While British women were to come to the rescue of Indian women due to their shared womanhood, social class and race tempered that alliance. British ladies always appeared as "superior gendered authority, as better women."[44] Thus, these educative activities helped the colonizers establish their moral superiority in relation to the natives and deepen the reach of the colonial state.

Over time, Indian elites began to view missionary educative interventions with suspicion, particularly as elite Indian women began to convert to Christianity. The threat of conversion dampened the enthusiasm for *zenana* visitations. The *Aligarh Institute Gazette*, a journal with a predominantly Muslim elite readership, for instance, pleaded its (presumably male) readers to not allow mission ladies into their houses.[45] To address this threat, as well as to reform Muslim women according to their own visions, Muslim social reformers put forth their proposals for women's education, which I will explore in detail in chapter 2. These social reformers differed in their allegiances to the British and their social class interests mediated their views on women's education. Suffice it to say that, from their perspective as well, women's superstitious religious practices and customs were viewed as remnants of the past that threatened the survival of the Muslim community or *quam*,[46] and therefore they too called on women to reform their ways. Some Muslim social reformers advocated for an education that introduced women to Victorian norms of domesticity, while others set out to forge distinctly Islamic education for women. Either way, education was to signal familial respectability, engender civilization, and correct the mistakes made by Muslims in the past.

Thus, from Christian missionaries and Muslim social reformers of the past to women's rights advocates and development practitioners today, a range of different social groups have converged on the figure of the Muslim woman/girl. This figure has functioned to incite fear of societal degeneration as well as hope for the future. She is passive but embodies energy and power, which if not harnessed properly through education, can spell the destruction of society. However, when educated appropriately, she can inaugurate familial, national, and civilizational progress. Thus, the education of Muslim women and girls has been intricately linked with governing them and molding them into ideal subjects, an argument that this book explicates.

Governmentality and Education

I trace the shifting constitutions of the ideal educated female subject across three moments to illustrate how they align with ever-changing rationalities for the government of populations and individuals. Foucault advanced the concept of governmentality to explain the ways in which modern European nation-states administered and managed their populations.[47] He later expanded the definition to include practices that "constitute, define, organize and instrumentalize the strategies that individuals in their freedom can use in dealing with each other."[48] Governmentality, then, directs us to consider the ways in which individuals take up particular knowledges, practices, and behaviors from within a field of possibilities, and willingly self-govern according to particular rationalities. The "art of governing" then entails guiding individuals toward desired practices that make them simultaneously more obedient and productive. In this way, power is exercised not only through coercion but also through engendering self-regulation and self-surveillance.

Given the didactic nature of the enterprise of education, it is not surprising that scholars have analyzed educational projects for inducing specific modalities of self- and populational governance.[49] Indeed, colonial interventions did not just entail economic and political exploitation, but also cultural domination and an active erasure of local/indigenous knowledge ecologies.[50] Within the European project of empire building, education was a technology of colonialist subjectification, as it represented the colonized to themselves as inferior when compared to Europeans.[51] Consider Edward Said's recollection of his schooling experience: "the tremendous spiritual wound felt by many of us because of the sustained presence in our midst of domineering foreigners who taught us to respect distant norms and values more than our own. Our culture was felt to be of a lower grade, perhaps even congenitally inferior and something of which to be ashamed."[52] Education—defined as including not only formal school curricula, pedagogies, and spatialities, but also hidden curricula and pedagogies enacted outside school contexts—then, is one of the key social practices through which dominant rules of society, as well as strategies for self-disciplining, are established and reproduced. Such practices in turn sediment particular relations of power and exploitation.

In the context of colonial India, the British viewed education as a means not only to create workers for their expanding bureaucracy but also to socialize the native elite into English tastes and ways of thinking.[53] As noted earlier, some of the earliest interventions in education can be traced to the Charter Act of 1813, which in addition to creating an opening for missionary educative enterprises, also allocated one hundred thousand rupees annually for "the revival and improvement of literature, and the encouragement of the learned natives of India."[54] Over the next twenty years, there was debate around which kinds of literatures—indigenous/vernacular or western—should be circulated, until Lord Thomas Macaulay decidedly moved the debate in favor of western literature through the English Education Act in 1835. While vernacular languages continued to be studied and taught, the English language shared an equal and oftentimes greater status. Furthermore, a cursory glance at Macaulay's famous *Minute on Education* (1835) shows that English models of schooling were introduced to create a cadre of people who could serve as cultural intermediaries between the British and their Indian subjects as well as staff the colonial bureaucracy. In 1837, Persian was abolished as the court language and was replaced with English, and, by the 1850s, English became the primary language of business.

The British were largely interested in university education and less so in primary and secondary education, as the former helped produce the translators and clerical staff needed for municipal governments. When Urdu departments were added to institutions of higher learning, they were viewed as providing a pathway to western cultural mores for Indians. The English versus Urdu debates, according to South Asian historian Margrit Pernau, were about "whether the cultural transformation [of the natives] could be brought about effectively through English, or whether the primary objective should be 'to make the improvement and cultivation of the vernacular tongue go hand in hand with the promulgation of the thoughts and ideas, the solidity of reasoning and freedom of enquiry of the European world.'"[55] The establishment of Urdu departments and patronage for translations from English to Urdu fit this broader objective of transformation of Indian thought and knowledge. Over time it was determined that mass education in the vernacular, too, should be provided, although the government remained less committed to funding it. Wood's Dispatch of 1854 called for providing higher education in English to the elites and basic education in the vernaculars to the masses. This policy shift led to the establishment of institutions such as departments of education in each province, as well as teacher-training schools, government colleges, high schools, and middle schools.

The British had thus far let the Indians undertake the civil administration of the colony; however, much of this changed after the War of Independence of 1857 (or what the colonizers termed as the rebellion or insurrection against the East India Company). While both Muslims and Hindus revolted, it was primarily Muslims who bore the blame.[56] For instance, Henry Harington Thomas, an official of the Bengal civil service, wrote in a pamphlet entitled the *Late Rebellion in India and Our Future Policy* (1858), "Hindoos were neither the contrivers nor the primary movers of this insurrection."[57] To halt future unrest, he went on to elaborate the role of education in producing a cadre of people that would hold favorable views of the English:

> The general introduction of our own language seems, to my view, the most certain way to bring the natives nearer to the Government. Once [we] let them speak and understand English, and they will begin to think in English, and to have English aspirations. They will discover in due time, that the British Government, though vexatious, and unintelligible to common Oriental minds, is superior to the Mahomedan after all, and the rising generation might yet appreciate those advantages of our administration, to which their fathers had been obstinately blind.[58]

Muslims, then, emerged as one of the key target populations that had to be molded in specific ways to align with the British. If we are to understand empire as "practices of power,"[59] as Partha Chatterjee argues, we can read the formal and informal educational practices of the British during the colonial period as playing an integral role in the governance of subjects. Indeed, Henry Harington Thomas proposed education in the English language and literature not only as a means of producing a subject population that was amenable to British rule but also one that appreciated British cultural superiority and, hence, would set out to reform its own barbaric ways: "Their growing familiarity with our language, and their acquirement of our literature, would render their relapse to barbarism impossible; their predilection for torture and massacre would be soon eradicated."[60] From 1857 onward, then, the medium of higher education in India steadily became English, with a focus on European literature. The elite Muslim social classes who had access to employment and resources under the Mughal rule were slow to adapt to the new administration. Hence, civil administration gradually shifted from Muslims to Hindus. Furthermore, Krishna Kumar observes that British education policies not only established knowledges worthy of study but also transferred teachers and curriculum from community life to state control.[61] Colonial institutions then became arbiters of authority and upward mobility. Access to colonial education, however, was mediated by race and social class. An education code introduced in 1883, for instance, "restricted nearly all secondary schooling for girls, and the funding for teacher training of women, to Eurasians and Europeans only."[62] Race and social class interests continued to mediate the colonial state's ventures into education.

It is in this context that male Muslim social reformers, anxious about their own declining status and lack of access to wages and patronage, called for reorganizing their institutions of learning and set out to professionalize themselves. Women emerged as a key discursive space in and through which social reformers articulated their visions for a new social order. This included calls for improving women's religious practices, contribution to the household, and relations with men and children, all to be accomplished through proper education. In the next chapter, I will show that a diversity of views about "the woman question" circulated at the turn of the twentieth century. For now, it is crucial to recognize that in the post-1857 context, with the introduction of British institutions of learning and their preference for English language and literature, different groups of Muslims set out to engage with critical questions about their own identity and futures. These questions were in turn linked with concerns about appropriate knowledges for Muslims and their modes of transmission, and Muslim women emerged as a key node in and through which these concerns were sorted out.

After the establishment of Pakistan, too, women continued to be a central discursive site through which social issues were debated. During the 1950s and 1960s, Pakistan was embroiled in questions about national identity, economic development, and modernization, and ideas about ideal educated subjects emerged at the nexus of those concerns. As I will show, women were posited as "daughters of the nation" and/or "scientifically inclined mothers" of future generations—all in the service of the patriarchal family and the nation. Schools were viewed by some as hospitable and by others as suspect. Likewise, in Pakistan today, contestations around school curricula and the classed outcomes of schooling show how the enterprise continues to make possible some subject positions while erasing others. Significantly, with the institution of mass schooling taking central stage in the development of youth, other societal institutions such as the family and religious institutions find themselves clamoring for a role in the moral development of young people.

GENEALOGY IN FEMINIST RESEARCH

A turn toward the archive is not a turn toward the past but rather an essential way of understanding and imagining other ways to live in the present.
KATE EICHHORN[63]

I started writing this book to denaturalize the assumptions about the figure of the Muslim girl—and relatedly, about Islam, Muslim men, Pakistan, and education's emancipatory promise—that have attained an almost commonsensical status in/ through international development discourses. An effective way for me to do this was to trace how education, girlhood, and womanhood are not static, rigid formations but effects of social negotiations, which necessarily means that there is an inherent diversity in what constitutes an ideal educated Muslim girl. Significantly, there could never simply be one ideal given how diverse our societies and their investments are. Hence, I decided to write a genealogy of the educated Muslim girl, focusing in particular on discourses internal to colonial India and Pakistan. In doing so, I hope to throw into question the universals produced not only by transnational development regimes but also institutions internal to Muslim societies. A genealogy further enables me to show that meanings around educated girlhood have shifted over time. Deploying these analytics then calls on us to investigate the relations of power that propped up particular visions of ideal girlhood in the past as well as in the present.

Genealogies are philosophical and historical examinations that elaborate the ways in which knowledge-making practices intersect to produce/erase subject positions. In this way, genealogies are not traditional histories or teleological narratives of progress; they do not have singular origins, but multiple beginnings and middles. They are rhizomes[64]—a collection of roots that have no beginning or end per se, and which go off in different, unpredictable directions. As a genealogist, I highlight how things become, but while doing so hope to highlight the fluidity and productivity as opposed to accomplished and stable objects/subjects. The practice of genealogy, informed by poststructuralist thought, directs me to consider practices of language and circulation of power that bring particular representations into effect. I ask: "under what conditions and through what forms can an entity like the subject appear in the order of discourse; what position does it occupy; what functions does it exhibit; and what rules does it follow in each type of discourse?"[65] In other words, a genealogy calls for decentering the subject and focuses instead on the concrete practices that produce that subject.[66] As a genealogist, then, my intention is not to discover some essential characteristics about the Muslim girl, but to investigate the different appearances of this girl and inquire into how she comes into being, the webs of discourses in which she is entangled, and the ways in which her constitution shifts over time. These shifts are an effect of power relations. Thus, in order to appreciate how certain subjects become intelligible and others deviant or unthinkable, we have to explore the nexus of power/ knowledge. Genealogy is also attentive to the recurrence of discursive tropes, "not in order to trace the gradual curve of their evolution, but to isolate the different scenes where they engaged in different roles."[67] In the context of my book, notions of respectability sutured onto middle-class sensibilities as well as ideal religious performances are some concerns that recur but perform different functions across time and in relation to women and girls from different social classes.

It is with these methodological lenses that I trace the subjects who become recognizable as "educated Muslim women/girls," as well as those who are marked as being outside the pale of recognition. Significantly, I argue that at any given moment in time, we find multiple articulations of what it means to be an educated woman/girl vying for dominance.

Assembling an Archive

A genealogy constitutes its own events because it is a narrative that has a political purpose.[68] For each of the periods under consideration, I have assembled cultural texts (linguistic and visual) that enable me to piece together dominant visions of ideal and failed woman-/girl-subjects. These include magazine articles, government documents, speeches by politicians, didactic novels, advertisements, television shows, research reports, focus group transcripts, and marketing materials of development campaigns. Together, these texts signal some of the prominent discursive connections of their time. Many elements of these archives can be described as being part of the public culture, which Akhil Gupta defines as "a zone of cultural debate conducted through the mass media, other mechanical modes of reproduction, and the visible practices of institutions such as the state."[69] Public culture is one of the most salient modalities for the discursive construction of the educated girl/woman. I will take a moment here to explain the kinds of texts I take up in each of the chapters and their affordance for my project.

In chapter 2, which focuses on the turn of twentieth century, I begin by mapping some of the ongoing debates about women's education by centering the political writings, speeches, and advice novels of prominent Muslim social reformers, who were predominantly men. These texts help to ascertain some of the prevailing anxieties and concerns, not only about women and their education, but also about the impending economic decline in the context of the expansion of the colonial state. I then draw on women's writings that appeared in periodicals, specifically *Ismat, Tehzib-e-Niswan,* and *Khatun,* and the didactic novels written by the pioneer female author/editor Muhammadi Begum, namely *Sughar beti* (Refined Daughter; 1905), *Sharif beti* (Respectable Daughter; 1908), and *Hayat-e-Ashraf* (The Life of Ashraf; 1899). While male social reformers' writings enjoyed healthy circulation, this was not so for women's writings, which often appeared in meagerly funded periodicals, still in their infancy during the early decades of the twentieth century. These periodicals, in fact, were not even considered worthy of digitization and archiving until very recently and, thus, have been largely neglected in the official writing of history.[70] I examine these periodicals because they formed one of the discursive sites where *ashraf* (respectable) women engaged with each other. Their writings, thus, provide an additional layer of understanding about the project of *making* women/girls at the turn of the twentieth century.

In chapter 3, while continuing to work with women's periodicals, I include additional documents such as national education policies, newspaper advertisements, political speeches, and a qualitative study conducted with girls, entitled the *Educated Pakistani Girl*, by Asaf Hussain in 1963. These texts illuminate ideal (gendered) citizen-subjects needed for the project of nation building, modernization, and development. When I arrive at the present moment (chapter 4), I outline the ideal girlhood established in and through transnational girls' education campaigns and complicate it by drawing on findings from focus group conversations conducted with girls, teachers, and parents in a city in South Pakistan, during the summer of 2015. I take these interviews to be performative, where my interview subjects narrate their educational trajectories and desires, and in doing so provide yet another glimpse into ideal educated girlhoods. I stay in the current moment in chapter 5 and examine two television shows aired in Pakistan in 2011 and 2012, which are based on Nazir Ahmed's *Mirat-ul-uroos* (The Bride's Mirror; 1869), taken up in detail in chapter 2. These televised productions afford me the possibility of tracking how concerns around gender and education have transmuted over a century. The final chapter of the book outlines overlapping storylines that emerge across the moments and sites centered in this book.

While I engage with a broad range of texts, this book is not about them. That is, I make no effort to understand the texts' (and their authors' or narrators') "true" meaning. I am more interested in the social conditions within which the texts become possible and intelligible, what the texts do, and what they produce. This approach enables me to examine discourses about women's and girls' education across different moments, not to determine causal links or to be comprehensive but to explore their connections and ruptures with other discourses that I am concerned with, such as the discourse on *sharafat* (respectability), class and religious performances, and nation building. As a genealogist who has commitments to transnational feminist and postcolonial theories, I trace the ways in which calls for education are linked with other calls—for inaugurating civilization, reproducing class sensibilities, signaling respectability, boosting economic growth, enacting modernity, or curating religious identity. In the process Muslim women and girls are called on to acquire the type of education that can enable them to effectively deliver on these societal projects.

Analyzing the Archive

While political speeches and texts might seem to be a logical choice for a genealogy, in that they provide a glimpse into the then prevailing political regimes, literature seems less so given the apparently fictive nature of the enterprise. However, I am influenced by Lee Quinby, who elaborates on the value of literary works for genealogy.[71] She notes that literary texts often engage with, and elaborate on, key issues of their time, and have also served as a disciplinary technology of colonization. Genealogies that take up literature then teach us about attitudes toward ongoing issues, as well as how literature partakes in establishing dominant regimes of truth. Indeed, post-structural scholars do not take such texts to represent essential truths—texts are not autonomous;[72] rather they "tell stories,"[73] and often multiple stories depending on the positionality of the reader. This view of literature is productive for me, as I examine texts written or commissioned by British colonial officers, religious *ulema*, modernists, and nationalists, who had different approaches to education, religion, and men's and women's roles in society. Furthermore, their differential access to resources also translated into varying abilities to produce and transmit knowledge.

Methodologically, examining these texts entails attending to the personal, social, and historical contexts within which the authors created them.[74] It also entails exploring the audiences imagined by the text, and what the text *does* in relation to opening up and foreclosing subject positions. This method of engaging with texts by attending to the knowledge regimes within which they circulate has been described as by Wendy Hesford as "intercontextuality": "To read intercontextually is to identify in a composition or performance the internal references to other texts or rhetorical acts, to become reflexive about the social codes and habits of interpretation that shape the composition or performance's meaning and that it enacts, and to comprehend how texts are formed by the institutions and material contexts that produce and through which they circulate."[75]

Enacting this method entails attending not only to the internal references of the texts but also placing them in the longer histories of cultural and social articulation, exploring the assumptions and knowledges that they draw upon, and how they move about in the world. For instance, colonial officers from the Public Instruction Offices in North India often contracted Muslim writers to author books about women's education. They were also active in selecting books that aligned with their views and assigned them as official textbooks in public schools. Nazir Ahmed's advice novel, *Mirat-ul-uroos* is one such text that received praise and monetary prizes from M. Kempton, who was the director of public instruction of Northwestern Provinces from 1862 to 1878, and also the lieutenant governor of Northwestern Provinces.[76] Such moves often antagonized the *ulema*, who wanted a different kind of education for women. In *Bahishti zewar* (Heavenly Ornaments; 1905), Ashraf Ali Thanawi (a well-known religious scholar) lists Nazir Ahmed's book as one that should be banned. The texts, then, have a life beyond themselves. They provide a glimpse into the ongoing contestations around women's and girls' education. Significantly, the autobiographical and biographical texts that I take up in this book, written predominantly by women, are particularly well positioned for this form of inquiry and analysis. As texts that sought to locate the personal within the social and political, they become generative spaces for me to examine what was experienced as a social reality, as well as to obtain insights into a new reality that the authors sought to establish through the very practice of writing.

The texts are also useful in providing a glimpse into the making of social class. Bourdieu theorizes class not only as income levels and economic opportunities, but also as aesthetics, language, and consumption practices.[77] Elsewhere, Jane Kenway and others argue that class is always in the making;[78] it is articulated, disarticulated, and rearticulated through connections with race, gender, nation, and ethnicity. The task of the researcher, then, is to examine how class-based solidarities, aesthetics, preferences, rituals, and hostilities are produced. In the book, readers will observe how social class is made through women's practices, which are in turn shaped by notions of respectability. In other words, it is the respectable woman who is the vanguard and symbolic representative of her social class. However, this woman is fashioned differently as class aesthetics change over time and space. As Kenway et al. note, "to study class is to . . . certainly identify longstanding practices, repeated patterns of behavior, the role of custom and convention. Importantly, it is not only about identifying such repetition but is also about identifying the effort of class invention, ingenuity and imagination."[79] The texts taken up in this book provide a peek into how women's education is expected to engender particular class sensibilities and aesthetics, while cautioning them against others.[80]

Engaging with Women's Narratives

There are multiple ways in which women's narratives have been taken up in genealogical projects. The first entails recuperating women's experiences and voices, and adding them to the long-standing narratives of history produced predominantly by men. This strategy sees "woman" as a stable, knowable category and views the endeavor of adding women's voices as a corrective. In doing so it produces a women's record that runs parallel to narratives of men. The second approach, however, takes gender as an analytical category and traces how gender and sexuality organize social life.[81] This approach views women's voices as part of broader assemblages, linked with race, class, and religion, and providing partial perspectives. Joan Scott has named these approaches as writing "women's history" versus "gender history," respectively.[82] I locate this book within the field of gender history to illuminate the operation of gender as a discourse in and through which negotiations and contestations around class, religion, and nation building take place. Even as I recover the first-person writings of Muslim women from the turn of the twentieth century and include Pakistani girls' narratives from 2015 (in chapter 4, as findings from focus group interviews), I view them as yet another kind of "text," which provide a partial glimpse into ongoing knowledge regimes. They are a *part* of my broader archive, although I recognize that this part has been neglected in official writings and, hence, seek consciously (and laboriously) to bring it into our conversation. As this book shows, Muslim women's writings from early- or mid-twentieth-century Pakistan do not radically depart from the ongoing rationales, concerns, and investments that were felt by men of similar social class and geographical locations. Indeed, women writers were embedded in their social and cultural milieu, resisting as well as acquiescing to reforms aimed at them. Their writings, then, tell stories about the dominant knowledge regimes and hint at both individual and communal interests.

A fortunate consequence of writing this genealogy is also that it disrupts present-day certainties about the silence of Indian Muslim women of the past. Such assumptions have enormous representational power in current collective imagination. Tropes of the "silent, uneducated Musalman woman who was/is married early and/or lives in polygamous households at the mercy of hypersexual Muslim men" continue to inform international discourses on girls' empowerment and education, as well as western foreign and domestic policies. Deploying women's narratives from the past interrupts these certainties by showing women to be fully human and political subjects. Furthermore, as Azra Asghar Ali notes, the lack of understanding about the voices of Indian Muslim women presents a key gap in our knowledge of how Muslim women's spaces opened up in the twentieth century.[83] This book hopes to address that gap.

Like any study, mine too has its limitations. The focus on particular moments, decades, texts, and themes entails downplaying or ignoring others. I do not discuss events in other time periods that have had an effect on how we have come to recognize and imagine educated female subjects. This opens me up to the critique of periodization, where particular events and time periods are marked as representational in the life of a nation or community. However, since this book is a genealogy, my objective has been to make a political argument about the figure of the educated girl. I am interested in broader systems of reasoning about women and girls that entail inclusions and exclusions, and help to produce particular kinds of subjective experiences among women and girls. It is these motivations that have informed my selection of texts, periods, and events.

Forging *Sharif* Subjects

In 1906, a young woman named Sayyida Jamila moved to Delhi with the support of her uncle to acquire medical education at a madrasa linked to a women's hospital. Her relatives pressured her immediate family to stop her. They argued that only lower status/caste (*ajlaf*) women left the protected space of the home. For respectable (*ashraf*) women like Jamila, it was enough to acquire knowledge of the sharia (religious injunctions) at home. Jamila responded to this criticism through an article, which was published in *Ismat* magazine.[1] She resisted her relatives' narrative by citing several sayings (*hadith*) of Prophet Muhammad and argued that it was incumbent upon both men and women to acquire knowledge (*ilm*); that there were two types of *ilm*—bodily and religious—both of which were necessary according to the Prophet. She explained that it was essential for women to learn medicine so that they could tend to other women in ways that male doctors could not. She also berated Muslims for falling behind in this endeavor, noting that other ethnic groups (*quam*) have continued to acquire broad education.

Jamila's story succinctly illustrates the competing notions of appropriate knowledges and educative spaces for respectable women that circulated at the turn of the twentieth century in colonial India. This period is marked by increasing anxiety on the part of the *ashraf* (singular, *sharif*) social classes, who had previously enjoyed privileges in the Mughal courts but after the entrenchment of the British rule were now struggling to preserve their social status. Women and their practices emerged as a prominent discursive space in and through which religious reformers, modernists, nationalists, and even women themselves contemplated their desired futures. This discourse was connected to concerns about women's mobility (Jamila had left her home), knowledges deemed appropriate for women (Jamila wanted to pursue education in medicine), and engagement in paid work (Jamila wanted to work as a doctor), which in turn had implications for their status as respectable (*sharif*) subjects. Thus, the nature of women's education—in particular, *what* should it be about, *where* should it happen, and toward what ends—became a topic of intense debate. In this chapter, I trace these ongoing discussions about women's education at the turn of the twentieth century in order to unpack concerns around social status, class, and gendered spaces. Specifically, I examine political speeches, advice texts, novels, and women's writings in Urdu periodicals. While I focus on the narratives of Muslim men and women, it is crucial to remember that these debates were shaped by the colonial experience, which I discussed in chapter 1.

GENDER, SOCIAL CLASS, AND RESPECTABILITY

During the early nineteenth century, Muslims were divided broadly into two social classes: the *ashraf* (distinguished/respectable) and the *ajlaf* (the low-born or common).[2] The former often included members of the nobility, aristocracy, scholars, and the landed elites, and the latter, traders and artisans. These categories mapped onto Muslims who had migrated to India versus the local converts, with the *ashraf* being Muslims of foreign ancestry, particularly Arab, Persian, Turkic, and Afghan. Cultural elements such as dress, etiquette, aesthetics, familiarity with Persian and Urdu, and the art of elegant conversation marked a person as *sharif.*

The economic power of the *ashraf,* however, came under pressure as the British colonial state expanded in India. While earlier, the British had sought alliances with local rulers, after the rebellion of 1857, they shifted to direct administration, which precipitated the decline in resources such as stipends, employment, and other privileges that *ashraf* Muslims had enjoyed. Furthermore, changes in inheritance laws and pensions/tributes left many families with limited resources. The British also created new educational institutions, which provided opportunities for upward mobility to groups that were previously excluded from the *ashraf* social class. Likewise, the establishment of the railway system proved opportune for traders who prospered. Hence, in the post-1857 context, we observe a reconfiguration of the social groupings, specifically a disaggregation of the *ashraf* into nobility (linked to the Mughal court), the "new *ashraf,*"[3] and the rest of the population. According to South Asian historian Margrit Pernau, the "new *ashraf*" came to include scholars, landed elites, as well as enterprising traders and merchants. The nobility was increasingly viewed as irrelevant. One of the ways in which the new *ashraf* established their distinctiveness was through a redefinition of *sharafat* (respectability). To be *sharif* no longer meant being linked to an aristocratic culture; instead, *sharafat* was signaled through one's social practices, which included hard work, religiosity, and self-discipline.[4]

These trends were accompanied by a radical reconfiguration of urban spatialities under the British.[5] Indian historian Faisal Devji elaborates on how the spaces where the *ashraf* men had exerted influence such as the administration, the courts, and the mosques, underwent extensive change under the British, reducing elite Muslim men's authority.[6] For instance, the British instituted their own legal system, leaving only family law to be regulated by Muslims. Furthermore, since religion was privatized, the *ulema* were also beginning to lose their public authority. Against this reconfiguration of public spaces, focus shifted to the space of the home. Relatively unregulated in the past, the home now surfaced as comprising the potential to redefine Muslim identity and norms of respectability. It is precisely in this context that women were transformed from being seen as causing *fitna* (chaos), embodying uncontrollable sexuality, and not being appropriate for raising children, to becoming the upholders of familial morality, domestic managers, and mothers of future citizens.[7] It was believed that women could be reformed through education, and in doing so, perform *sharafat*. Women's languages, religious practices, learning, relations with each other and with the opposite sex, mobility, and engagement with waged work, all came under intense scrutiny. In other words, women were brought into tighter circuits of control and surveillance.[8]

One element of this surveillance entailed reforming women's religious practices and bringing them closer to orthodox Islam. This in turn amplified the need to define and codify Islam, a task that proved to be extremely difficult, given the diversity of Muslims in colonial India. Since "customary law" was accepted as a legitimate source of sharia, there existed multiple stances on issues such as *purdah*, inheritance, and polygyny. However, customary practices were increasingly marked as un-Islamic by some Muslim reformers who advanced their own understandings about proper Islam. Hence, in this period we also observe an intense effort to codify Islam, one in which, alongside the *ulema,* the newly emerging trader/merchant classes participated as well by actively funding mosques, building schools, disseminating religious texts, and undertaking other pious endeavors.[9]

These contestations had real consequences, particularly for women from the nobility who had previously enjoyed active roles in the lives of their families as well as in political and economic domains. Family networks signaled social status and women had played important roles in cementing these networks through marriages and maintaining relations, including participating in rituals and festivals. Pernau notes that "the woman of the highest rank generally held uncontested sway in the women's quarters"[10] and in relation to a young bride, it was the husband's mother, rather than the husband himself, who held authority. Measures were also in place to ensure upper-class women's financial security through property and exclusive use of the dower (*mahr*). Given the exclusion of men from women's spaces, women had developed a unique form of speech, known as *begmati* (ladies' language). This language included figurative terms and expressions that were linked to women's everyday practices.[11] The broader shifts that took place during colonial rule, including changes in property ownership and inheritance, led to many transformations in women's roles.

A popular didactic novel, *Mirat-ul-uroos* (The Bride's Mirror; published in 1869) written by Nazir Ahmed (d. 1912), succinctly illustrates these dynamics. This novel also outlines how a broad range of women's actions came to be linked to familial respectability. In the novel, Nazir Ahmed employs the characters of Akbari and Asghari, two sisters married to two brothers, Akil and Kamil, as foils against each other to explicate the performance of an ideal educated Muslim female subjectivity. Asghari has elementary reading and writing skills, is an expert at household management, and abides by "proper" Muslim practices—that is, she does not engage in superstitious customs or excessive rituals. Due to her training and intelligence, she is able to create a happy and harmonious home for her husband and in-laws. Ahmed narrates several episodes where Asghari's ability to read and write enables her to forestall inconvenient situations. Over time, Asghari goes on to establish a successful madrasa at her home for the girls of her neighborhood. Even though etiquette restrains her from charging her students fees, she is able to extract personal benefit from the institution, including securing a good marriage proposal for her sister-in-law, using monies made from selling students' products to decorate the rooms where she holds classes, as well as utilizing gifts from students to maintain relations in the neighborhood.

In contrast, Asghari's older sister, Akbari, is unable to maintain her household even though her husband makes a decent income. She is impulsive and does not preserve class boundaries. For example, she mingles with the rich as well as the poor, and shares personal details with them. To mark such cross-class familiarity as inappropriate for *sharif* women, Ahmed shows that Akbari gets swindled by a *hajjan* (a women who had recently returned from performing the *hajj*/pilgrimage). Akbari neither has the acumen to stay away from such charlatans, nor the basic literacy skills to detect their frauds. This is in contrast to Asghari, whose social aloofness and distant attitude toward women from lower social classes is praised by Ahmed. Asghari intentionally avoids contact with women from non-*sharif* backgrounds and invites only *sharif* girls to her home-based madrasa. Clearly Akbari's and Asghari's actions articulate their social class and status, securing or unraveling claims to *sharafat*.

In Asghari, then, we find a performance of what Ahmed deems to be an ideal *sharif* subject, one who reproduces her own and her family's social standing. And, it is Asghari's education that enables her to manage her household competently, as opposed to Akbari, who exposes herself and her husband to extreme hardship because she does not relate to the world in a way that an educated woman would. Ahmed goes into detail about the type of education that Asghari received. Her training includes the study of the Quran, literacy (in the languages and mathematics), skills (*hunar*), etiquette (*saleeqa*), proper religious practices, and household management (*khana-dari*). This broad education takes place within the confines of the household. Asghari, in turn, imparts similar training to other girls from the neighborhood. In addition to reading skills, she teaches them *duniya ka kaam* (affairs of the world), which includes skills necessary for managing a household (such as sewing, cooking, dyeing clothes, and organizing ceremonies). She also teaches *Muntakhab al-hikayat* (a selection of didactic stories) for her students' entertainment. Ahmed advocates this kind of education for women if the Muslim *quam* intends to reclaim its status.

As alluded to earlier, *Mirat-ul-uroos* was written in a context when the Muslim aristocratic families were undergoing radical changes as a consequence of losing their prior positions of authority within the Mughal administration. The British increasingly excluded Muslims from the army, revenue collection, and political offices, and the rise of Hindus within those institutions left elite Muslims in a real and imagined precarious position. It also put pressure on the opportunities afforded to women for education. In the preface of *Mirat-ul-uroos,* Nazir Ahmed notes that even though it is not a custom in India for women to read and write, many women from *sharif* families especially in large cities know how to read the Quran and other texts. Indeed, Ahmed's own family in Delhi was one such family. Since *sharif* Muslim women practiced seclusion, they were often educated at home by their fathers, brothers, and/or visiting *ustanis* (female teachers), who were usually the wives and daughters of the *maulvis* (religious functionaries). However, with the deteriorating economic position of *ashraf* Muslims in North India, limited incomes were available to retain teachers. This led to a severe decline in the ability of Muslims to hire female teachers at a time when their demand was high.[12] In addition, while there had existed an extensive system of private and public patronage as well as endowments (*waqfs*) for boys that facilitated the establishments of *maktabs* and madrasas, the regulation of *waqfs* by the British administration severely limited the availability of funds for such educative enterprises. All in all, the local systems of knowledge transmission in place for both boys and girls came under extreme strain, as the colonial administration entrenched itself in India. These trends were accompanied by explicit and implicit policies by the British administration to direct funds toward English education,[13] and to strengthen English as the language of the government.[14] That Persian language was abolished as the language of the administration by the British in 1837 led to further economic marginalization of many *ashraf* Muslims.

Against this background, the genre of didactic novels in Urdu emerged as a critical site for educating Muslim youth, especially young women, of which *Mirat-ul-uroos* was one of the earliest.[15] Nazir Ahmed, for instance, notes in the preface that he wrote *Mirat-ul-uroos* as an advice text for his own daughters in order to reform their thoughts and improve their habits. Ahmed himself belonged to the socioeconomic group that had to professionalize in order to secure employment and resources under the raj. Hence, his writings seem to represent the active efforts of Muslims of the "new *ashraf*" to reproduce/sustain their privilege by simultaneously distancing themselves from the nobility and becoming more enterprising. Two thousand copies of his book were acquired to be distributed to English schools; a hundred thousand copies were sold over the next few years.[16]

Nazir Ahmed's text was one articulation among a cacophony of ideas about education for women and girls that emerged from the mid-nineteenth century through the turn of the twentieth century. Pointedly, while there was consensus around reforming women, there were differences particularly in relation to the content and space for women's education. These differences can be mapped onto social class as well as varying assumptions about women's social roles. Significantly, as this chapter will show, women too participated in this discussion. However, before delving into women's writings, I will review the dominant elements of the debate on women's education shaped largely by male social reformers. I am less concerned about providing a comprehensive overview and more interested in tracing the contours of this debate. Therefore, I center select Muslim reformers and their writings in order to represent some elements of the ongoing public discussions. I have chosen reformers who belonged to different religious interpretive traditions, had different levels of association with the British, and differed in their views about women's education.

WHAT SHOULD WOMEN KNOW?

Muslim social reformers differed on which knowledges were necessary for women, as well as the spaces where women could acquire these knowledges.[17] These perspectives, often advanced by male social reformers, set the contours of the public discussion on this topic. Female authors writing in periodicals or speaking at women-only political gatherings were in some ways engaging with, responding to, and critiquing what their male counterparts were calling for. Broadly, there were those who believed that all kinds of knowledges that were considered appropriate for boys were relevant for girls as well; those who thought that knowledges imparted in English schools were out of the question for *sharif* girls and that Muslims had to devise their own institutions and curricula for them; and others, who believed that elementary literacy skills acquired at home were adequate for girls. These different perspectives on what knowledges girls should acquire appear to reflect the reformers' visions of how the *ashraf* could maintain their status in what was seen as an increasingly precarious environment.

The prominent Muslim scholar and education reformer Sir Syed Ahmed Khan (d. 1898) argued that it was not necessary to invest in the public education of women. While of the opinion that Muslims needed to study the English language and western sciences in order to recover their status in India, Sir Syed emphasized the education of boys over girls. Sir Syed was the leader of the Aligarh Movement, which sought to reinvigorate Muslims in the subcontinent in the aftermath of the decline of the Mughals and the War of Independence of 1857. Much of his effort was aimed at establishing educational institutions. In 1864, he founded the Scientific

Society and in 1875, a school in Aligarh called the Muhammedan Anglo-Oriental College, which in 1911 became the Aligarh Muslim University. While Sir Syed advocated for a broad education for men, he did not think that education beyond the religious sciences was necessary for girls, or that separate schools had to be established for them. Sir Syed subscribed to the "trickle-down theory,"[18] whereby educated men would be able to educate their wives, sisters, and daughters at home, who in turn might educate their sons. That was indeed the norm in *sharif* families. The training of the fictive character of Zubayda Khatun, featured in prominent Indian Muslim poet and writer Altaf Hussain Hali's (d. 1914) *Majalis-un-nissa* (Gatherings of Women), gives a glimpse into women's education at home: "By the time I was thirteen, I had studied the *Gulistan* and *Bostan*, *Akhlaq-e-muhsini*, and *Iyar-e-danish* in Persian, and in Arabic the necessary beginning grammar, in arithmetic the common factors and decimal factors and the two parts of Euclid's geometry. I had also studied the geography and history of India, and had practiced both *naskh* and *nasta'liq* calligraphy and could copy couplets in a good hand. At that point, my father began to teach me two lessons a day. In the morning we read *Rimiya-e-sa'adat* and in the evening *Kalila wa dimna* in Arabic."[19]

Zubayda Khatun had been educated enough that she was able to train her son in elementary Urdu, mathematics, and the Quran before sending him to school. In her case, then, education was linked with personal fulfillment and some contribution to the family. It is precisely due to this reason that Sir Syed said, "the present state of education among Muhammadan females is, in my opinion, enough for domestic happiness, considering the present social and economic condition of the life of the Muhammadans of India."[20] Furthermore, Sir Syed was keenly aware of the hypocrisy of the colonial critique of Muslim women's position in India. On one occasion, he noted that although, "England greatly favors the freedom of women, yet when its laws are examined, it is obvious that the English consider women quite insignificant, unintelligent and valueless."[21] He explained that in England women cannot "hold responsibility for any legal instrument" without the husband's consent and that prior to 1870 property gained through inheritance as well as its profits belonged to the husbands.[22] He further observed that while there may be "excess" of *purdah* in India, there are other kinds of excesses in Europe as well. Sir Syed represents that moment in the history of Indian Muslims when they were beginning to lose their privileged positions. Sir Syed could still imagine *sharif* men as being responsible for the development of both the private and public spheres—the masters of both domains—if they acquired western knowledges. Indeed, in Altaf Hussain Hali's narrative, Zubayda's son is advised to engage with classical sciences only to the extent that they are helpful practically. Instead he is to acquire English, the language of the new rulers.[23]

By the late nineteenth and early twentieth centuries a wave of social reformers emerged who adamantly believed that educating women at home, government schools, or Islamic schools was necessary in order to strengthen the Muslim *quam* and harmonize relations within the family. Education, they believed, would make women better wives and mothers, and enable them to take over the management of their homes as men left to look for work under the new administration. This is a distinctly new subject—woman as the home manager, as a companion, and as a child-rearer—which came into being as a consequence of the rapidly changing political and social contexts of Muslims in North India. Some reformers even made allowances for women to engage in paid labor to be able to support their families economically. These different subject positions called for different kinds of knowledges and spaces for the educative enterprise.

To understand the prevailing conditions of *ashraf* women's education we can consider Syed Shamsuddin ibn Miansaheb Qadri's short pamphlet entitled, *Risala talim-niswan* (Pamphlet on Women's Education), published in 1895. Qadri, was the deputy education commissioner/inspector and his writings provide a glimpse into some of the emergent concerns around women's education. The author begins by lamenting the current conditions of the *quam,* and nostalgically recalls the times when his ancestors (Muslims) had high status in *ulum wa fanun* (knowledges and skills),[24] which in turn signaled the high status of Islam. He goes on to argue that the welfare of nations depends on the *talim wa tarbiyat* (education and nurturing) of both men and women. The *Risala* is composed of several didactic stories. It tells us about the efforts of Zeb-un-Nissa, who used to write the alphabet on different toys so that her daughter could learn it while engaging in play. It narrates the story of a girl, Husunara, whose parents did not educate her even though they were well-off. Husunara was later married to an *ilm dost* (friend of knowledge), who upon finding out that his wife is not educated expresses amazement.[25] The author notes that the hearts of educated and uneducated people often do not find harmony with each other.[26] In fact, "for an uneducated woman to be in an educated man's house is hell for him in this world."[27] We clearly see emergent ideas about companionship and happiness in marriage in relation to women's education.[28] These ideas get taken up by other reformers as well. In addition, the notion that women are bearers of civilization is also salient in the *Risala.* Qadri argues that it is important for women to be educated because if men are uneducated then the effects of that remain limited to them but if women are *baywakoof* (foolish) then their children suffer as well.[29]

By the turn of the twentieth century, within *sharif* circles, the question around women's education was no longer one of whether or not women should have an education. It revolved mostly around the knowledges required for women and the ideal location to transmit them. Mumtaz Ali (d. 1935), a prominent advocate of women's education and founder of the women's journal *Tehzib-e-Niswan,* called for a broad education of women, which included the study of religious sciences as well as reading and writing. In his work *Huquq un-niswan* (Women's Rights), published in 1898, he argued that since God had given women equal intellectual faculties as men, they deserve access to the same education.[30] He countered his critics, who believed that too much education would lead to vulgarity in women by noting that any education that did so could lead to the same vulgarity in men as well.[31] He then went on to present a strategy for expanding women's education through establishing a women's newspaper and publishing a list of novels suitable for study by women.[32] He believed that an education would enable women to develop the skills necessary for becoming better, more interesting companions for their husbands. His articulation for the need for companionship within marriages seems to be premised on the complementarity between the male provider and female housewife, which led him to prioritize women's roles as wives and their ability to fulfill their domestic responsibilities. Women, hence, needed to acquire knowledges that could help them become domestic managers and interesting companions. Mumtaz Ali's is a distinctly elite position, which assumes division of labor along gender lines. Such divisions were not possible for Muslims from lower economic classes. The social reformers who focused on those social classes, hence, elaborated a different vision for women's education. In fact, concern for women from low-income social classes is most visible in the calls for education advanced by another prominent leader, Sir Sultan Mahomed Shah Aga Khan (d. 1957).

Sultan Mahomed Shah Aga Khan III was born in Karachi, in today's Pakistan, on November 2, 1877.[33] He became the forty-eighth imam of the Shia Ismaili Muslims at the age of eight on the passing away of his father, and went on to establish himself as an influential political leader, not only in colonial India but also on the international scene. In addition to facilitating the establishment of the Muhammadan Anglo-Oriental College at Aligarh, he worked closely with the leaders of the Pakistan Movement as well as the British administration to secure the recognition of Muslims as an independent political entity. In 1902, he was appointed to the Legislative Council set up by Lord Curzon, and in 1906, he was elected as the first president of the Muslim political organization, the All India Muslim League. He remained active on the Indian political front throughout his life but over time increasingly took on international policy-oriented tasks, including serving as the president of the League of Nations for a brief period.

While of similar views as Mumtaz Ali, the Aga Khan argued for women's education, not only for the purpose of discharging responsibilities in the domestic sphere as bearers of civilization, but also for becoming economically independent from their male relations and acquiring personal happiness.[34] In his text *India in Transition,* published in 1918, the Aga Khan notes that one of the reasons due to which reforms for women's progress had been slow was because they had been motivated by the end purpose of service to the other gender and not for women themselves. He suggests that "the constant argument has been that of the necessity for providing educated and intelligent wives and daughters, sisters and mothers, for the men . . . the time has come for a full recognition that the happiness and welfare of the women themselves, must be the end and purpose of all efforts towards improvement."[35] In fact, with respect to his own followers, the Ismaili Muslims, he noted, "I am trying to guide our young women's lives into entirely new channels. I want to see them able to earn their living in trades and professions, so that they are not economically dependent on marriage, nor a burden on their fathers and brother[s]."[36] A Muslim leader with strong ties to the British administration and extensive exposure to social movements in Britain and America, the Aga Khan argued for universal and compulsory access to education for the masses, and worked with the British government to instate legislation that would make primary education compulsory for both boys and girls.[37] As the spiritual leader of Shia Ismaili Muslims, who were a minority interpretative tradition in Islam and were primarily from the non-*ashraf* classes, the Aga Khan was concerned with a population that was often poor and did not have the resources to partake in home-visitation or home-based educative efforts.[38] We can, thus, assume that it made most sense for the Aga Khan to call for changes in the government's policies that would affect the *ashraf* and non-*ashraf* alike.

Relatedly, since the Aga Khan hoped to improve the economic well-being of his followers, he welcomed women's participation in economic activities. He, therefore, did not want education for girls to stop with basic literacy or elementary religious knowledge, and emphasized that "all knowledge in the world should be open to girls."[39] To increase his female followers' mobility, he banned the *purdah,* noting that "the free social and intellectual part played in the life of Arabia by Imam Hussain's daughter, Sakina, and by the daughter of Talha and the great grand daughters of Khalifa Abu Bakar can be contrasted with the position of women in the 19th century."[40] In his *Memoirs,* published in 1954, he notes, "in my grandfather's and my father's time the Ismailis were far ahead of any other Muslim sect in the matter of the abolition of the strict veil, even in extremely conservative countries. I have absolutely abolished it; nowadays you will never find an Ismaili woman wearing the veil."[41] In this regard the Aga Khan was indeed an outlier when compared to his peers; even Mumtaz Ali, while advocating the toning down of the strict *purdah* observed by Indian women,[42] was neither in favor of its abandonment nor for the integration of women in the public school system. What we have, then, is a reformer whose investment in a particular social class of Muslims moved him to articulate a vision of education that led to greater mobility for his female followers. However, while condemning *purdah* among his followers, the Aga Khan was careful not to fall into the Orientalist trap of seeing *purdah* as a social ill, as the British did. In a letter to the *Times* on August 8, 1919, he disagrees with Lord Southborough's denial of suffrage for Indian women on the grounds that Muslim women in *purdah* would not be willing to go to the polling booths. He argues that "*purdah* ladies go into the law and registration courts all over the country, and give evidence in relation to the transfer of property,"[43] and that women's electoral franchise is an issue of justice.

In contrast, another key Muslim reformer, Ashraf Ali Thanawi (d. 1943), of the Deoband madrasa (funded by the "new *ashraf*"),[44] was unwilling to compromise on the prevalent practices of seclusion and, hence, argued for increasing women's basic literacy skills just enough so that they were able to communicate with the outside world and engage in the practice of religion. Thanawi was an influential religious scholar, whose juridical as well as other writings provide a glimpse into this scholarly class's efforts to retain their authority in a changing political context.[45] He wrote numerous texts, one of which entitled, *Bahishti zewar* (Heavenly Ornaments), published in 1905, is considered one of the most influential Urdu books in Muslim South Asia, with the highest number of editions.[46] The text introduces women to Islamic norms and provides a curriculum of sorts, so that women could address their educational needs without leaving the *zenana*. The text is also a discursive effort at constructing women as the guardian of Islamic morality, and clarifying what it meant to be an educated *Muslim* woman.

Bahishti zewar calls on women to reform their corrupt/superstitious practices and provides detailed guidance on religious rituals, duties, laws, and etiquette. Thanawi elaborates on acceptable relations between men and women, nuances of public transactions such as loans, contracts, and property ownership, and the rights of men and women according to Islamic law, among other things. He also makes space for women to undertake certain economic activities (such as making mango pickles), which could help them secure some economic independence. He employs the text to impart basic literacy skills to his female readers as well. Recognizing that his text was of an introductory nature, Thanawi encourages women to study advanced religious sciences. However, he does not propose a plan for women to accomplish this. As noted earlier, the *zenana*-school system was limited in what it could offer women in terms of educational enhancement. Women, therefore, would have had to leave the *zenana* in order to obtain the advanced knowledges that Thanawi proposed. However, by showing a strong preference for seclusion, Thanawi limited his own proposal. While *Bahishti zewar* deals with women's issues, according to Islamic studies scholar Muhammad Qasim Zaman, its broader function seems to be to establish the ulema's authority to guide Muslims in a time of extensive religious contestation.[47] Thanawi's text betrays anxieties around new forms of femininities that reformers such as Nazir Ahmed, Mumtaz Ali, and the Aga Khan were advocating; in fact, Thanawi lists Nazir Ahmed's book as one that should be banned. His is, then, an effort to provide an alternate figuration of educated femininity that could respond to the changing social context while still maintaining the religious practices that he deemed to be appropriate.

If one analyzes the different knowledges that were deemed appropriate for women from the perspective of the kinds of subjects that they sought to produce, it becomes clear that they are informed by different conceptualizations of societal needs and women's roles in fulfilling those needs. The curricular proposals put forth by Thanawi, Sir Syed, and Ahmed call for an educated subject whose education is to advance familial, and to some extent communal, interests. It is a subject who understands her responsibility to reproduce familial respectability and willingly pursues it. While Thanawi opens up space for women to acquire specialized knowledges—religious knowledges being historically restricted to elite Muslim men—and, hence, appears as egalitarian, his proposals are delimited by his preference for seclusion and lack of institutionalized spaces for Muslim women to acquire said knowledges. The Aga Khan and Mumtaz Ali, on the other hand, call for knowledges that might allow for the recognition of a woman's personhood. They imagine a subject who pursues education for her interests, thinks about her own economic independence, and knows and fights for her rights (after all, Mumtaz Ali's seminal text was entitled *Huquq-un-niswan,* or Women's Rights). This is especially the case in relation to the Aga Khan who gave a range of directives to his followers in order to enhance their economic welfare. Education, then, was to produce a sense of individuation in this subject and a discernment that might allow her to balance familial and communal interests with personal desires.

As I have suggested earlier, the concerns of the male reformers seem to be inflected by their own social class as well as the social groups for which they advocated. Whereas the Aga Khan may have called for women's education to increase their independence from patriarchal control, Mumtaz Ali's call for educated wives as better companions *reformulated* patriarchal control. These overlapping, yet distinct, educated subjectivities are what become a point of negotiation at the turn of the twentieth century. Women, too, participated in these discussions—an aspect that has remained understudied thus far. My examination of women's writings shows that the gender of the authors did not lead to radical departures; women's writings, thus, are part of the same knowledge regime.

WOMEN'S WRITINGS

While "Muslim women" appear as central objects of concern and reform in both colonial and nationalist discourse, official histories of Muslims in India often do not include women's own voices.[48] The dominant image of the Indian Musalman woman of the eighteenth and nineteenth centuries is one of being uneducated, silent, and secluded. However, as the evidence below will show, Muslim women were not silent objects of reform projects but actively engaged in them. Unlike their male counterparts, however, their work was often featured in periodicals, dairies, reformist literature, interviews, letters, and pamphlets—writing products that have not been considered worthy of preservation. These texts, however, give us important clues about the political and social culture of the period, as well as the dominant idioms in and through which life was lived and imagined.

Women's periodicals began to appear in many languages in colonial India around the mid-nineteenth century. These periodicals were part of a broader range of written materials, such as didactic novels, pamphlets, and *dastaans* (stories) that were increasingly becoming available due to the accessibility of the printing press. While male social reformers established most of these periodicals at the time, many took care to note the valuable partnership, sometimes co-editorship, of their wives or other female relatives. That these periodicals provided an opportunity to both men and women to educate women is evidenced by their public goals as well as their titles. For example, *Mu'allim-i-Niswan* means "Women's Teacher" and *Tehzib-e-Niswan* can be translated into "Women's Cultural Upbringing." While often men also wrote in the periodicals (sometimes even writing *as* women), the periodicals did provide women an avenue to engage with each other in multiple ways. Through the periodicals women obtained information about the activities of the British administration and Muslim social reform movements; shared child-drearing and domestic management practices; provided interesting leisure reading materials; explained cultural practices of women from other parts of the world; and practiced their writing skills and shared personal news. In the periodicals women also expressed their views on the then contested topics such as *purdah/* veiling, marriage, polygamy, right to vote, Age of Consent laws, women's dress, and education.

While this book focuses on Urdu periodicals and novels, women's writings were emerging in other languages too. In the context of colonial India, for instance, Padma Anagol has analyzed women's press in the Marathi language to illuminate the ways in which women put forth their critiques of Indian society and gender relations.[49] Anagol notes, "writing gave women the opportunity to *recast themselves* as modern women, rather than being *recast by men,* thereby preparing themselves for the rapid changes brought by the colonial world" (original emphasis).[50] She argues that it is crucial to explore the agency of women as a group in order to correct dominant portrayals of the historical moment. Other scholars have chosen to focus on individual women's lives. For example, Tapan Ray-Chaudhuri and Geraldine Forbes examine the memoirs of Haimabati Sen, a female doctor who challenged medical hierarchies,[51] Tanika Sarkar has written about the first Bengali autobiographer, Rashsundari Debi,[52] and Elora Shehabuddin has explored the work of Rokeya Hossain and her fictional text *Sultana's Dreams.*[53] Sarkar has also explored women's periodicals from Bengal to examine why Muslim women were written out of official Indian nationalist histories in the first place.[54] She argues that Brahmo/Hindu women often constructed Muslim women as the "backward" other to bolster their own image as "liberated/modern": "representation of Muslim women as 'backward/victimised' were intimately related to the production of the category modern 'ideal Indian woman' as Hindu, upper caste/middle class and the category 'Muslim' as predominantly male, violent, dissolute and 'medieval' in late colonial Bengal."[55]

Likewise, scholars concentrating on the Middle East have also found it productive to engage with women's writings in the periodicals. Marilyn Booth, for instance, examines over five hundred biographies published in Egyptian newspapers and magazines between 1892 and 1949 to highlight women's participation in negotiating modernity and nationalism.[56] She argues that by examining the biographies, we can gain insights into "what women were doing, not simply to hear the oratory of male intellectuals debating 'women's status.'"[57] Likewise, Beth Baron's work on women's periodicals published in Egypt at the turn of the twentieth century also shows the dynamism between producers and consumers of early women's press.[58] She shows how the new literary medium was a productive platform for a voracious readership to interact with each other and with editors. My work, with its focus on North Indian Muslim women's journalistic writings in Urdu, then, adds to this scholarly tradition.

Women's Magazines in Urdu

The earliest women's periodicals in the Urdu language are *Akhbar-un-Nissa*, which was issued in 1887 under the leadership of Sayid Ahmed Dehlavi, and *Mu'allim-i-Niswan*, published in 1892 by Maulvi Muhibb-e-Hussain. I was unable to find any issues of these two magazines. However, the third major periodical, *Tehzib-e-Niswan*, issued in 1898 under the editorship of Sayyid Mumtaz Ali (1860–1935) and Muhammadi Begum (1878–1908) from Lahore, has been preserved in private collections, which I was able to obtain. The next major, albeit short-lived, periodical was *Khatun*, published from 1904 to 1914 from Aligarh under the leadership of Shaikh Abdullah (1874–1965) and his wife, Wahid Jahan (1886–1939), although the former was much more involved as Jahan took up the responsibilities of administering a girls' Normal School and then a hostel. *Parda Nashin*, edited by Mrs. Khamosh, was published in 1906; *Ismat* followed in 1908, published from Delhi by Rashid al-Khairi. *Ismat* is the only magazine from this time that has survived to the present time.

During the early decades of the twentieth century, an increasing number of periodicals began to be published under the editorship of women. *Sharif Bibi*, edited by Fatima Begum, in 1910; *Zillus Sultan*, which was the official journal that expressed the views of Sultan Jahan the Begum of Bhopal, edited by Muhammad Amin Zuberi in 1913; *An-Nissa*, edited by Sughra Humayun Mirza, from Hyderabad, in 1919, who also went on to publish *Zeb-un-Nissa* from Lahore in 1934; and, *Hamjoli*, published in the 1930s under the editorship of Sauida Begum Khwishgi. The literary landscape thrived, with women not only taking up editorships but also authoring the majority of the articles in these periodicals. Soon after publishing the women's periodicals, both Mumtaz Ali and Rashid al-Khairi set out to publish a periodical explicitly for children and girls—*Phul* (for children) was published by the former in 1910 and *Bannat* (for girls) by the latter in 1927. Rashid al-Khairi also published a journal entitled *Tamaddun*, aimed at men with the objective of changing their views about women's education. *Tamaddun*, however, was short-lived, from circa 1911 to 1916.

In this chapter I make the early issues of *Tehzib, Ismat,* and *Khatun* the primary object of my inquiry, given their prominence. South Asian historian Gail Minault has called these three periodicals the "the big three"[59] of the Urdu language. She also argues that "for the study of the lives of middle class Muslim women in *purdah* and movements for their social and educational reform, women's magazines in Urdu are essential."[60] The prominence of these periodicals was confirmed during my interviews with librarians at the University of Karachi, Mushfiq Khawaja, Bedil, and the University of Punjab. Locating these magazines has been difficult as archival preservation efforts in the past often ignored women's writings.[61] Most issues are in private collections or, in some cases, at university libraries. I was able to secure a large number of issues by visiting public and private libraries in Pakistan during the summer of 2015. Specifically, I review *Tehzib* issues from 1906 (earliest available issues) to 1913, *Khatun* issues between 1906 (earliest available issues) to 1914, and *Ismat* issues from 1910, 1911, and 1919.[62]

In addition to women's journalistic writings, I also draw on two didactic novels— *Sughar beti* (1905), and *Sharif beti* (1908)[63]—and a biography, *Hayat-e-Ashraf* (1899), written by a pioneer female editor and writer, Muhammadi Begum. I bring them into dialogue with *Mirat-ul-uroos* (1869), by Nazir Ahmed, discussed earlier. These texts explicitly set out to do the pedagogical work of delineating ideal performances of Muslim womanhood and girlhood. While Nazir Ahmed's work has been discussed extensively, Muhammadi Begum's writings are still understudied since her work has not circulated in the same ways that Nazir Ahmed's has. Engaging with these novels enables me to elaborate key issues of the time and explore how literature partakes in establishing dominant regimes of truth.

Tehzib-e-Niswan, Khatun, and Ismat

Tehzib-e-Niswan (hereafter *Tehzib*), a weekly, was first published in 1898 in Lahore and was edited by Sayyid Mumtaz Ali and Muhammadi Begum. Both had established themselves as pioneers in thinking and writing about women's education and reform. Mumtaz Ali was a younger contemporary of Sir Syed Ahmed Khan, and it was known that Sir Syed did not completely agree with his views about women. In fact, Mumtaz Ali waited to publish his book, *Huquq-un-niswan,* until after the death of his mentor.[64] Mumtaz Ali was educated at the Deoband madrasa and English-medium schools, an educational trajectory that would become increasingly common for many *ashraf* men. His wife, Muhammadi Begum, was educated at home, where she learned to read the Quran and keep household accounts, develop her Urdu language abilities, and acquire the domestic management skills of sewing and cooking.[65] She was a prolific writer and, in addition to several short stories, wrote books on poetry, cooking, and housekeeping. She is undoubtedly one of the earliest Muslim female public writers in the Urdu language.

Tehzib was published with the explicit purpose of providing reading material for women. It included a diverse range of writings—articles discussed etiquette, relations with in-laws and husbands, childcare, housekeeping, recipes, news about parties, and announcements about upcoming events such as fundraising drives. Authors also expressed their opinions on ongoing debates such as *purdah*, polygamy, and wasteful expenditures at weddings. The periodical adopted language that would be comprehensible to women who had elementary reading skills. *Tehzib's* weekly format encouraged conversations among women. The letters to the editor offered another space for women to communicate with each other, seeking or offering advice, voicing opinions, or simply sharing personal news with their *behnain* (sisters). *Tehzib*, then, allowed for the emergence of a transregional community of *sharif* or *tehzibi behnain* (respectable or cultured sisters). Over time, *Tehzib* also published news about women's conferences and reproduced speeches. The journal remained active through 1949 under the leadership of various editors, including women.

Khatun was published from Aligarh between 1904 and 1914, and was edited by Shaikh Abdullah, the then secretary of the women's education section of the All India Muhammadan Education Conference,[66] and his wife, Wahid Jahan. Abdullah founded the journal as the voice of the All India Muhammadan Education Conference. The journal, therefore, provided a review of the activities of the Conference, including speeches, news of committees on women's education sponsored by the government, and information about other conferences and rallies. It had the explicit purpose of improving the landscape of women's education in addition to providing high-quality literature for women to read.[67] Its editors wanted to encourage a rigorous conversation about women's education, which included sharing their own views about how women's education could be institutionalized as well as the resources that were needed for this endeavor. Every issue of the journal opens by clarifying the purpose of the journal, specifically that it seeks to "spread education among women and to engender a knowledge-oriented disposition in educated women."[68] In an article appearing in *Khatun* published in 1906 the editors note that this endeavor will not be successful without men's attention, and the magazine thus highlights for men the need for women's education and the drawbacks of not attending to it.[69] *Khatun* imagined an audience that was already relatively literate, and therefore, did not make the concessions around writing style that *Tehzib* did. In addition, it envisioned its audience to be involved in politics and/or belonging to the social classes that had resources to raise funds for women's education. These characteristics, at the turn of the twentieth century, were shared primarily by *ashraf* men who were often the patrons of the Muhammadan Education Conference. Hence, the journal did not shy away from including writings by men for men on the topic of women's education. In fact, Shaikh Abdullah's editorials are one of the key spaces where we learn about the contemporary efforts for women's education.

Khatun, thus, was one of the key sources for me to learn about the British administration's efforts (or lack thereof) for Muslim women's education as well as the efforts of the Muslim *ashraf* classes. For example, the third volume of *Khatun*, published in 1906, provides a glimpse into the earliest efforts toward the institutionalization of women's education. Readers who needed female teachers had access to free advertisements;[70] profits from the journal's sale were used to create scholarships for poor and orphan girls; and the female readers were urged to purchase the journal as a form of self-help. Early issues of *Khatun* include a large number of calls for funding girls' schools and feature the names of those who donated funds or in-kind support for women's education. Book reviews and serialized stories were also included in the journal.[71] Altaf Hussain Hali's famous poem "Chup ki daad" (Justice for the Silent) was first published in *Khatun* in 1905.

Ismat, a monthly magazine, was issued from Delhi and is the only magazine that is still published in present-day Pakistan. Its first issue appeared in 1908, under the editorship of Rashid al-Khairi, a social reformer who also published extensively on the topic of women's education and rights in the form of didactic novels and fictional stories. Al-Khairi studied up to matriculation at the Delhi Anglo-Arabic School and was related to the well-known social reformer, Nazir Ahmed.[72] The cover of *Ismat* outlines that it is aimed at *sharif hindustani bibiyan* (respectable Indian women). The magazine featured serialized stories, editorials, commentaries on news, short articles, recipes, embroidery patterns, letters to the editor, poetry, and announcements for new books. While al-Khairi was the primary editor until his death, some issues were edited with Sheikh Akram and Mrs. Sheikh Akram as well.[73] *Ismat's* language was conversational, much like *Tehzib's.*

I view these periodicals (journalistic writings) as cases that give insights into the fractured production of the ideal womanhood. In other words, while the male social reformers—whose writings had greater circulation than women's writings—constructed ideal female educated subjects, such discursive productions inevitably erased the diversity of women's lived experiences. Attending to women's magazines sheds light on the kinds of contestations and negotiations that male-produced models created in women's literary cultures. Here we find that women often had multiple views on the topic of education, and intensely debated the appropriate knowledges, purposes, and spaces for education. The differences often emerged from women's divergent socioeconomic backgrounds. This is not to say that women departed radically from male social reformers' views. That, in fact, is not the case. What these periodicals, however, do show is the process of the very *making* of the educated subjects who were the object of the male social reformers' concerns. It shows that the production of the educated, *sharif* subject was not inevitable or straightforward. It was discussed and debated, and sometimes even rejected, by women. Thus, exploring the understudied genre of women's writings in Urdu periodicals helps to understand that women were not silent objects of reform projects but actively engaged with them.

A CONVERSATION AMONG *ISMATI BEHNAIN*

As noted earlier, in most cases, the debates around Muslim women's education were initiated by men and were aimed at women. *Khatun,* for instance, includes a plethora of evidence for this. Many of the articles are written by Shaikh Abdullah, who, as the secretary of the women's section, was at the forefront of attempts to establish schools for girls and provide training to female teachers. Likewise, Rashid al-Khairi also stressed reforms for women through his writings. In many cases, male reformers called on other men to advance reforms for women. For example, in *Ismat,* al-Khairi issued a call to Muslim preachers to take up the task of advocating for women to improve their lives.[74] In elaborating the rational for establishing *Tamaddun*—the magazine aimed at men—he argued that since men will not read women's magazines (like *Ismat*), in order to reach men they have to establish a magazine only for men;[75] and that *Tamaddun* will secure the rights of wives from husbands.[76] By the turn of the twentieth century, however, women emerged as key participants in this conversation—as writers and editors.

Consider the conversation that ensues among the daughter of Maulvi Bashiruddin (often writers who practiced *purdah* did not reveal their first names and wrote as "daughter of" or "mother of"), Begum Saheba Rizvi, and Sayyida Asghari Begum that takes place across two issues of *Ismat* in 1911, where they respond to each other's views on education. The daughter of Maulvi Bashiruddin, in her article entitled "Talim niswan" (Women's Education),[77] outlines the two sides of the debate on the issue of women's education: those who are against it and those who want the same education for women as that for men. The latter entails going to English schools and studying the curriculum determined by English standards. The author notes that since these discussions are about women, they, too, should pay attention to them. She discredits the first group by noting that since Prophet Muhammad said, "to acquire *ilm* (knowledge) is *farz* (duty) on all Muslim men and women," Muslims do not have to attend to those who argue against women's education. However, she then goes on to critique those who are in favor of English schools and provocatively asks: "What kind of education did the Prophet guide us to acquire?" To her, it is that which allows one to become a better Muslim. She then explains what this entails: women should learn to read and write in order to understand their *din* (faith); be able to send letters to their father, husband, and relatives; keep calculations about domestic chores (budget); and be able to address the everyday illnesses of their children and care for them. In short, this educated subject has knowledge of religion, elementary literacy skills, and can effectively manage her household. Any educative endeavors that do not yield such a transformation in women would be constituted as a failure. Indeed, this is precisely why the author claims that the books and novels that are taught in "English schools" are not useful as they divert women's attention to stories and fiction. Such knowledges do not fulfill the purpose of enabling women to improve their practice of religion or domestic management skills, and thus cannot be considered worthy. The author produces a dichotomy between English versus Islamic knowledges. While she advocates that women should get an education, English knowledges, often represented by novels and stories, are deemed unnecessary and even harmful. Readers will recall that this line of reasoning is very similar to that proposed by Ashraf Ali Thanawi.

In response to this article, Begum Saheba Rizvi wrote a clarification on behalf of those who supported women's education outside the *zenana*.[78] She notes that advocates like her do not believe that girls should go to English schools but to schools organized and managed by Muslims. Giving her own example, she explains that her grandfather, who was active in the women's education movement, said that it was not appropriate for Muslim girls to attend English schools due to the teaching of Christianity. Rizvi notes that Muslim girls should only join Muslim schools. The author goes on to express her grievance at the current status of the Muslim *quam* and their lack of attention to women's education. She sees this as a departure from the past, when both men and women were educated, and women excelled at many endeavors. This reference to the past is significant because it was a rhetorical strategy used by many writers, including male writers discussed earlier in this chapter. Feature articles on the lives of Muslim women of the past—such as the wives of Prophet Muhammad as well as his daughter, Fatima—were written time and again in women's periodicals to inform the readership of the long tradition of women's learning in Islam. The preponderance of such articles signals an effort to reclaim education as legitimately Islamic. The authors believed that Muslim women of the past were indeed "educated," and hence proposed that it was possible to obtain an education without attending English schools or compromising one's traditions and norms. In asserting that Muslim women of the past were intellectually accomplished and practiced proper Islam, *Ismati behnain* forged this very possibility for themselves as well.

Rizvi, however, opposes the curriculum proposed by the daughter of Maulvi Bashiruddin by noting that more substantial education was required for women, which included chemistry, literature, geography, astronomy, and history, in addition to religion. Elementary knowledge of religion, which allowed one to only study a book or two translated into Urdu (as the daughter of Maulvi Bashiruddin had suggested) was not useful. Rizvi's calls are reminiscent of Mumtaz Ali and the Aga Khan, who, too, called for broad-based education for girls. She further observes that the fact that girls do not have relevant reading materials (and hence read novels and stories that do not align with their culture and customs) is a result of men's lack of effort in making such literatures available to women, as well as the widespread support for only elementary education of women. The author concludes by calling for the establishment of an Islamic (*Islami*) girls' school.

In the same issue of *Ismat*, Sayyida Asghari Begum also responded to the article written by the daughter of Maulvi Bashiruddin. She notes that the restriction of women's education to only the study of *hadith* and *fiqh* was limiting. She explains that Muslim women in the past had been extremely accomplished and cites the example of the daughter of Prophet Muhammad, Fatima, as being a renowned poet. At the same time, she agrees with the daughter of Maulvi Bashiruddin, that "the company of missionary ladies is poisonous for our uneducated women."[79] She proposes that if women were to set aside some of their earnings for the establishment of *Islami* schools and colleges then it would not be necessary for them to go to English schools and colleges, or read inappropriate texts. She calls on male reformers to attend to women's education and raise funds as they had been doing for the establishment of the Muhammedan Anglo-Oriental College.

I have included this brief exchange among three women across two issues of *Ismat* to illustrate the vibrant conversations that were taking place among women on the topic of women's education. These dialogues resist the impression that the discourse on women's education was only shaped by men. While it is true that women called on men to attend to their needs, it is also significant to acknowledge women's own contributions to this debate. Importantly, this conversation exemplifies three different but overlapping visions of an educated subject. The daughter of Maulvi Bashiruddin sees the purpose of education as producing proper Muslims and, hence, emphasizes the acquisition of religious knowledges. Her proposal excludes the study of the English language and English literatures, as she does not envision such subjects to play a critical role in women's everyday lives. Both Rizvi and Asghari Begum call for a broad-based education that includes the study of the sciences, because they believe that if Muslim women were to reacquire their prominent positions in the world (similar to that held by Muslim women of the past, as they imagined) then they would have to partake in all available knowledges. However, they do not see English schools as the ideal location for education, as such spaces introduced ideas that were "poisonous." These fears were often associated with the preaching of Christianity in English schools as well as the study of what they considered as irrelevant literary texts written by western authors. All three writers draw on the discourse on religion to legitimize their stances. What we have then is a glimpse into *ashraf* women's negotiations around education, which also reveals the kinds of roles that they envisioned for themselves and other women of their social class.

The tensions across these different articulations of appropriate knowledges for women are also a reflection of the opportunities for livelihood that were available to women of different social classes. This becomes clearer in Muhammadi Begum's (1878–1908) didactic novels.

CURRICULUM FOR *SHARIF* DAUGHTERS

Muhammadi Begum's *Sughar beti*, published in 1905, is a meticulous and detailed account of how young girls should comport themselves in their everyday lives. Begum decided to write this text after completing *Rafiq uroos* (Friend of the Bride), which was aimed at married girls ("biyahi larkiyoon").[80] She wrote *Sughar beti* for "unmarried, young-aged, girls" ("kuwari, kam umer larkiyoon").[81] The author paints a picture of a young girl living in a *sharif* household and how she

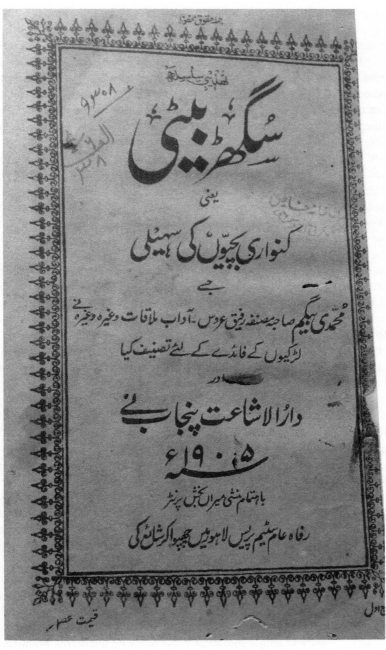

FIGURE 1. Cover page of Muhammadi Begum's *Sughar beti*.

should operate in all aspects of her life so that she excels in both *din* (faith) and *duniya* (world). The text's tone is that of a familiar friend, as the author addresses the reader using personal pronouns (such as *tum*, "you"), which helps to achieve a sense of intimacy. It also marks the reader as a *sharif* girl and the author as her well-wisher, an advisor. Muhammadi Begum shares several personal anecdotes to further establish a sense of kinship with the reader.[82] In one instance, she mentions an event from when she was sixteen years old and wanted to have a new set of clothes. The fabric the shopkeeper sent over to her, however, was see-through. She returned it, asking for thicker cloth to maintain her *haya* (shame). Much like *Mirat-ul-uroos*, *Sughar beti* sets out to be a comprehensive advice text for young girls and, in this way, is useful to explore the construction of the ideal *sharif* daughter-subject.

The text includes the story of the "ignorant girl" (*ghafil larki*) against whom the ideal girl becomes legible. The *ghafil larki* is careless, impulsive, and wasteful. She misses her morning prayers, forgets to pick up her jewelry after washing herself, fails in examinations, drops hot food on herself, and burns herself. She creates difficulties for herself and her mother. She repeatedly fails to perform an educated subjectivity not only due to her inability to read or write but also due to her failure to be a thoughtful member of the family. Ideal girlhood, in this case, is accomplished in the context of the patriarchal family and falling short of one's responsibilities in that domain marks one as a failure.

In contrast, the ideal girl possesses an awareness of God, respects and loves her parents, elders, and teachers, and successfully performs her myriad roles within the patriarchal family. Muhammadi Begum provides detailed advice on how to perform this subjectivity of the good daughter (*beti*): "do not annoy your parents to fulfill your desires for play and *asaish* (luxury)";[83] "girls should help their mothers with household chores";[84] "my dear girls, if you are clever and are able to work, then you should provide rest to your mothers. Take over the work they are doing."[85] The author goes on to explain how to sit in the presence of adults, particularly, fathers;[86] to put on *orthni* (covering) when brothers or father enter the *zenana;* and, to respect them (*tazeem*). The author also discusses personal hygiene, dress, and play. She advises girls to learn housekeeping (*khana-dari*) from their mothers but to also keep an eye out for books and other resources from where they can learn how to manage their future households. In fact, Muhammadi Begum herself wrote a book entitled, *Khana-dari* (Housekeeping).

The ideal girl is also not enticed by English norms. Muhammadi Begum advises girls to not take up the English dress because those who do are laughed upon by both their own *quam* and the English:[87] "we should continue our *quami* dress and if there are any faults we should correct them."[88] Here *quam* signifies the specific religious, class, and ethnic community that made up the *ashraf.* Muhammadi Begum urges girls to try to learn how to read and write. She argues that these skills are important so that girls can communicate with their parents and siblings after marriage and are not dependent on others. Significantly, as Muslims, she deems it incumbent upon girls to learn the Quran and know its meaning. She also advises girls to improve their writing skills, because "good writing can become a source of income for poor girls." However, literacy appears as only one component of a girl's broad-based education. Other elements include proper disposition and etiquette, as well as household management.

Another key aspect of education for Begum is learning the *hunar* (skills) of sewing, embroidery, and cooking.[89] The author emphasizes that both rich and poor girls should learn *hunar* because in times of difficulty one can meet their requirements with *hunar*. She argues that it is all the more important for women to know *hunar*, because if bad circumstances befall a man, he can always find manual labor (*mazdoori*) but such kinds of work are not available for women: "*hunar* is a blessing and all humans should seek it all their lives."[90] The author also likens *hunar* to wealth, which cannot be stolen. While women's monetary contribution to the household was still a nascent idea and did not enjoy wide support—after all, working for money was not a practice that *sharif* women undertook—given the changing economic contexts of the *ashraf,* these expectations had to be revised. Muhammadi Begum appears to be playing a role in destigmatizing both work undertaken at home so that families did not have to hire servants as well as income generation by *sharif* women. Her novel *Sharif beti* is a clear example of this rethinking of *ashraf* women's roles in the home and beyond.

In *Sharif beti,* Muhammadi Begum sets out to address girls from low-income but respectable families. Published first in 1908, the book was republished in 1912 and then again in 1918. *Sharif beti* is the story of a ten- or eleven-year-old girl, Sharif-un-Nissa—also called Sharifun, whose family descends into poverty after her father's death and her mother's subsequent illness. The text traces Sharifun's early life to show how she overcomes myriad forms of hardships while forging new pathways toward respectability. This text was quite successful, with a thousand copies printed in 1908, a second edition of another thousand copies in 1912, and then a similar number in 1918. Sharifun is *parhi likhi* (someone who can read and write), knows the Quran, was taught Urdu and Farsi by her younger brothers, and has the *hunar* of sewing and cooking. These knowledges, taken as a whole, mark her as a subject who is intelligent, thoughtful, and resourceful. The text illuminates Sharifun's resilience and work ethic in sustaining her mother and younger brothers over several years. In addition to taking up the work of sewing, Sharifun eventually opens a madrasa for girls at home, and becomes financially secure.

The text seeks to reform ideas around paid work, gender, and respectability. There is a strong thematic focus in the book on destigmatizing paid work for women and girls, and marking those girls who engage in such work as respectable. It seems that Muhammadi Begum believes that Sharifun's subject position will become commonplace in coming years as Muslim households in Lahore specifically, and North India more broadly, cope with the changing economic and social

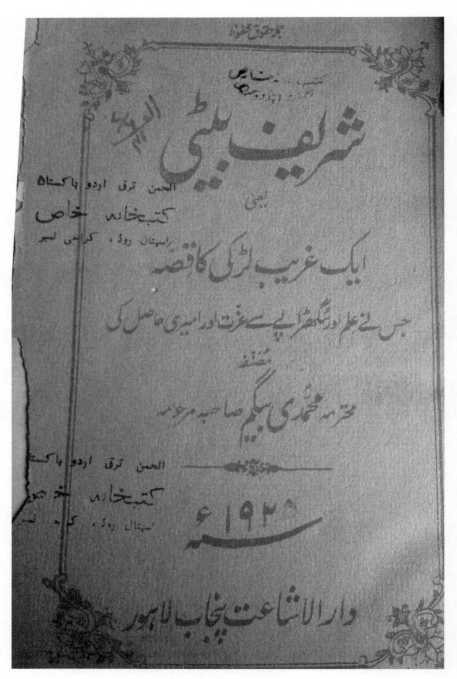

شریف بیٹی

انجمن ترقی اردو پاکستان
کتب خانہ خاص
اسپتال روڈ، کراچی نمبر

ایک غریب لڑکی کا قصہ

جس نے علم اور سگھڑاپے سے عزت اور امیری حاصل کی

مصنفہ

محترمہ محمدی بیگم صاحبہ مرحومہ

انجمن ترقی اردو پاکستان
کتب خانہ خاص
اسپتال روڈ، کراچی نمبر

سنہ ۱۹۲۵ء

دار الاشاعت پنجاب لاہور

FIGURE 2. Cover page of Muhammadi Begum's *Sharif beti*.

environment. She thus argues that to work for pay is not an *aeb* (fault). Even so, there exists a strong undercurrent in the text whereby it is assumed that working for money should be reserved only for dire situations. Such exceptions show Muhammadi Begum's struggle with competing requirements of respectability and economic precarity.

For instance, we learn that since respectable women did not work, after the death of her husband, Sharifun's mother goes to great pains to ensure that Aman-ma (their servant who used to bring them piecemeal work) did not disclose their identity to any potential clients. Likewise, when her mother falls ill and Sharifun has to take over the management of her household, she, too, privileges secrecy. She even declines offers for tutoring girls in the neighborhood in order to protect her identity. Later in the novel, we observe that Aman-ma convinces Sharifun to take up teaching in order to provide for herself and her brothers. Furthermore, Begum marks only particular kinds of work—where requirements of *purdah* could be maintained such as sewing, teaching, and nursing at home—as acceptable. This selective sanctioning continues to reproduce class boundaries because it was often not possible for lower-class women to maintain seclusion.

Muhammadi Begum's attempts at figuring out ways to reproduce *sharafat* during these economically constrained times are visible in her text, *Hayat-e-Ashraf*. In it she traces the life of another *sharif* woman who has to leave the *zenana* to earn an income upon the death of her husband, and is successful in doing so while maintaining *purdah*. One could also read the novel as showing how a woman significantly stretched the limits of acceptable practices of *purdah* when her circumstances demanded it.

Hayat-e-Ashraf

Hayat-e-Ashraf was compiled by Muhammadi Begum and includes not only Muhammadi Begum's account of Ashraf-un-Nissa's (d. 1903) life, but also articles written by Bibi Ashraf herself, in which she describes her efforts to learn reading and writing,[91] as well as the writings of Bibi Ashraf's daughter, Jafari Begum. *Hayat-e-Ashraf*, then, is a piece of writing that bears the imprint of three different women. I therefore view it as a palimpsest, layered with multiple performances of educated selves. While these different kinds of writings—letters, poems, articles—have a life of their own, they are also brought together by Muhammadi Begum, who complied them as a didactic text for young girls' reading pleasure. In the context of this chapter, *Hayat-e-Ashraf* can be viewed as a case study—the specificities of Bibi Ashraf's life circumstances, her efforts to educate herself, her desire to maintain *purdah*, her struggle for economic survival, and her staunch religious practices, are all aspects that help to ground some of the trends that I have discussed thus far. Furthermore, the text also helps to frame discussions about women's mobility and spaces for education, which will be discussed next.

Bibi Ashraf was born in 1840 in a Shia Muslim family in Bahnera, a small community in Bijnor, Uttar Pradesh. *Hayat-e-Ashraf* traces her life from birth to death;

however, as noted earlier, Muhammadi Begum chooses to include Bibi Ashraf's own words to elaborate some periods of her life. In particular, Muhammadi Begum reproduces two articles written by Bibi Ashraf, which were first published in *Tehzib-e-Niswan* in 1899, sketching her childhood. These first-person accounts provide us a glimpse into prevailing attitudes about women's reading and writing at least within the *ashraf* families of North India. Instead of finding the oppressed, silenced, victimized Muslim girl, we find a resourceful Ashraf, who through the help of her grandmother, encouragement of her father, and creative maneuverings, overcomes the hindrances of her mother's death, lack of teachers, as well as obstacles created by an uncle and an aunt, to learn how to read and write. Significantly, Bibi's Ashraf's writings give us insights into the functioning of *maktabs* for girls and the kind of curriculum available to them. The key hindrances for women's education in *Hayat-e-Ashraf* seems to be limited support from some (not all) members of the family, lack of qualified female teachers, and insufficient availability of literature/reading materials. Yet, the text is replete with examples of a thriving culture of learning among girls. Indeed, as I will elaborate below, Jafari Begum writes a poem expressing her sadness at the conclusion of her madrasa education.

Bibi Ashraf informs us that girls in her *biradari* (extended family or tribe) were taught to read for a long time, although teaching of writing had been opposed. Her own mother knew how to read the Quran and Urdu books, and it was expected that she, too, would obtain such an education. She notes that her grandfather had hired a female teacher for ten rupees per month, plus food and clothing. The teacher taught the six girls in Bibi Ashraf's household, but over time twenty to twenty-five girls from the neighborhood joined them. Hence, it became a kind of *maktab* (small school).[92] In addition to reading the Quran, the students learned how to cook and sew.[93] The teacher (who was also of similar social status—being a *sharif pathan*), however, did not know the Urdu language, and even after searching for an Urdu teacher, one could not be found.[94]

Soon, the teacher remarried—a practice (widow remarriage) that was not deemed acceptable in *sharif* households at the time.[95] This was read as a personal insult by Bibi Ashraf's grandfather, who then disallowed the teacher to teach his female relations. He was no longer willing to admit a stranger into his household. Bibi Ashraf and the other girls thus were left without a teacher. She recalls that many of the girls continued to learn from their mothers; at that time, however, her own mother fell sick, and soon passed away: "my mother was more sad about my not being able to study than her own illness."[96] This sentiment again points to the desire for learning that women of different generations seemed to have had, and the ability of older women to teach their children. Bibi Ashraf's mother was a *marsiya khwan* (a reciter of Shia elegies that commemorate the martyrdom of the grandson of Prophet Muhammad, who was a Shia imam)—pointing to women's rich oral cultures. At the time of her mother's death, Bibi Ashraf had completed seven out of thirty volumes of the Quran, and upon her grandmother's urging,[97] set out to complete the rest on her own. While there were many positive role models in Bibi Ashraf's life who urged her to read and write, we also learn about her uncle and aunt, as well as "other ladies" who discouraged her.[98] It is precisely due to this reason that she had to devise alternate, creative ways to continue her study, this time to learn the Urdu language.

Bibi Ashraf decided to obtain devotional texts from her relatives and used to sneak up to the roof during the afternoons, when others were sleeping, to copy the texts.[99] She creatively used everyday materials, such as grill ash, to produce ink, the lid of the water pot as a container for the ink, and twigs from the broom to write with. She tricked her grandmother into securing paper for her. Bibi Ashraf was delighted to be able to copy these texts—she recalls: "The happiness of that time is beyond words."[100] However, she could not read what she wrote. That is when she encountered a teacher in the most unexpected of circumstances. As she recalls, a younger male relation once asked her to help him with Quran lessons. While helping him, she found out that he knew the Urdu language and asked him to teach her. He refused, noting that he did not have the time and that she would not understand the book anyway.[101] At that point, Bibi Ashraf threatened him: "if you don't teach me, I will not teach you either."[102] This convinced the cousin, who began teaching her Urdu. He was, however, soon sent off to Delhi to study but Bibi Ashraf persisted and continued to draw on what she had learned to complete the Urdu language book on her own. She became so adept at Urdu that other women asked her to write letters on their behalf.[103] During the conflicts of 1857, her father—who worked in Delhi—could neither visit them nor write to them for a year and half. When peace was restored, her grandmother asked her uncle to write a letter on their behalf. Bibi Ashraf, however, also wrote a letter to him. Upon reading that letter, her father was extremely pleased—so much so that he sent a reward for her and praised the letter for elaborating not only the conditions of the family but also other events: "This letter gave the pleasure of reading a newspaper and history. I read it once every day."[104] Needless to add, Bibi Ashraf's paternal uncle was not happy.

I have traced Bibi Ashraf's experiences of learning and reactions from family members to highlight the specificity of girls' efforts to learn. On one hand, we have the figures of the mother, grandmother, father, and grandfather, who encouraged her to varying degrees, and on the other hand, the paternal uncle and aunt, who did not. These specific stories contradict sweeping interpretations about Muslim women and their families of the past. This does not mean that women did not have difficulties. Boys and men had far more opportunities than women: Bibi Ashraf's father was educated and worked as a lawyer; her husband was afforded an education at the Delhi College that enabled him to become an assistant professor of

Arabic and Persian at the Government College in Lahore; even the young male cousin who taught her Urdu was sent off to Delhi for education. What is interesting to note, however, is that there were figures who supported women's education, and that women creatively navigated other restrains.

It is this education that served Bibi Ashraf well upon the death of her husband when she had to provide for herself, her children, and four to five young relatives who were part of her household. Early on, she drew on her skills of sewing (including lacework) to sustain her household;[105] later, she took up a teaching job at a semi-government school in Lahore, Victoria Girls School, where she eventually became the head teacher and continued to work until her death in 1903. One of the key storylines in the text is that of Bibi Ashraf's ability to live respectably by drawing on her education and not compromising on religious practices and social norms, especially *purdah*.

Muhammadi Begum allocates significant space in the text to note that even though Bibi Ashraf worked in a school, she maintained the norms of *purdah*. Bibi Ashraf also ensured that proper arrangements for *purdah* were made for her students in the classrooms,[106] as well as during pick-up and drop-off (in the form of a *doli*—a mode of transportation for women that was covered to ensure that outsiders could not see the passengers inside). Her tenure at the school proved so successful that the school's reputation went from being one where *sharif* families would not send their girls to a school that now required seven *dolis* to transport *sharif* girls.[107] Relatedly, we also find recurring mentions of Bibi Ashraf's devotion to her Shia religious practices. She organized *majalis* (religious gatherings) every Muharram, was regular in fasting and prayers,[108] and distributed food to poor women. Bibi Ashraf also had excellent domestic management skills, which included living within her means, keeping a clean house, and being adept at cooking and sewing. This discursive representation of Bibi Ashraf serves the function of illuminating for the reader what an educated Muslim female subject could look like. The areas that Muhammadi Begum chooses to highlight—practice of *purdah*, performance of religious rituals, and *khana-dari*—were some of the prominent issues under discussion during that time as *sharif* families were concerned about the changes that education might bring about in the lives of their womenfolk. An ideal educated woman then was pious, an expert domestic manager, and could make a living if unfortunate circumstances befell her without seriously threatening the prevailing norms of her social class.

While Bibi Ashraf was able to perform this womanhood, there was less agreement on whether it was a real possibility for the majority of Indian Musalman women. Some reformers believed that women and girls should be able to leave the *zenana* to attend schools, either in the neighborhoods or even English schools; others saw the space outside the *zenana* as corrupting and therefore, a threat to familial respectability. Either way, *ashraf* women's movement in public spaces was undergoing negotiation.

SPATIALITIES OF *SHARAFAT*

In the *zenana, ashraf* women enjoyed relative freedom from the male gaze. This allowed for contact with women across socioeconomic classes and provided secrecy to some extent. In these spaces women were "in charge" of many things, including arranging marriages, prescribing the rituals and etiquettes around birth, visiting elders, and organizing feasts.[109] Women formed friendships and provided each other with support. For some *ashraf* women, as Bibi Ashraf's story shows, the *zenana* also was a place of learning. Girls often studied with tutors arranged for them in their homes or at their friends' homes. In *Hayat-e-Ashraf,* Muhammadi Begum reproduces some letters and poems written by Bibi Ashraf's daughter, Jafari Begum. One such poem, written upon the conclusion of Jafari Begum's time at the girls' *madrasa,* gives us a glimpse into the solidarity that girls experienced in such environments.

In the poem Jafari Begum calls her classmates *hamjholiyan* (friends) and *behnain* (sisters).[110] She recalls the different kinds of activities that they undertook, from poring over maps and copying texts to learning to cook and sew. We get a sense of intense friendship among the girls; for instance, whenever Jafari Begum had to take time off from the madrasa other girls complained that the place felt empty (*sunsaan*).[111] The poet also expresses nostalgia for the time she spent in the madrasa with her friends.[112] Similarly, Bibi Ashraf notes how her eagerness to learn Urdu was the result of the time she spent in such spaces. When she was young she would observe other women read aloud from books during the *majlis* held every Thursday and during the month of Muharram: "all women from the *kunba* (extended family) knew Urdu very well."[113] It was in such gatherings that the desire to learn the language sparked in Bibi Ashraf. In fact, it was also women from this broader *biradari* (tribe) who lent her the books of devotional literature that she would sneak up to the roof and copy.

Over time, however, both the colonial officers as well as Muslim reformers became suspicious of the *zenana.* Hidden from the male gaze, the *zenana* had allowed princely women to engage in politics while avoiding surveillance from British administrators.[114] As Barbara Ramusack notes: "Since the British did not have direct access to the *zenana* or women's quarters, they were particularly anxious to reduce the influence of Indian women, whom they stereotyped as superstitious and of doubtful morality. Here the British conflated their Oriental concepts of the exoticism of Asian women, especially an uncontrolled sexuality and lack of intelligence, with British disdain for alternative sources of identity for young princes."[115]

Likewise, Muslim reformers, such as Thanawi, while advocating the practices of seclusion and *purdah,* had embarked on an effort to reform the *zenana* by installing men in charge. We observe this gradual transformation of the *zenana* in *Mirat-ul-uroos,* where Asghari constantly looks to her father, Durandesh Khan, for guidance. Durandesh Khan had sent her a letter upon her marriage, which included instructions on how she should conduct herself. She read the letter at least once a day, even if it was not necessary. When in need of advice, Asghari often wrote to her male relations to come to her rescue. In other words, it was men who prescribed the appropriate ways of managing the household, and women implemented their visions.

This reconfiguration of women's spaces is not unique to colonial India. Afsaneh Najmabadi observes a reconstitution of women's spaces in Iran as well, where calls for greater participation of women in public spaces decreased the privileges that they had enjoyed in homosocial spaces.[116] Likewise, Lila Abu-Lughod critiques the elite Egyptian reformer Qasim Amin's calls for educating elite women and girls to improve their domestic management skills as another effort to "impose on women a new form of industriousness and new standards of household work that are more demanding of their time, keeping them bound to the home rather than permitting them time to visit."[117] The anxieties around women meeting each other emerged in the context of colonial India as well. The ideal *sharif* woman did not engage in frivolous relations with lower-class women, as is clearly visible in *Mirat-ul-uroos*. Similarly, Muhammadi Begum's protagonist in *Sharif beti*, Sharifun, and her mother take care not to disclose their financial difficulties to their neighbors.

This suspicion of women's activities and cross-class exposure also had an impact on the debate around ideal spaces for women's education. Could women leave the *zenana* to attend English schools? Islamic (*Islami*) schools? Neighborhood (*mohalla*) schools? What would be the implications of such movements on the practices of *purdah*? How would class distinctions be maintained? After all, it was only *ajlaf* women who moved extensively in the public spaces. Indeed, as the president of the Muhammadan Education Conference, Mamtajul Mulk Khalifa Sayyid Muhammad Hussain of Patiala, noted in 1905, "while all educated families agreed on the importance of educating girls, there were still differences in *how* and *where* that education should be given."[118]

Mrs. Abdullah, the coeditor of *Khatun,* was acutely aware of such anxieties and their implications for women's education. During the inaugural Ladies Conference in December 1905, she made a speech in which she noted that those who were against women's education often saw women's *mil jhol* (interactions) with fear.[119] They dreaded that their daughters and daughters-in-law, if educated, would become like the women in America and Europe, whom they viewed with suspicion. However, Mrs. Abdullah assured the audience that Muslim women in Turkey and Egypt were also educated and continued to meet with each other, and had not engaged in any offensive habits (*kharabiyan*)—after all "why would *kharabiyan* emerge when *sharif* women are meeting together?" She argued that "men have extended the injunctions for *hijab* and *purdah* to call for restrictions on women's movements; however, that is changing as some men see such rituals as excessive." She went on to observe that there were also women who believed that not meeting other women (*mil jhol*) preserved their *sharafat*—"women believe that *sharafat* is within the four walls of their homes and people outside it are not *sharif* and, hence, do not deserve to be engaged." However, Mrs. Abdullah proposed that education would bring about a change in such forms of thinking. In other words, education would reform Muslims so that institutions such as public schools, too, could emerge as viable spaces for respectability. Mrs. Abdullah sought to advance women's education by allaying fears that entering new educative spaces or leaving the *zenana* might lead to corruption in women. She articulated activists (much like herself) who were already in these spaces as *sharif.* This move was crucial because Mrs. Abdullah was part of the group that called for separate schools for girls. In fact, she and her husband established a Normal School in 1906, which later also included a hostel. She and her sister dedicated much of their lives to these schools. Other women, such as the Fairzi sisters and the Begum of Bhopal, were also active in establishing and/or raising funds for such institutions.[120] Redefining the spatialities of *sharafat* in this manner was significant in order to encourage girls' participation in such schools.

It is in this environment that Muslim reformers became particularly interested in establishing schools that represented their values. During the meetings of the All India Muhammadan Educational Conference, a forum established by Sir Syed Ahmed Khan in 1886, some leaders proposed that a more concerted effort should be made to establish institutions for women's education. In the third annual meeting of the conference in 1888, it was resolved that Muslims should set up *zenana maktab* (female schools) "strictly in conformity with the traditions and respect of the respectable and well-bred Mohammadans, and in accordance with their religious injunctions."[121] While Sir Syed rejected these proposals in 1889 and again in 1891, after his death in 1899 a number of leaders in the conference marked it as a priority. That year the conference passed a resolution for setting up a girls' school in the capital of every province, and the next year called for preparing appropriate books for Muslim girls. The 1905 Muhammadan Education Conference was another key platform where different visions for women's education were debated and discussed. Here, a major proposal was the establishment of a boarding school for girls. In the presidential address at the conference, Mamtajul Mulk noted that various groups had divergent preferences for how girls should be educated and called on the attendees to work on these multiple pathways.[122] Those who were willing to give education privately should do so, and those who could create madrasas should do that as well. Hence, there was a recognition and acceptance of multiple points of view on the issue, which took into account preferences that reflected social class interests as well.

Many social reformers set out to establish schools in the late nineteenth and early twentieth centuries. These efforts included Munshi Muhammad Qasim's school in Bangalore, established in 1867; Amina Khatoon's school in Baroda, in 1895; the Aga Khan III's effort to establish schools for girls, in 1905, in Gwader and Mundra; the Aligarh Zenana Madrasa, established by Shaikh Abdullah and Wahid

FIGURE 3. Girls at a convent school, ca. 1873. (Figs. 3–6 retrieved from Native Pakistan website, http://nativepakistan.com/photos-of-karachi [accessed January 23, 2018]).

Jahan in 1906; and Rokeya Hossain's school in Calcutta in 1911, among others. Such schools were often supported by elite Muslims such as the Begum of Bhopal and the numerous other Muslim women who sent donations to Shaikh Abdullah and whose names appeared in the issues of *Khatun*,[123] through grant-in-aid awarded by the British administration, and/or funds raised within Muslims communities through *farmaish* (exhibitions) and *meena bazaars* (women's shopping spaces).[124] Christian missionaries, who also had *zenana*-visitation programs in place since the early nineteenth century, primarily ran the government schools.

Figures 3 through 6 depict the different kinds of schools operative at the turn of the twentieth century. Even a cursory comparison of the photographs gives us a glimpse into the anxieties around the changes that English education might have introduced. In figure 3, for instance, girls who attend Christian missionary schools are donning English/western clothes and there are paintings of Jesus and Mary on the wall. In comparison, girls in figure 4 seek to maintain *purdah,* are learning the Urdu alphabet, and in addition to the female *ustaani,* there also appears to be a male guardian present. Likewise, in figure 5, girls appear to be wearing dresses, which later became a target of admonishment (as the next chapter will show).

FIGURE 4. A vernacular girls' school, ca. 1873.

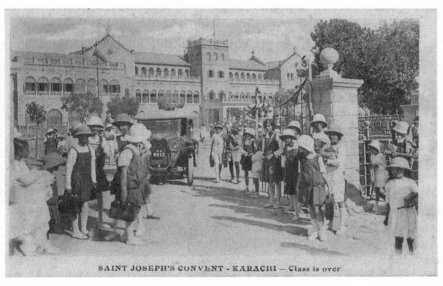

SAINT JOSEPH'S CONVENT - KARACHI — Class is over

FIGURE 5. St. Joseph's Convent School for Girls, established in 1862.

SAINT JOSEPH'S CONVENT - KARACHI — Drawing Class

FIGURE 6. A drawing class at St. Joseph's Convent School for Girls.

A large number of *purdah*-observing women did not want to send their daughters to government schools. Hence, during the Ladies Conference of 1905, a key resolution was passed to establish a Normal School in Aligarh for training teachers who would teach *sharif* girls at home.[125] This demand for teachers came from elite Muslims, and fundraising efforts, too, drew on the support of these Muslims. Such efforts and activism for women's education continued and strengthened during the early decades of the twentieth century as a greater number of associations advocating for women's education were established. For example, Anjuman-Islamia (Association of Islam) was formed in 1876 and set up a girls' primary and secondary school; Anjuman-i-Muslim Khawateen (Association of Muslim Women) was established at Nagpur; and, in 1908, Sir Muhammad Shafi founded Anjuman-i-Khawateen-i-Islam (Association of Islamic Women) in Lahore with Begum Shafi as the president.

While in the discussion thus far we observe a consensus around the need for women's education and an effort to devise multiple avenues for women to obtain education, this was still an elite phenomenon. Literacy among women was below one percent,[126] and according to the reports collected by the Muhammadan Educational Conference, female education was the lowest priority of the British government. For example, in an editorial in *Khatun* in 1906,[127] we learn about the details of a committee set up by the British on women's education. After six months, the committee submitted a report to the government noting that while the government had promised in August 1905 to reserve budget for women's education, it had not yet done so by the following year. The editor, Shaikh Abdullah, expressed his disappointment at this inaction by the government. He noted that even after recognizing its responsibility towards girls' education the government did not do anything: "Until now it was argued that Hindustani people do not want to educate their women, and that's why the government did not want to raise the issue. However, that is no longer the case. Thousands of people want to educate their daughters and sisters, then why is the government not helping and leading us and is being lazy? A cultured government no longer has any excuse."[128]

ATTACHING RESPECTABILITY TO WOMEN'S PERFORMANCES

South Asian historian Sanjay Seth provocatively asks that if by the turn of the twentieth century there was an agreement around the need for educating women, why then was there still so much discussion about this topic?[129] In this chapter I have shown that women's education was a topic of extensive discussion because it was linked with notions of familial *sharafat*. While there was an agreement that women made the ideal site to display familial social status, there was less agreement on *which* kinds of performances of women would signal this *sharafat*. It is against this background that different articulations about women's knowledges and spaces for education traced in this chapter become meaningful. They point to an effort by Muslim reformers, both men and women, to *make* good middle-class wives and mothers, as well as potential future workers. It is an effort that transformed women's homosocial spaces, which had encouraged cross-class contact and alliances as well as kin-based activities, into a space where men were increasingly in charge. Eventually the *zenana* would be replaced by the nuclear family, under the control of the father/husband.

These trends crystalized group boundaries along class lines. Whereas in the past, elite as well as poor women were considered the weaker, corruptible sex, and hence excluded from the domains of men, now, *ashraf* women were able to participate in at least some public spaces and knowledges previously restricted only to men. Lower-class women still could not access the kinds of educational opportunities that have been reviewed in this chapter and constituted the *other* of *sharif* women. In other words, women from the nobility and new *ashraf* social classes were able to reinscribe their *sharif* status through education, but women from lower-income classes who were omitted from previous ethnic/class-based definitions of *sharafat* continued to be excluded. Indeed, in Nazir Ahmed's *Mirat-ul-uroos,* while both Akbari and character of the *hajjan* appear as subjects whose conduct does not conform to the expectations of ideal womanhood, only Akbari is portrayed as a salvageable subject (as she later reforms her ways). The *hajjan* who belongs to the lower class continues to appear as a failed subject. Likewise, the *ghafil larki* (ignorant girl) of Muhammadi Begum's *Sughar beti,* too, can be rescued via education because after all she is still a *sharif larki.*

In the next chapter, we will observe that the tension around appropriate knowledges for women continues to persist in post-independence Pakistan, where those who were educated in convent/missionary schools come to be marked as failed subjects. There is a resounding call for the newly established nation to produce a new kind of educated citizen-subject, one who is grounded in local languages and religion, and will participate in the development of Pakistan. The discourse on *sharafat* which helped define ideal orientations to self, others, family, and religion, now is linked with the discourse on ideal Pakistani citizen-workers, performing the same functions of defining orientations but now also including those toward the nation and waged work.

Disaggregating the Girl/Woman

Before moving on to the next chapter, I want to pause and note here that I read the turn of the twentieth century as a moment that launches the disaggregation of the category of the woman/girl. As noted in the first chapter, Ruby Lal has observed that while during the early decades of the nineteenth century we can detect a female figure engaged in playful activities who can be read as a "girl," this figure morphs over the course of the century into a composite of girl-child/woman.[130] Girls come to be invoked primarily as future wives and future mothers. The texts that I have surveyed in this chapter from the turn of the twentieth century show instances where the girl-child/woman is articulated outside the discursive frames of future wife and future mother as well. Women's writings provide evidence of multiple and complex female figures: engaged in play (*Sughar beti; Hayat-e-Ashraf*), as students (Sharifun and her students; Akbari's students; Bibi Ashraf), and as contributors to household income (Sharifun). There appear subjects who are willing to travel and live in boarding schools to acquire an education, who are transforming the space of the home into a madrasa, and who decide to work in the public sphere as teachers, political activists, and editors. These subjects understand their circumstances and engage with them in a thoughtful manner. Their education often includes the study of the Quran, seminal texts in Arabic, Persian, and Urdu, and domestic management skills as well as skills that could potentially be monetized. They are economically dependent on their male relations but can put together a meager income in dire circumstances. In some cases (such as that of Bibi Ashraf), they may also be able to find employment within the colonial administration.

The archives explored in this chapter, thus, begin to add layers to the dominant characterizations of the girl-child/woman as a future mother and future wife. The Muslim girl-child/woman of the turn of the twentieth century is a future domestic manager, future mother, and future wife but also a student, traveler, editor, writer, and activist. Furthermore, as we move forward to the 1920s (a period not taken up in this book), periodicals such as *Phul* (first edition, 1910) and *Bannat* (first edition in 1927), and novels such as *Musalman larkiyoon kay liyay* (For Muslim Girls), published by Khuwaja Banoo Saheba in 1929, among others, specifically invoke terms such as *larki* and *bachi* in addition to the usual dominants terms of *niswan* and *khatun* that circulated in the nineteenth century. These texts, written for the girl's (*larki*) reading pleasure, to teach her elementary language skills and prepare her for married life, also bring into being these very subjects. Indeed, as the twentieth century progresses, we observe the consolidation of the category of "girl" as she becomes one of the most prominent sites of monitoring and regulation through the expansion of mass schooling.

3

Desirable and Failed Citizen-Subjects

The print advertisement in figure 7, from 1962, features the newly launched national airline, the Pakistan International Airlines (PIA). It signifies the early efforts of the state of Pakistan to modernize and develop, while enlisting its citizens, both men and women, to participate in the nation-building project. The ad boasts the airline's competent staff—pilots and hostesses—but in the process naturalizes women's caregiving roles. While PIA's pilots have received specialized training, its hostesses are simply extending the caregiving services that they have been providing within the patriarchal home for centuries to now the aviation industry. This formulation also serves another purpose: it calls on women to join the aviation industry without seriously disrupting established norms of femininity.

Upon its founding, Pakistan faced myriad challenges from territorial disputes with India and limited economic and administrative resources to a weak democratic structure. Millions of refugees from India had to be rehabilitated, which put intense pressure on the government. The country inherited meager educational and industrial institutions and, hence, immediately launched into building these resources in order to become competitive. Discussions about modernization, linked with technological and scientific advancement, as well as questions about the role of Islam in the new nation, consumed the emerging bureaucracy, state leaders, and newly created citizens. The moment also called for a clear articulation of an ideal Pakistani citizen-subject. Therefore, we find extensive discussion on the topic, which includes not only political discourses and visualities but also attempts by the citizens themselves to define what it means to be a "Pakistani." The figure of the educated female citizen-subject emerges as a meaningful discursive space to map out the different tensions, hopes, and desires that circulated during this moment.

on the world's most
interesting airline

our pilots have been
trained for years...

our hostesses,
for centuries.

Why fly to London on a Pakistani plane? One reason: PIA pilots are
talented. They're experienced, Pakistan and American licensed. They're
good. So are our hostesses. They've been taught by their mothers (who
were taught by theirs and so on) that serving guests beautifully is a
pleasurable duty. Want something? Look up. Your hostess is at your
elbow. Come join us. We fly Boeing 707 jet flights to London, Rome,
Beirut, Tehran and Karachi. Have your travel agent book you aboard.

PAKISTAN INTERNATIONAL AIRLINES WHERE PEOPLE TO FLY WITH
608 Fifth Avenue, New York 20, New York / LT 1-0600

FIGURE 7. PIA advertisement, 1962: "On the world's most interesting airline, our pilots have been trained for years . . . our hostesses, for centuries."

Specifically, in this chapter, I examine the articulations of educated female subjects during the early decades after the political establishment of Pakistan (roughly
1947–67). I review education policy documents published by the government of
Pakistan; speeches by politicians; *Ismat* issues published between 1948 and 1963;[1]
Tehzib-e-Niswan issues published in 1948 and 1949;[2] an academic study entitled *The
Educated Pakistani Girl*, written by Asaf Hussain and published in 1963; as well as
archival photographs. The sources centered in this chapter focus primarily on West
Pakistan (today's Pakistan) and were written in the Urdu or English languages.[3]

The ideal educated girl of this period emerges at the nexus of discourses on
nation building, modernization, and religion. Education was meant to shape girls
into ideal citizen-subjects—an articulation that was gendered. Women and men
were expected to perform different duties to advance the state's agenda of development and modernization. Women were idealized primarily as mothers of future
citizens or as daughter-workers (like the hostesses in figure 7). In addition, particular kinds of educated female subjects were deemed to be undesirable for the emerging nation, including girls who were enamored by the West and its cultures. Thus,
women and girls were cast as either modern or as failed, with the state participating
in the production of these definitions through its institutional policies as well as
discursive support for particular representations of femininity.

A NATION-IN-THE-MAKING

British colonizers had tried to make sense of the diversity in India by categorizing
its population along religious lines through practices such as the census and cartography.[4] These categorizations, over time, were taken up by Indians themselves,
who moved away from their syncretic Hindu-Muslim (Hindustani) cultural history
and language, and toward distinct nationalist groups, calling for separate home-
lands.[5] Upon the conclusion of the First World War, for instance, a pan-Islamist
movement, the Khilafat Movement, called on the British to protect the caliphate
in Turkey and united Indian Muslims to rally behind this cause. Divisions along
religious lines were further exacerbated by the intransigence of the Indian National
Congress to award constitutional protections to Muslims, as well as the steady
conflation of "India" with "Hindu."[6] By the 1930s, the Muslim League emerged as
the political party that represented the interests of all Muslims. It capitalized on
Congress's refusals to admit religious distinctions and proposed a separate homeland for Muslims. Even though the leadership of the Muslim League was composed of liberals such as Muhammad Ali Jinnah and Liaquat Ali Khan, the party
drew on religion to create a broad alliance across different factions of Muslims.
It was during the 1940 session of the All India Muslim League that the "Lahore
Resolution" first articulated the political demand for the formation of autonomous
states where Muslims were in a majority. The Indian National Congress rejected
the plan and clashes between the Congress and the Muslim League continued until
the establishment of Pakistan in 1947.

Pakistan, which comprised of Muslim-majority states and parts of Bengal and Punjab (divided along communal lines), was imagined as the land where ordinary Muslims would live prosperously and have economic opportunity. The official proposal for Pakistan, however, remained distinctly clear of religious ideology. After all, Muhammad Ali Jinnah, the president of the Muslim League, was a secularist and did not intend to mix religion and politics. When the Muslim religious scholars or *ulama* tried to insert religious ideology (specifically the role of Islamic law or sharia) in the proposals for Pakistan, Jinnah remained firm on his stance, stating: "Whose Shariah? Hanafis? Hanbalis? Sha'afis? Malikis? Ja'afris? I don't want to get involved. The moment I enter the field, the *ulama* will take over for they claim to be experts and I certainly don't propose to hand the field over to [them] . . . I am aware of their criticism but I don't propose to fall into their trap."[7]

However, soon after the establishment of Pakistan, Jinnah passed away in 1948 and the *ulama*, who before the partition had sided with the Indian Congress over the Muslim League, now sought to influence the trajectory of the new nation of Pakistan. In this context, questions around how Islam should be taken up by the nation-state became prominent: Is Pakistan an Islamic state or is it a state for Muslims? How should religion be part of the nation's discourse? What is the role of sharia? Furthermore, the early establishment officers drew on religious ideology to mask the ethnic and linguistic diversity of what came to be known as Pakistan. The state, thus, emphasized its common religious identity to bind its diverse population. After Jinnah's death, the prime minister of Pakistan, Liaquat Ali Khan, explicitly solicited support from Islamist elements. The "Objectives Resolution" passed in March 1949 referred to Islam as the "religion of the state" and noted that the "principles of democracy, freedom, equality, tolerance and social justice as enunciated by Islam shall be fully observed."[8] The newly emergent nation was drawing on the discourse of Islam to establish its distinct identity. This orientation was also visible in the realm of language policies, personal laws, and—what I am concerned with—educational policies and curricula.

During the 1950s, as the state set out to establish its industries, attend to the needs of its citizens, and neutralize the threat of recolonization by India, it became increasingly authoritarian and centralized. South Asian Studies scholar Saadia Toor observes that the state adopted repressive policies against those who opposed centralization.[9] Furthermore, this decade was marked by heavy U.S. influence in the country. Since the British had aligned with India, Pakistan sought assistance from the United States (after failing to capitalize on preliminary interest from the Soviet Union), and the United States found it beneficial to engage with Pakistan in order to contain the Soviet influence.[10] The United States was interested in "using the Karachi-Lahore area of Pakistan as a base for air operations against the USSR and a staging area for forces engaged in the defense or recapture of Middle Eastern oil areas."[11] Over the years, Pakistan received economic and military assistance from the United States. In addition, the United States was allowed to set up secret intelligence bases and conduct surveillance work. Hence, during the 1950s, Pakistan became "America's most allied ally."[12]

This alliance, however, had destabilizing effects for Pakistan, as the United States encouraged undemocratic and conservative tendencies in the country. It saw religion as a cultural bulwark against communism and, thus, favored a strong central government that allied with particular interpretations of Islam to unify its diverse population. The CIA-backed Pakistan Committee of the Congress for Cultural Freedom, for instance, hosted seminars, talks, and published materials that marked Islam as the potential middle road between capitalism and communism.[13] Furthermore, instead of encouraging democratic practices in the nation, U.S. officials, drawing on modernization theory, argued that a strong military would be best positioned to lead Pakistan onto the path of modernization, a move that clearly aligned with its own objectivities of curbing the Soviet influence. Hence, in 1958, with American support, the military general Ayub Khan (1958–68) came into power through a coup. Although the ruling party—the Muslim League—was already demonstrating authoritarian tendencies, under Ayub, Pakistan underwent greater centralization. While this period saw the growth of industries, the income gap widened. Ayub's pro-business policies created a welcome environment for tourists, foreign businesses and investments in Pakistan; however, the elite retained the profits. The Kashmir war between Pakistan and India in 1965 proved to be a turning point in the U.S.-Pakistan relationship. The United States did not provide much assistance to Pakistan during the war, instead placing sanctions on the nation while India continued to receive assistance from Moscow. This was viewed as a stab in the back by many authorities in Pakistan. Ayub thus decided that while it was prudent to maintain relations with the United States, it was also critical to establish relations with other major powers, including Muslim nations.

Meanwhile, the state continued to draw on the language of Islam to construct a homogenous population. To ensure that the *ulama* provided an interpretation of Islam that was inline with the state's modernizing agendas, an advisory Council of Islamic Ideology was proposed in the Constitution of 1962, which together with research undertaken by the Islamic Research Centre provided religious interpretations that were pro-development. Educational institutions, too, were to play a critical role in modernizing the populace through training in the sciences and technology, as well as by forging citizens who exhibited a modern relationship to the state and Islam.

Education for Modernization and Citizenship

At the time of Pakistan's independence, it is estimated that 85 percent of the population was illiterate, more so in the rural areas.[14] Education policy in the newly independent state followed some of the broad contours set by the colonial administration—such as maintaining the office of the Ministry of Education and education departments at central and provincial levels—as well as the objective of developing key economic sectors of the nation. The British had a functionalist view of education, which was concerned with producing a critical mass of subjects who could run the colonial administrative apparatus and respond to the needs of the colonial economy. The bureaucrats in post-independence Pakistan drew heavily from this approach. Education scholar Ayaz Naseem notes that "the main aim of the educational policy was to create a class of administrators (the civil bureaucracy) and a labor pool that could keep the economy of the new state in line with the demands of the peripheral capitalist system."[15] At the same time, public education was also a key mechanism through which a homogenous citizenry could be produced out of the diverse elements that now formed Pakistan. A review of the early education policy documents as well as speeches by politicians and educators gives us a glimpse into this purpose of education: to produce a Muslim worker-citizen-subject.

During the first National Education Conference, which was held in Karachi from November 27 to December 1, 1947, Muhammad Ali Jinnah emphasized the need to institute an educational system that would make Pakistan competitive with the rest of the world. He noted: "There is no doubt that the future of our State will and must greatly depend upon the type of education we give to our children, and the way in which we bring them up as future citizens of Pakistan. . . . We should not forget that we have to compete with the world which is moving very fast in this direction."[16]

From the beginning then, there was a desire for the nation to obtain a competitive edge, which led to an emphasis on advancing technological and scientific knowledges. As Jinnah explained, "There is immediate and urgent need for training our people in scientific and technical education in order to build up our future economic life, and we should see that our people undertake scientific commerce, trade and particularly, well-planned industries."[17] In addition, education was also seen as crucial preparation grounds for creating a democratic citizenry. As Fazl-ur-Rehman, the federal minister of education, noted in 1953: "It goes without saying that the existence of a large bulk of illiterate population constitutes a grave menace to the security and well being of the state. There is now general agreement that in its own interest the state should provide for its boys and girls universal compulsory and free basic education which is the primary requisite training in democracy."[18]

Earlier in 1948, he had argued that the education system would also transmit universal Islamic values in the populace:

> The need for radical reorganisation of the education system to accord with national requirements and aspirations cannot be emphasised too strongly. It also needs no arguing that the education system in Pakistan should be inspired by Islamic ideology emphasising among many of its characteristics those of universal brotherhood, tolerance and social justice. . . . The education system in Pakistan has therefore to embody and reflect those ideals which have been shaped and molded by Islam, [which] far from being a set of dogmas and rituals is a positive philosophy of life and pervades all

aspects of human activity. It is, therefore, imperative that so fundamental an activity as education should be inspired by the spirit of Islam.[19]

Education, then, from the very outset was described as a critical apparatus of the state that would enable it to compete economically, create a democratic citizenry, and impart the proper spirit of Islam. Therefore, literacy became one of the key sites for investment by the state. During the first National Education Conference it was proposed that universal primary education would be achieved within twenty years. However, it soon became apparent that such a target was improbable due to the lack of teachers. Hence, the National Plan of Educational Development of 1951–57 changed the focus to providing teacher-training institutes. While not much progress was made on this front either, the general rhetoric around education remained linked with labor needs and the progress of the nation. The government of Pakistan's five-year plan for 1955–60, for instance, notes:

> Primary education is essential to prepare citizens for the discharge of their democratic and civic responsibilities and to provide them with equal opportunities for economic and cultural advancement. It is essential to the nation as a base for the entire structure of secondary and higher education from which will come leadership in all walks of life and support for technical development in agriculture and industry.[20]

The plan also declared that, "owing to inadequate attention to the scientific and industrial development of the country in the past, a false prestige has been assigned to literary attainments rather than manual dexterity and pride in craftsmanship and technical accomplishment."[21]

A major effort to reorganize the educational system of Pakistan was undertaken during the early years of General Ayub Khan's regime. Ayub's government placed a high priority on education for its capacity to usher in modernity. He established a Commission on National Education, which prepared a report in 1959 that incorporated suggestions made by earlier commissions, conferences, and five-year plans. The Report of the Commission (which was also known as the Sharif Report) proposed curriculum reforms that would enable the development of "basic skills in reading and writing and arithmetic, a liking for working with one's own hands and high sense of patriotism."[22] It also noted that the educational system should produce workers needed for the economy, including the executive class, supervisory personnel, and skilled clerical workers.[23] The second five-year plan (1960–65) also described the intimate connections across education, national identity, and economic growth-driven development. Thus, education was to produce worker-citizens and launch the nation into industrial modernity. As Ayub Khan said during a Curriculum Committee meeting in 1960, "Of all the reforms we have initiated in the last 20 months . . . the reconstruction of the education system is the one closest and dearest to my heart. No economic planning, social progress, or spiritual enlightenment can make such headway without [a] sound, solid and realistic base of good education."[24]

Pakistan's educational agendas were also influenced by foreign elements via aid and technical expertise. Since the introduction of science and technology was assumed to be a key practice through which the nation could modernize, a number of polytechnics were established with foreign technical assistance.[25] Furthermore, changes in agricultural management were made in consultation with the British government.[26] A number of foreign agencies and academic institutions, including UNESCO, the Harvard Development Advisory Service,[27] and the Ford Foundation took an active interest in curriculum and teaching in Pakistan. For instance, the U.S. Educational Foundation, one of the Fulbright commissions, was established as early as 1950 in Pakistan. The commission responsible for the 1959 Sharif Report included representatives of western universities such as Cambridge, Indiana, Oklahoma State, Michigan State, Chicago, and Columbia, and foundations such as the Ford Foundation and the Carnegie Institute.[28] Education scholar Shahid Siddiqui critiques this foreign involvement in the Sharif Report by noting the distinct lack of representation of Pakistanis: "Two out of the four experts engaged in the preparation of Pakistan Education policy were foreigners, i.e. Dr. Herman B. Wells, President of Indiana University, Bloomington, USA, and Dr. John C. Warner, President Carnegie Institute of Technology, Pittsburgh, USA. The two other Pakistani experts, Dr. I. H. Qureshi and Dr. Abus Salam, were also engaged in teaching in foreign university—Dr. Qureshi at Columbia University, New York and Dr. Salam at Imperial College, London."[29] Siddiqui observes that these relationships were particularly fruitful for foreign universities as they set up research institutes in Pakistan where their faculty could engage in research and teaching. Ford Foundation's ambitions in Pakistan's education sector have also been documented, whereby some officials of the foundation offered to help with the architecture of Islamabad in order to gain favors for longer-term involvement in Pakistan's educational future.[30] This reliance on foreign monies and expertise has continued to the present, as I elaborate in the next chapter. It is against this background that I analyze the state's calls for girls' education.

While girls' education received attention across all the official education policy plans, in the second five-year plan it was particularly noted that,

> of the 4.7 million children presently attending primary schools, only 1.1 million are girls. Clearly, girls must be provided with much greater opportunities for primary education. This will be done both by admitting girls to more of the existing primary schools, and by ensuring that where separate facilities are required a much larger proportion is assigned to schools for girls.[31]

During the same time period—on November 8, 1961—a conference that brought together government officials as well as educators (a detailed overview of which is available in *Ismat*),[32] called for women's education to enhance the workforce, but also noted the lack of teachers and facilities as key hindrances. It seems that, while girls' education was always on the agenda, limited resources prohibited any

FIGURE 8. Teachers attending to first- through fourth-grade students in a village near Lahore (December 1947). Photo by Margaret Bourke-White / The Life Picture Collection / Getty Images. Reproduced with permission.

FIGURE 9. A teacher teaching at the Sind Moslem College; female students are seated behind the wall, which functions as *purdah* (December 1947). Photo by Margaret Bourke-White / The Life Picture Collection / Getty Images. Reproduced with permission.

significant progress. Figures 8 and 9 show some of the educational spaces that were operative in the new nation.

More broadly, the Pakistani state institutions saw women primarily through two registers: nation building and development/modernization. In the former case, women's bodies came to be bound intimately with the national project of reproducing Pakistan's citizenry—biologically as well as culturally; and with regard to the latter, middle-class women were seen as an untapped workforce whose productivity was needed for the development and modernization of the new nation. Since low-income women were already active in the informal economy, it was middle-class women who were the focus of the state's attention. The emergence of these subject positions for women coincides with the increasing professionalization of mothering, which in turn was an effect of the popularity of the scientific disciplines of psychology and social work.

DESIRABLE SUBJECTS

The Sharif Report called for women's education to make women function better within the patriarchal family and contribute to the patriarchal state: "For it is the home-makers of the nation who can best instill the values of order and beauty in the consciousness of the rising generation."[33] Furthermore, the report identified areas of study and professions deemed appropriate for women, or those that might come "naturally" to them:

> elementary homecraft, needlework, tailoring, weaving, cooking and home and child-care. It is suggested that vocational centers for women should teach nursing, teaching, photography, typing, textile printing, commercial cooking, hospital aid, dietetics, nutrition expertise, textile design, supervision of village aid hospitals, supervision of bursary schools, midwifery, child psychology, household management, interior decoration, and for national emergency situations women should learn to become stenographers, typists, clerks, secretarial workers and telecommunication operators.[34]

Such didactic messages from the state also circulated through other channels, such as mass media linked to its industries, particularly the tourism and aviation industries. In addition to the advertisement reproduced in figure 7 earlier in this chapter, here is another one published in the *Pakistan Times* in 1966 (fig. 10). With the caption "Pakistani girls make good daughters—no wonder they make such good Hostesses," this ad was placed by the recently founded national airline. In the ad, a woman appears to be discharging her traditional role as an adept caregiver. The ad notes, "affection for the young, respect for elders and the desire to be helpful, hospitable and gracious . . . make-up every daughter of Pakistan." So, the Pakistani woman makes an ideal airhostess and can be "Pakistan's Ambassador in many countries abroad."

In this vein, it should not be a surprise that Pakistani women were also used as a symbol to bolster tourism, simultaneously alleviating the anxieties of

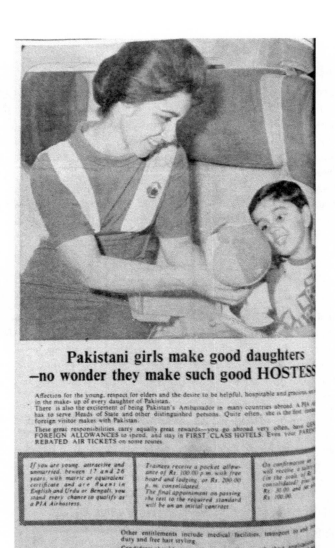

**Pakistani girls make good daughters
—no wonder they make such good HOSTESS**

Affection for the young, respect for elders and the desire to be helpful, hospitable and gracious, are in the make-up of every daughter of Pakistan.

There is also the excitement of being Pakistan's Ambassador in many countries abroad. A PIA Airhostess has to serve Heads of State and other distinguished persons. Quite often, she is the first contact a foreign visitor makes with Pakistan.

These great responsibilities carry equally great rewards—you go abroad very often, save generous FOREIGN ALLOWANCES to spend, and stay in FIRST CLASS HOTELS. Even your PARENTS get REBATED AIR TICKETS on some routes.

If you are young, attractive and unmarried, between 17 and 26 years, with matric or equivalent certificate and are fluent in English and Urdu or Bengali, you stand every chance to qualify as a PIA Airhostess.	Trainees receive a pocket allowance of Rs. 100.00 p.m. with free board and lodging, or Rs. 200.00 p.m. consolidated. The final appointment on passing the test to the required standard will be on an initial contract.	On confirmation as Airhostess will receive a salary (in the scale of Rs. ... consolidated) plus Rs. 30.00 and ... Rs. 100.00.

Other entitlements include medical facilities, transport to and from duty and free hair styling.

Candidates should appear in person along with their applications, passport size photograph and Certificates-Testimonials in original at the following programme:—

Station	Date	Time	Place
Rawalpindi	13-9-1966	1000 Hrs.	Office of the District Manager, Flashmen's Hotel, Rawalpindi
Lahore	12-9-1966	1000 Hrs.	Office of the District Manager, Shah Din Building, The Mall, Lahore

PIA PAKISTAN INTERNATIONAL AIRLINES

FIGURE 10. An advertisement for the Pakistan International Airlines published in the *Pakistan Times* in 1966. Photograph taken by Pippa Virdee, and reproduced with permission. Available at: https://bagichablog.com/2017/01/30/pia-the-jet-age-and-working-women (accessed January 24, 2018). The newspaper, the *Pakistan Times,* was closed in 1996.

FIGURE 11. Tourism promotion posters featuring women. The poster on the left, "Hunza at World's End," is based on a 1953 *National Geographic* article and photograph.

predominantly North American and European tourists heading to developing countries for holiday, and feeding into masculinized fantasies. Women represented safety, congeniality, and promised access to beauty and nature. In a poster published by the Ministry of Commerce in the 1960s, with the caption "See Pakistan . . . Hunza (Pakistan) at World's End" (fig. 11), we see an image of a fair-skinned, blue-eyed woman holding flowers.

This poster was based on a 1953 photograph taken by Franc and Jean Shor for the *National Geographic,* for their article entitled "At World's End in Hunza: This Strange Shangri-La near the Himalayas Has Few Laws or Taxes and No Army; Bridegrooms Take Mother on the Honeymoon."[35] The photograph depicts "a Hunza woman [as she] knits homespun yarn with needles of modern plastic." Readers are reminded that the *National Geographic* magazine is notorious for eliciting a colonizing and voyeuristic gaze, as well as for essentialized representations of non-western subjects. [36] In the poster above, Pakistan's northern areas are transformed into an exotic land, ripe for exploration.[37] Analyzing the portrayal of brown women in the *National Geographic,* Moon Charania observes that such images reenact "an old Orientalist fantasy of the mysterious character of the East and of the brown woman, simultaneously repulsive and tantalizing. . . . She, as a metaphor for land, becomes available for Western penetration and knowledge."[38]

In the posters published by the Ministry of Commerce of Pakistan, too, we observe similar dynamics at play, where women are featured to seduce the (male) traveler. In a 1963 poster published by Pakistan's Department of Tourism (also in fig. 11), women appear alongside exotic animals and archeological finds.

In addition to being enrolled in both representational and manual labor to advance the nation, women were also deemed to have a critical role in the reproduction of future citizens of Pakistan. A speech by Aquila Barlas Saheba, the chairman of the department of sociology at the University of Karachi, at the Literature Association Rally in London hints at this.[39] In this speech, which is reproduced in a 1948 issue of *Ismat*, Barlas notes that the project of "building the nation should start with the education and upbringing [*talim wa tarbiyat*] of women since it is in their laps that future politicians, scientists, poets and soldiers will be raised." Likewise, the then minister of education for Pakistan, in an article entitled "Women's Education," published in 1949 in *Tehzib*, notes that since the next generation of Pakistanis will be raised by women, women's first responsibility is to be teachers to their children.[40] The new, educated female subject, then, is imagined as a mother-teacher. Readers will recall that similar rationales for preparing the next generation were advanced at the turn of the twentieth century; however, what is different now is that mothering is being linked increasingly to scientific knowledges, which transforms those women who are unable to partake in schooling due to their social class into potentially bad/underperforming mothers.

In order to properly discharge the responsibilities of mothering toward the next generation of Pakistanis, women had to be trained in the sciences. The minister of education for Pakistan in the same article in *Tehzib*, for instance, calls on girls to obtain an education in the field of psychology, so that they may apply this knowledge to their children. During this time (in 1948), a women's magazine entitled *Nafsiyaat* (Psychologies) was also launched, which contained articles explaining scientific ways to raise children, with such titles as "Your Child's Future" and "Interpreting Dreams" (1948, no. 1); "Child and Punishment" and "A Child's Psychological Life" (1949, no. 1); "The Effect of Films on Youth" (1949, no. 2); "Educational Psychology" and "Social Psychology" (1950, no. 2). Elsewhere, we find advice for women to prepare healthy domestic environments for children that draw on the latest knowledge of healthcare and commercial products. Consider the following advertisements in *Ismat*. In figure 12, mothers are advised to prepare food in Dalda oil in order to improve their children's health. The ad begins with a conversation between a mother and a doctor hovering over a sick child. The doctor says, "To keep children healthy, it is important to feed them food cooked in pure oil." The mother is then shown inquiring from a shopkeeper about such a product, who advises her to use Dalda. In the next three frames we learn that her family—composed of the son and husband—are enjoying their meals cooked with Dalda, with the child asking for seconds and the father commenting on how tasty the food is. In larger font we learn that "Dalda provides strength and is pure oil." Significantly, the ad also notes that

FIGURE 12. An advertisement for Dalda oil. *Ismat* 92, no. 4 (1954): 56.

during the production process, "it is never touched by hands" and hence arrives in a sealed package "fresh and pure and therefore favorable for health."

Figure 13 cautions pregnant women against germs that they may contract during their delivery. This advertisement for Dettol, an antibacterial product, features

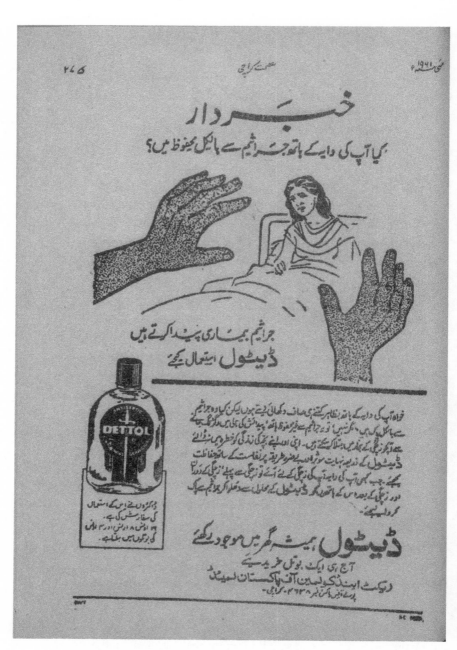

FIGURE 13. An advertisement for Dettol. *Ismat* 106, no. 5 (1961): 54.

a pregnant woman who appears to be threatened by the dirty hands of the mid-wife. The ad opens with "Beware—are your midwife's hands safe from germs?" The ad calls on women to ensure that before, during, and after the delivery, midwives wash their hands with Dettol: "Don't put your own and your child's life in danger."

And, in figure 14, a substitute for mother's milk is introduced. The ad begins with complimenting the child featured in the ad as "cute as well as healthy," and goes on to explain that this is the result of "a mother's love, her nursing, and Ostermilk's attributes." The ad details the several ways in which this milk "is an excellent substitute for a mother's milk." It contains iron to produce enough blood in children, and vitamin D to strength children's bones and teeth. Indeed, "wise mothers raise their children on Ostermilk."

All of these advertisements discursively produce the figure of the educated mother as one who is concerned about the health of her children and draws on modern, scientific knowledge to design safe environments for them. To do so, however, she must also become a discerning consumer. After all, these ads promote particular consumer products. In their study of modern girlhood across the world, Weinbaum and others observe that commodities were intricately linked to the expression of modern femininity. Particular commodities were marked as appropriate for the consumption of the "modern girl." These often included products that enabled them to fulfill their duties either in relation to the family (buying childcare and home-improvement products) or the state (partaking in savings). This insight finds resonance with Satish Deshpande's work in the context of India as well.[41] Deshpande notes that mid-twentieth-century constructs of citizenship in India were linked to patterns of consumption and production. Members of the elite and modernizing middle classes emerged as the vanguard of the new nation because their consumption aligned with modern domesticity and the productivist paradigm of citizenship. By consuming the right kinds of products, the Pakistani woman, too, was to relate to the nation and the family in ways that promoted their development; in the process, she expressed her modern, class-based identity.

The national discourse that sought to transform women into workers and consumers was primarily aimed at middle-class women who had the financial means to acquire an education and other commodities in the first place. Most Pakistanis lived in extreme poverty in rural areas and were illiterate. The professionalizing discourse that produced the "working daughter of the nation" or the "scientifically inclined mother" was not aimed at them. Poor and peasant women were often already engaged in the informal economy, and lacked both the monetary and cultural resources necessary for accessing emerging consumer products.

For-profit corporations, on the other hand, aspired to transform all kinds of women into consumers. Consider the following print advertisement of a private bank, which features a woman in burka (fig. 15). Even as it positions the burka-clad woman in the time-space of the past by constructing her in opposition to the

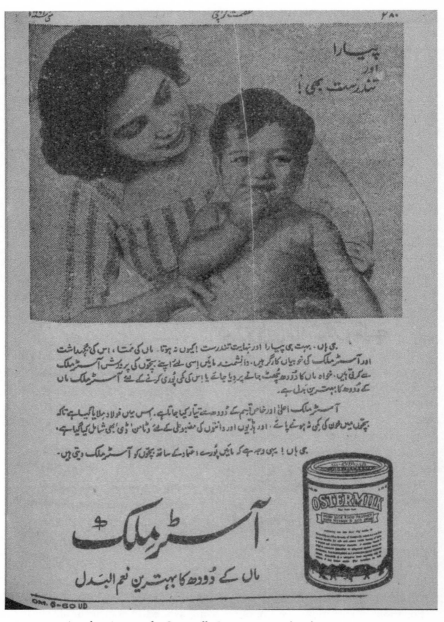

FIGURE 14. An advertisement for Ostermilk. *Ismat* 106, no. 5 (1961): 59.

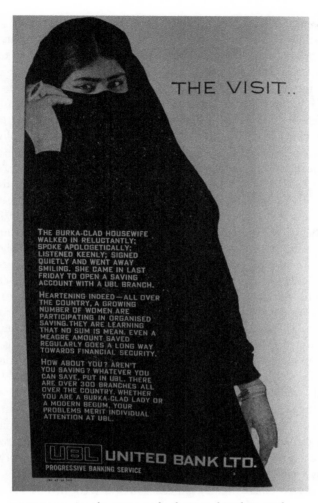

FIGURE 15. An advertisement for the United Bank Limited,
which appeared in *She* magazine, Pakistan, on February 15, 1967.
Photograph taken by Liam Kelley. Reproduced with permission.

"modern begum," it sees her as potentially adding value to the nation as a consumer
and, hence, is willing to overlook her "nonmodern" expressions of piety. Burka-
clad or not, women are called on to transform themselves into consumer-citizens
by participating in "organized savings," a critical need for the emerging nation.

Insights from women's periodicals further clarify the class dimension of the
discourse on women's education and their role in nation building via waged work.
While the state viewed women's labor as critical for national progress and drew on

the language of "duty" and "responsibility," women from low-income backgrounds often saw such work as a "necessity" in the precarious postindependence environment and even resented it. Bilquis Ahmed Shafiq, writing for *Ismat* in 1949, for instance, notes that after independence she feels that women have to take on more burdens to improve the welfare of their families.[42] Similarly, Shaista Suharwardy, in her article "What Is Woman's Work?" in *Ismat* in 1954, observes that while recent essays in the magazine discuss women's responsibilities to contribute to the family's income, they fail to highlight the difficulties of such work.[43] She observes that the debate seems to suggest that it is women's choice to work outside the home; whereas, in reality, dire circumstances have compelled women to do so. The author cites the example of many families who, after migrating from India to Pakistan, have had to rely on women's employment in order to make ends meet. In some cases, men are not able to get jobs, have become disabled, or have died. She further notes that while earlier women were taken care of in extended family systems where income and expenses were shared, that is no longer the case. She thus sees work as a "burden" rather than "responsibility" or "duty," terms often used by state institutions. Recognizing these new realities of women, Suharwardy calls on the government to take active measures to ensure that it becomes possible for women to engage in paid work in safe working environments. She calls for modifying school curricula to account for the fact that girls will likely not stay at home and must be educated to work alongside men if need be. In other words, she envisioned schools as transforming women's relationship to paid work. Authors such as Suharwardy highlighted the class dimension that was often erased in national discourses on women's education and work.

Even as the state called on women to take ownership on the domestic front and participate in the economic development of the new nation, it circumscribed their empowerment by constant appeals to men to continue to watch over women. Consider the following advertisements for the Pakistan Savings Certificate scheme published in *Ismat.*

The first advertisement (fig. 16), published in 1954, is entitled "Danai" (Wisdom) and uses second-person pronouns to address the father:

> Wisdom . . . As an intelligent and farseeing father, it is your responsibility to educate your children so that they are prepared for life's hard work. It is important to plan and save for education from the beginning. Savings Certificates are issued for precisely this reason, so that you have the ability to save money. You can save your money by buying these certificate and can earn an interest on them too. By doing so you not only prepare for your children's education but also contribute to the country's material resources, so that more educational institutions can be established in the country . . . or else, you know that uneducated people are a burden on their family and the nation. Lack of education is the biggest hindrance. Save money and invest in Pakistan Savings Certificate.

FIGURE 16. An advertisement for Pakistan Savings Certificate scheme. From *Ismat* 92, no. 4 (1954): 55.

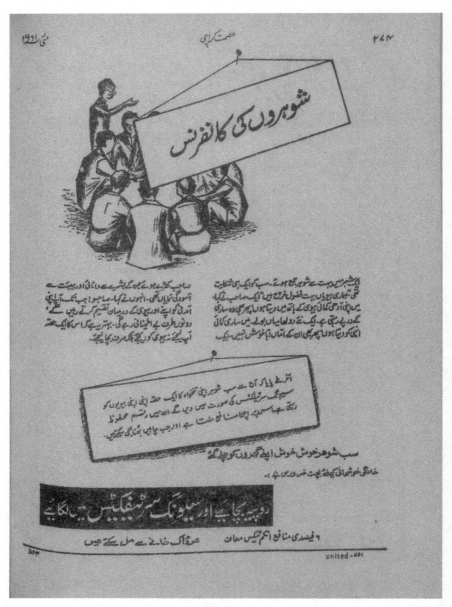

FIGURE 17. An advertisement for Pakistan Savings Certificate scheme. From *Ismat* 106, no. 5 (1961): 53.

The visuals of this advertisement stand out. In bold letters the word "Wisdom . . . " is juxtaposed with an image of a man. A much smaller image of a man and a woman appears on the other side. The reader immediately associates wisdom with men, that men are in charge of the family and so must think and plan for its financial and educational future. What is most peculiar about this advertisement is that it is in a women's magazine but is addressed to men ("as a father . . . you"). There is, thus, an implicit logic that even though women will most likely read this magazine, they too, will comply with the normative view that men are wise and guardians of the home. A 1961 advertisement (fig. 17), captioned "Husbands' Conference," draws on a similar logic but is much more explicit in its marking of women as inferior:

> Many husbands gathered in a city. Everyone had the same complaint: "Our wives are very spendthrift." One man said, "I give half of my income to my wife but even then it is not enough." A newlywed said, "I give all my income to her, even then her parents are not happy." A wise man stood up and said, "*Sahebo*, until you keep distributing your income between yourself and your wife, both sides will be uncomfortable. It is better to neither keep the money yourself nor give it to your wife but to save it." Finally it was decided that all husbands will give a portion of their income to wives in the form of a Savings Certificate. This way the amount will be protected, it will earn interest, and whenever it is needed, it can be monetized. All husbands returned happily to their homes. For domestic happiness, savings are necessary . . .

In this advertisement again, while it is signaled that men rely on women to run the household, there is little trust in women's ability to manage the finances. Women are spendthrift and regardless of how much income men earn, it is never enough. Thus, the ad calls on men to take charge by avoiding giving women liquidity. After all, when women don't have the cash, they won't be able to spend! This logic again establishes husbands as thoughtful leaders of their homes, who can guide their families to prosperity *in spite* of their wives. Women are called on to play a part in familial and national projects, but, given their natural (rather, naturalized) shortcomings, they need to be managed and controlled by both men and the state.

FAILED SUBJECTS

The demarcation of failed subjects was also a crucial aspect of the discursive project of defining successful performances of educated, Pakistani, Muslim subjectivities. Asaf Hussain's book *The Educated Pakistani Girl* (1963), provides an intimate portrayal of Pakistani girls during the 1950s, and his categorizations of his interview subjects as *purdah-nasheen* (those who wear the veil), "modern," and "ultramodern" give us insights into this discursive project. *The Educated Pakistani Girl* is an interpretation of a mixed-method study conducted by the author. Hussain had collected data from a hundred "educated" girls between the ages of eighteen

and twenty-five; for the purpose of the study, he defines "educated" as having completed the tenth grade or beyond. While Hussain is mostly concerned with girls'
views about love, marriage, and sex, what is most interesting to me is the discursive construction of the "educated Pakistani girl." I highlight some findings from
the text, as well as girls' own statements, to illustrate how both being too religious
and "ultramodern" came to be seen as inappropriate performances of an educated
girlhood. In other words, these performances were at odds with the performance
of citizenship and religiosity demanded by the new nation of Pakistan.

Hussain categorizes girls along a continuum of backward to progressive, from
purdah-nasheen to modern to ultramodern. He has a clear preference for what
he sees as the middle ground—the "modern Pakistani girl." He sees the *purdah-
nasheen*s as "misfit[s] in a developing society"[44] because they partake in what
he sees as a regressive practice (the *purdah*), believe in the superiority of men,
and find coeducation to be distracting. He also observes that the *pardah-nasheen*
girls were not able to provide an answer about how they could be helpful to their
nation. Likewise, Hussain sees the ultramodern girls or "teddy girls,"[45] who were
enamored with the West, as also not performing the kind of girlhood conducive
for the nation's progress. They were "born and bred in rich, well-to-do, influential
families" and represented the "gloss of the educated westernised gentry."[46] They
were "bored with this country" because its people "[are] narrow-minded, customs
are outdated, religion is stringent, the country is underdeveloped, the masses are
illiterate, and so the question of serving it does not arise."[47] Yet, because they could
not visit the West easily, they brought the West to Pakistan through practices such
as flirting or casual relations with men, dancing at parties, and being fashion-con-
scious.[48] As Hussain notes, "the ultramoderns find it very convenient to copy the
Western mode of living, thinking it to be superior, forward and 'cultured.'"[49]

It is the "modern girl" that Hussain sees as the ideal citizen that the nation can
depend on. This girl demands equal rights—as one informant notes, "A country
can only develop when both (men and women) have equal rights so that they
can participate equally for the improvement of the country";[50] and another says,
"Women should be treated according to the law of human rights established by
the UNO."[51] They are interested in coeducation so that they can work with men
and support their families: "co-education should be encouraged. Keeping boys and
girls apart makes them come close and meet secretly and they are misled";[52] and
"co-education is good in a way because it teaches the sexes to walk shoulder to
shoulder."[53] They appear to have an approach to gender relations that is in the service of familial and national projects, rather than personal sexual fulfillment and
pleasure (like the ultramodern girls) or a rejection of relations with men that would
be detrimental to the national developmental project (like the *pardah-nasheen*).

On citizenship, the author notes that modern Pakistani girls are not like "the
living dead . . . the *purdah-nasheen*s, but have a deep-seated urge to help their
sisters, their people and their country."[54] Girls themselves noted: "I would like

to do something for the uplift of Pakistani women struggling in the quagmire of illiteracy and primeval darkness";[55] "Give village aid, teach cleanliness and social uplift in order to bring up children properly";[56] "I am interested in teaching and would like to see our women educated and cultured. It is my wish to help to create good sense and liking for art. There should also be an educational campaign for the masses."[57] Whereas the ultramodern girl is depicted as belonging to the upper/ elite social classes, the modern girl is middle-class. She is interested in getting an education and working so that she can support her family. She displays proper commitments to the nation—as a transmitter of national culture and a biological reproducer of national subjects. She also monitors her sexual relations, and so, unlike the ultramodern girl, is not considered a threat to the nation. The foregoing constitutes a theorization of "modern" as leaving behind antiquated religious practices (in this case the *purdah,* gender segregation, etc.) and as being cautious about western social mores (represented by the ultramodern girl's habits). Hussain's articulation of the modern girl, then, is a new invention that is distinctly Pakistani and Muslim.

While these portrayals of girls by Hussain may be reductive, they do point to the discursive conditions within which the "educated Pakistani girl" emerges. They signal how the needs of the new nation, changing social and gender relations, as well as multiple articulations of Islam, created pressures for the articulation of a distinctly modern girlhood that was patriotic *and* Muslim. During the 1950s and 1960s Pakistan portrayed itself as a modern state that welcomed tourists, foreign businesses and investments, and established a large range of industries. During this period Ayub Khan invited several western state leaders to Pakistan to strengthen ties. In 1961, for instance, Queen Elizabeth toured Pakistan and in 1962 the first lady of the United States, Jackie Kennedy, visited as well (figs. 18 and 19). The self-articulation of the nation as "modern" and "progressive" also called for an articulation of a girlhood that, too, could display just the right combination of national pride and modernity. This is the girl that Hussain describes as the "modern girl," upon whom the nation could rely.

The discursive construction of the *pardah-nasheen* as a failed subject and the "modern girl" as the ideal subject was coproduced in western journalism about Pakistan as well. Consider the following photographs taken by Margaret Bourke-White and published in the January 5, 1948, issue of the *Life* magazine. They portray the multiple performances of womanhood at the inception of Pakistan, some of which are marked by the photographer as modern and others as implicitly backward. Figure 20, for instance, portrays a group of women who belong to the National Guard, practicing combat techniques. These women are named by Bourke-White as "modern Pakistan [*sic*] women," and are juxtaposed with women who observe *purdah* (fig. 21). Specifically, the caption reads: "Modern Pakistan [*sic*] women are symptomatic of the progress the new nation is struggling to make. Here, led by Zeenat Haroon, young members of the Sind province Women's

FIGURE 18. British Queen Elizabeth on a royal tour of Pakistan in 1961. Getty Images. Reproduced with permission.

FIGURE 19. First lady of the United States, Jackie Kennedy, visiting Pakistan in 1962. Getty Images. Reproduced with permission.

FIGURE 20. Sind Women's Guard, 1947. Photo by Margaret Bourke-White / The Life Picture Collection / Getty Images. Reproduced with permission.

National Guard meet to practice the use of the bamboo *lathi* in self-defense. But most Pakistan women still prefer the old custom, even to the veiled face."[58]

So, even at the inception of Pakistan, some subjects were already marked as inappropriate for the progress of the nation. The binary of modern versus religious hardened over time, as Hussain's book (published in 1963 but researched during the 1950s) reveals. Such binaries, however, were reductive. Certain of the most active women in the project for women's education were *pardah-nasheen*. Figure 22

FIGURE 21. Women in *purdah* going to a park, 1947. Photo by Margaret Bourke-White / The Life Picture Collection / Getty Images. Reproduced with permission.

FIGURE 22. November 1947, Women's Educational Conference. Photo by Margaret Bourke-White / The Life Picture Collection / Getty Images. Reproduced with permission.

shows a photograph taken by the same *Life* journalist during the November 1947 meeting of the Women's Educational Conference. Here, *purdah-nasheen* Khadeeja Ferozuddin, who was the deputy director of Public Instruction of West Punjab, leads the meeting in which she called for separate medical colleges for men and women. However, the caption in *Life* of a close up of Khadeeja Ferozuddin reads: "The Lady in the Lace personifies old customs and traditions connected with Pakistan's religion. Although this lady, Khadeeja Feroz Ud-din is deputy director of public instruction for the West Punjab, she opposes co-education. She veils her face and even hides her hands in gloves."[59] Such narratives leave the "modern girl" as the only site of possibility.

Hussain's survey and narrative illustrate the broad categories linked to girl-hood that were in circulation during the early decades after the establishment of Pakistan, as well as the kinds of investments about the nation, Islam, waged work, and family that marked women along the continuum of backward to ultramodern. One key threat to ideal girlhood was represented by English/missionary education.

THE LINGERING THREATS OF COLONIAL EDUCATION

In women's periodicals as well as policy documents and political speeches, we find scathing critiques of the kinds of subjects that English/missionary education was producing. Early on, the Advisory Board for Education of Pakistan (ABEP), which was established during the first All Pakistan Educational Conference, held in 1947, noted that education should be free from "an over-emphasis on the superiority of modern Western civilization, the glorification of its material achievements and the consequent relegation to a place of inferiority of Eastern cultures," as well as from "the pernicious results of Macaulay's system of education."[60] Elsewhere, Fazl-ur-Rehman, the then federal minister of education, concluded that Macaulay's system had led to the "dominance of alien influences in the textbooks, readers and juvenile literature," in such a way that "all traces of Muslim culture were deliberately excluded."[61] The concern with English education often took the form of anxiety about proselytization in schools, as well as a fear that the next generation would not learn its own language and culture. The Committee of the Punjab Education Department, for instance, contemplated changing the medium of instruction from English to Urdu since the English medium of instruction had "caused considerable mental strain."[62] Likewise, in June 1948, the Interuniversity Board also decided that English should no longer be the medium of instruction in the universities of West Pakistan and to adopt Urdu within four to five years.[63] A deeper exploration of women's periodicals explicates these anxieties around missionary education as well as the danger that its students presumably embodied.

Consider the conversation across three issues of *Ismat* in 1956 and 1957 about convent/missionary schools. We find that colonial legacies in education were seen as undesirable for the new nation of Pakistan due to their (real and imagined) corrupting effects on the nation's children. In an article entitled "The Convent School,"[64] written by Zubaida Zareen, the author notes that the movement for an independent Pakistan rested on claims that Muslims needed a separate homeland to sustain their language, culture, and religion. However, she laments that until now there has not been an agreement about a national language and English continues to have a strong influence through convent schools. She complains that such schools produce students who are enamored with the West and consider themselves superior to the average Pakistani child. She goes on to note that while only rich parents in the past sent their children to convent schools, now even middle-class families are doing so, concluding that "it is an inferiority complex that compels many Pakistani parents to do so." The author argues that such students will neither become English nor remain Pakistani; rather, they will be "*neem-angraiz*" (pseudo-English). She also criticizes the dress prescribed for girls in convent schools (recall figures 5 and 6 in the last chapter). She asks: "Why are we investing so much on this identity—is that why we created Pakistan?" Zubaida Zareen concludes by explaining that while she is not against learning from other nations, "Pakistan should also have its own distinct identity," and she cautions that "such Christian missionary schools will destroy our religion."

Zubaida Zareen's article represents a generational anxiety that consumed the emergent nation's citizens around independence: What will the next generation do with this new nation? What will be the place of Islam in the new nation? How can we preserve our values? There is a clear discomfort with the British legacies, especially educational institutions that prioritized the teaching of English and Christianity, as well as an anxiety around the indecision of the national leaders about declaring Urdu as the national language. As elaborated earlier, the British administration had given Christian missionary societies permission to establish schools across colonial India and the Muslim world more broadly. Such schools were often run by missionaries themselves in the hopes of "saving" native girls and women through conversion to Christianity. Furthermore, many graduates of these schools went on to teach in schools established by the government.[65] Zubaida Zareen's article elaborates anxieties about the religious conversion of those who attended such schools. We also observe a conflation of Muslim and Pakistani identity in the article: to be a good Pakistani is to be a good Muslim, and since convent schools emphasized Christianity they were viewed as a threat to both religion and the nation. For Zareen this threat materialized in the kinds of attitudes that these schools seemed to engender in its students: convent-school students thought of themselves as superior to other Pakistanis, were enamored with the West, and did not know the Quran; female students did not abide by normative dress codes, signaling a potential for crossing other social boundaries as well.

In response to this article, Mussarat Hamid, in *Ismat* (1956), argues that while she respects Zareen's views, "it is impossible in the current climate in Pakistan to pursue the study of the Urdu language when all higher education materials are provided in English" and when "Pakistan is dependent on the United States and England to advance its educational system."⁶⁶ The author then compares the state of government schools with convent schools, noting that the former often have a low quality of education. In such schools, children often engage in "cursing and bad behavior." So, she questions Zareen's argument about how such schools can teach ethics and culture. While Hamid agrees with Zareen that Muslim children should know religion, she thinks it is the responsibility of their parents (and not of schools) to impart such knowledge. Hamid then directs her attention to the state, critiquing it for a lack of effort to improve the quality of education. In Hamid's article we find a distinction between religious/moral and secular education that will congeal over the next decades in Pakistan, with the former being assigned to the "home" and the latter to the school. While Hamid argues that parents should take over moral instruction, she does not acknowledge the explicit and implicit presence of Christian morality in convent schools, which Zareen points out so painstakingly.

In the 1957 issue of *Ismat,* we find yet another article on convent schools written by Bushra Sultana Rohi Saheba that engages the two previous articles.⁶⁷ The author observes that while the state of public schools is bad, it does not mean that parents should send children to convent schools. The author provides pragmatic solutions to improve public schooling, such as by increasing teachers' salaries. However, like Zareen, she too worries that if children continue to go to convent schools, over time "Pakistanis will lose their culture, unity, and religion." She writes, "We will no longer remain Muslims. We cannot expect that our children get an education in convent schools and yet have the same kind of respect and understanding of religion that Muslim children have; that is not possible." The author clearly makes a connection between education and subjectivity, noting that an English education will not engender the kinds of values that she deems significant for Muslims. Like Zareen, Sultana Rohi also believes that studying in convent schools results in alienation from society because students begin to think of themselves as superior: "Instead of English, English-like Pakistani leaders are being born." She asks: "Should one sustain this destruction just because children will know how to speak English?" She thus calls for more efforts to improve government schooling.

This set of articles not only highlights the issues surrounding the educational legacy of the British but also the anxieties of an unknown future. Specifically, we observe an effort to delineate a distinctly Pakistani and Muslim subjectivity through an emphasis on national language, public schools, and religious practices, and the simultaneous marking of English and Christianity as threats to this subjectivity. These calls were situated in a wider landscape, where anti-Urdu and anti-Pakistan efforts were on the rise in neighboring India. For instance, after partition, the Hindu Mahasabha, the Jan Sangh, and the RSS demanded a Hindi-only policy in India. The calls to establish Urdu as the national language of Pakistan were to signal Pakistan's distinct culture and religion. This not only resulted in contesting the role of the English language in Pakistan—as the authors of Ismat did—but also the suppression of other dominant languages, particularly Bengali. Consider the words of Jinnah during a speech in Dhaka on March 21, 1948: "Let me make it very clear to you that the state language of Pakistan is going to be Urdu and no other language. Anyone who tries to mislead you is really the enemy of Pakistan. Without one state language, no nation can remain tied up solidly together and function. Look at the history of other countries. Therefore, so far as the state language is concerned, Pakistan's language shall be Urdu."[68]

According to Toor, to recognize the claims of Bengali would mean agreeing to the possible "cultural non-contiguity between the two wings [of Pakistan], which would undercut Pakistan's claims to nationhood"[69] and the very idea that Muslims shared the same culture and history. Opposition to convent schools, coed schools, and proposals for the inclusion of Urdu in the curriculum, hence, occupied a central place in the struggle for the meaning of Pakistan and Islam. And, women were a key discursive space for clarifying the negative effects of convent schools.

Consider an article entitled "The Curriculum of Women's Education" by Imam Akbar Abadi published in 1956 in Tehzib.[70] In this piece, the author laments that the contemporary curriculum of women's education is leading to shamelessness. He notes that while no one should be against women's education, the educated generation's assumptions about progress have transformed women into "Japanese dolls" (a reference to superficiality). He observes that the current curriculum makes women experts in writing afsaneh (short stories), reading and writing in the English language, and developing interests in dancing, but does not engender ethical and intellectual thought. The author argues that for a nation like Pakistan, a different kind of education is needed for women—one that enables them to learn ethics and compassion, independence and self-confidence, love for country and nation, and an understanding of their rights. Abadi, then, sees women primarily as citizens who are to serve the emerging nation through their contributions at home and perhaps also through waged work. Thus, education that does not enable women to perform these tasks appears frivolous to him. He emphasizes that the question is not whether or not women should be educated, but what kind of education should they have and how to discontinue the contemporary (English) education.

Suraiya Pardeen articulates similar anxieties around missionary education's effects on women in her article for Tehzib, "A Woman's Status and Responsibilities in Pakistan," published in 1948.[71] Pardeen gives the example of her own city of Abbottabad, where, though the majority was composed of Muslims, most schools and colleges had been established by Hindus or Christians. While Pakistan inherited the state-run primary and secondary educational system, this infrastructure was concentrated in urban areas and was predominantly run by Hindus who later left for India. In Karachi, out of the total thirty-five secondary schools, only half a dozen were managed by Muslims.[72] In this context, Pardeen laments, "Muslims had no choice but to send their daughters to study there." However, she goes on to criticize English schooling, saying that it is no longer sufficient to memorize a couple of English verses and call oneself *talim-yafta* (educated); the study of the Quran should be included in the curriculum so that people can become "real Muslims." Likewise, Rashid Siddiqui published an article in *Tehzib* in 1948 entitled "Today's Muslim Woman,"[73] in which he argues that today's *parhi likhi* (educated) women have been directed away from simplicity and toward fashion, and have become western-oriented: "over time western superficiality took over eastern *sharafat*."

Similarly, Fatima Begum Saheba, in her *Ismat* article "Our Girls' Education and Upbringing"[74] published in 1957, emphasizes that while women play a paramount role in the building and progress of the nation, they can also be the cause of its downfall. She laments that little attention is being paid to girls' education and observes that girls in schools and colleges do not wear appropriate clothes ("they wear tight clothes"), have short hair, laugh loudly, and desire to become like Christian women from Europe. They want to do well in men's sports, hate the Persian language, preferring the acquisition of English and French languages, avoid religious education, look down on *Islami* colleges, and are proud of missionary-school education. She proposes that all of this could have been prevented had girls been given religious education. Instead, girls learn to play the piano and dance because it is assumed that "the more modern, fashionable and forward-looking a girl is, the better her prospects for getting married into a rich household." To disrupt these beliefs, the author argues that the government should make it mandatory for children to learn the meaning of the Quran. She also proposes that housekeeping should be introduced in school curricula and that, in addition to the English language, Arabic should be made compulsory. She calls on other women to advocate for these curricular changes as well, and concludes with remarks that will continue to haunt the Pakistani educational system for decades: "So what if girls of the nation become lawyers, magistrates, judges, doctors, professors, and clerks? So what if they have B.A., M.A., Ph.D., M.B.B.S., L.L.B.? Only if they become real Muslim mothers will the Islamic Republic benefit."

Across these, and many other articles in the periodicals,[75] there is an acute sense that while convent education is producing both male and female subjects who do not have the ideal orientation and attitude toward the nation and religion, the stakes are higher when it comes to women since they symbolize familial *sharafat* and have the responsibility of nurturing the next generation. Suraiya Pardeen's binary of "western superficiality" versus "eastern *sharafat*" indicates these tensions. To be *sharif* entailed engaging in the proper practices of Islam and orienting oneself to others and family in ways that would be acceptable within a Muslim framework. This framework, however, was not clear or universally agreed upon by any means. There was extensive debate about what an education inspired by Muslim ethics would look like. An interesting set of articles in *Ismat* in 1948 illuminates this tension.[76]

It is a letter written by Mushtaq Ahmed Zahiri, addressed to Latifa Khanum, that elaborates how education inspired by eastern traditions (including Islam) is distinctly different from western traditions. The letter was a response to Khanum's earlier criticism of Zahiri, a regular contributor to *Ismat,* for being against women's education and independence (*azadi*). Since Zahiri often employed the language of religion, Khanum as a rebuttal provided evidence of Muslim women's independence in Turkey, Iran, and Egypt, as well as examples of Muhammad Ali Jinnah and his sister Fatima Jinnah. Zahiri's detailed response to Khanum gives us a glimpse into a kind of rationalization that is surprisingly prevalent in Pakistan today as well. It also lays out some of the sacrifices—especially in terms of sacrificing women's mobility and access to knowledge—that particular segments of society were willing to make to secure what they deemed to be proper education.

Zahiri argues that he does not oppose women's education—he is against the specific *kind* of education that had become dominant in the aftermath of the British raj. "Everywhere you look," he says, "you will find people who are greedy, only interested in accumulating wealth for themselves, and willing to cheat, lie, and loot others to get ahead."[77] He notes that the people who run Pakistan and Hindustan are educated but they take bribes, are unjust, and take advantage of others. This, he believes, is a clear indication of the results of contemporary forms of education. In contrast, Zahiri argues, *haqiqi talim* (real education) is one that "makes man human," so that he acts justly and fulfills his responsibilities. A human should not simply be invested in accumulating wealth and fulfilling his greed; he should, instead, fulfill his responsibilities to Allah, his parents, relatives, the poor, and orphans. This kind of education, Zahiri states, is necessary for both men and women. However, he notes that until such an education can be provided, it is prudent to stay away from contemporary forms of education, because if one is "influenced by English education then *haqiqi talim* loses its effectiveness." In contrast to English education, the author proposes that *Asia-i-talim* (Asian education) should be pursued because the latter is grounded in religion and ethics. Clearly, Zahiri believes that decidedly different values and morality are advanced by English and Asian education. The latter, in his view, is grounded in different epistemologies, an argument that is now, interestingly, being made by decolonization scholars as well. His proposals, however, do not lay out a plan to revise the current educational system and appear to cut off women's access to prevailing opportunities, a move that was resisted by Khanum, who called him out on it.

The writers in Urdu periodicals were aware that they had to work with the infrastructure of schooling from the colonial period and called on the state to take a more active role in building educational institutions. Thus, many articles focused on figuring out ways to modify the educational system in response to ongoing threats. This included contemplating the role of Islam in the educational system (as the Imam Akbar Abadi and Fatima Begum Saheba's articles illustrate) as well as exploring how distinctly Islamic values, morals, and traditions could be transmitted via schools. These public discussions around school knowledges led to many policy changes. The 1959 education policy, for instance, made it compulsory for a course on *Islamyat* (the study of Islam) to be taught up to the seventh grade (the 1972 policy extended this to tenth grade, and the post-1977 policies made it compulsory for eleventh and twelfth grades as well as professional colleges). The 1959 education policy also made provisions for teaching in Urdu. Over time, a number of public schools were established to meet the needs of the population; however, these schools emulated British models of schooling and did not resolve questions around religious/moral instruction.

Over the subsequent decades, a class-differentiated educational system emerged in Pakistan, with the rich sending their children to grammar/convent/missionary/private schools, while the poor did not have access to schools and the upwardly mobile middle classes strove to improve the public educational system and/or establish low-tuition private schools. The debate about private versus public schooling continued to take center stage. The 1966 Commission Report, for instance, outlined key difficulties with the private sector, and in 1972 the government nationalized all private schools except religious education institutions.[78] The 1979 policy, however, reversed this nationalization, followed by an encouragement of the private sector from 1992 onward.[79] This led to a rise in the number of private schools, which were again in the 2009 national policy deemed to be at odds with the public sector.[80] The government continued to invest in school infrastructure and saw an increase in enrollment rates. Net enrollment in primary school increased over time to 79 percent for males and 65 percent for females, and in secondary school to 40 percent for males and 29 percent for females (data from 2008–12).[81] Schools became the dominant site for Pakistanis to acquire an education. However, concerns around appropriate knowledges continued to be aired. Curriculum reforms also put pressure on madrasas to clearly define their curriculum as distinct from the government's, and in the post-9/11 context madrasas were stigmatized as international pressure on Pakistan increased.[82] Meanwhile, private providers of education grew rapidly, especially in the rural areas where they exploited the saturated market of low-waged teachers to gain maximum profit.[83]

IN THE SERVICE OF THE FAMILY AND THE NATION

Whereas in the last chapter I showed that women's education was assumed to transform them into subjects whose actions signaled familial respectability and social status, in the current chapter, we have observed that anxieties about the role of

Islam in the new nation, concerns about Christian proselytizing, and the national imperative to modernize and develop, created the context within which women's education took on new meanings. Women were not only to represent familial respectability, but now also to partake in the cultural and economic reproduction of the nation. The different discourses on women's education with their attendant knowledges presented in this chapter point to the multiple ideals of desired and undesired educated subjects that circulated in postindependence Pakistan. Both the *pardah-nasheen* and the "ultramodern/teddy girls" represented failed subject positions because they had not been able to form the ideal relationship to religion and the nation. In the case of the latter, it was the knowledges imparted at missionary/convent schools that were seen as wanting, and for the former it was the staunch disengagement with modern institutions (such as coeducational schools) that was marked as regressive. The ideal educated subject was one who engaged with the institution of religion in ways that did not hinder the modernizing project of the Pakistani state, ready to contribute to the development and economic growth of Pakistan and prepare future citizens. In other words, ideal girls were future "scientifically inclined mothers" or "daughter-workers." These subjects were brought into being through a range of practices, which included not only formal state policies that expanded school infrastructure and opened up specific industries to women, but also the articulation of women as natural caregivers and daughters of the nation through populational reasoning and curriculum.

Feminist historians have illustrated that in moments of political crises new roles become available/accepted for women. This also happened in the context of Pakistan. The nation enlisted women for its modernization project, making available to them new domains of economic activity. However, women's articulation as mothers and daughters prevented any major moves toward women's independence from the patriarchal family and state. Laura Bier traces similar shifts in women's experiences in the context of Nasser's socialist Egypt (1956–70).[84] She argues that while the state made available new work opportunities for women, it did not address the gender inequalities embedded in the Muslim Personal Status Law. There was, thus, a serious contradiction in the state drawing on feminism to mobilize women to participate in its development project without meaningfully disrupting the persistence of male control in the sphere of the family. These observations ring true in the context of Pakistan as well.

The Pakistani state acceded to conservative elements, sometimes even enshrining women's inequality in law. For instance, during the 1950s and 1960s, when the Pakistani state sought to reform Muslim laws that governed the family sphere, it acquiesced to the *ulama*'s demands that often strengthened men's control over women. The *ulama* dissented against the recommendations presented by the first commission set up to review Muslim family laws in 1955,[85] which led to a revision that was later implemented in the Muslim Family Laws Ordinance of 1961. While women gained some rights with regards to marriage, custody of children, divorce, and registration of marriages, the ordinance also set up an arbitration council that brought many areas related to women's lives (such as women's claims to maintenance) under state jurisdiction. Since then, family laws have continued to be a space for contestation between the state and *ulama,* with the state often acquiescing to the *ulama's* demands at the expense of women.

While this chapter focuses on the early decades immediately postindependence (1947–67), I will conclude by hinting at some of the ways in which notions of ideal woman/girlhood shifted in the succeeding decades before moving on to the contemporary period in the next chapter. General Ayub's regime ended with the rise of Zulfiqar Ali Bhutto (1972–77), whose socialist message resonated with low-income as well as educated middle-class Pakistanis. Bhutto was ousted by army General Zia ul-Haq in 1977, who ruled for ten years. During his tenure, the little space that women had gained in Pakistan was radically reduced, as he codified a conservative interpretation of Islam into law. Specifically, with the 1979 Iranian Revolution and Soviet encroachment in Afghanistan, Pakistan emerged as a front-line state for the fight against communism as well as Shia theocracy. The United States sought Islam as a bulwark against communism, and Zia aligned with the Wahhabi version of Islam proposed by Jamaat-e-Islami and Saudi Arabia to advance his otherwise illegitimate rule. Zia also intensified the decimation of left-leaning groups and movements.[86] Zia's Islamization policies reformed all domains of life through changes in laws, school curricula, imposition of dress codes, and a focus on piety in public and personal lives. The ideal woman of Zia's time was the caretaker of the home, who conformed to strict performances of public piety. Her dependency on the family and state was accomplished through various measures that institutionalized her secondary position in society. This included laws such as the Hudood Ordinance (which conflated rape with adultery), the Qisas and Diyat Ordinance (which privatized the crime of honor killings), and the Law of Evidence (which reduced women's testimony to half of that of men).[87] Women's organizations such as the Women's Action Forum, established in 1981, protested against such laws only to be violently suppressed. A domestically confined, sexually pure, and pious womanhood was codified as the ideal. The result has been a tightening of circuits of surveillance through legal measures.[88]

Zia's policies have had a lasting influence of pathologizing women's autonomy and placing them squarely within the domain of the Muslim home. The Hudood laws were not repealed until 2006, with the Women's Protection Bill; this bill, however, was declared as contrary to Islamic injunctions by the Federal Shariat Court in 2010. Qisas and Diyat laws are still in place. In addition, the dissipation of leftist movements during Zia's regime left much of the feminist agenda to be picked up by transnational organizations such as UN Women and international nongovernmental organizations, as the next chapter will show. Women's agendas advanced by such interests, however, have not only clashed with local sensibilities, due to different imaginations about ideal womanhood, but have also been critiqued for often being closely tied to promarket, neoliberal agendas, exacerbating women's exploitation. Yet they form the discursive context within which contemporary meanings of girlhood and womanhood are being shaped.

4

The Empowered Girl

Women and girls represent humankind's most valuable untapped natural resource.

BAN KI-MOON, *UN SECRETARY GENERAL (2012)*[1]

You arm a young woman with a decent education and you see her conquer the world.

MARYAM SHARIF, DAUGHTER OF THE PRIME MINISTER OF PAKISTAN, *LEADING THE WHITE HOUSE'S LET GIRLS LEARN INITIATIVE IN PAKISTAN (2015)*[2]

Investing in girls and women is not only the right thing to do for them as individuals. It's also the smart thing to do for economies.

JIM YONG KIM, *WORLD BANK PRESIDENT (2016)*[3]

On May 20, 2017, a member of the National Assembly of Pakistan, Musarrat Ahmad Zeb, claimed that the attacks on Malala Yousafzai were staged; she noted that, "I was approached for the same drama but refused as I was not interested in seeking asylum in another country. . . . My inner conscience has compelled me to spill the beans."[4] She went on to name different girls from Pakistan, particularly those succeeding in formal schooling, calling them "not Malala." In other words, as the argument goes, there exist a number of girls in Pakistan who struggle to obtain an education but have not attained the same kind of attention that Malala has. That Malala is not unique, that she should not be seen as an exception. Such sentiments have widespread appeal in Pakistan. When Malala's autobiography was published, the chief of the All Pakistan Private Schools Federation, Kashif Mirza, noted that while the 152,000 private schools had supported her when she was shot, they had now decided to ban her book: she "was a role model for children, but this book has made her controversial. . . . Through this book, she became a tool in the hands of the Western powers."[5]

What is it about Malala's articulation in Anglophone media cultures, and relatedly the kind of "educated girlhood" that she symbolizes and advocates for, that is so threatening? Why would some Pakistanis be *against* Malala but *for* the education of girls? What does this case reveal about the promises and anxieties attached to the figure of the educated girl in contemporary Pakistan? To explore these questions, I shift my focus back to the transnational discourse on girls' education that first drew my attention to this topic. I engage in a critical appraisal of the visions of ideal girlhood and the purpose of education posited in this discourse by situating it within the promarket, neoliberal turn that the development regime has taken during the past few decades. I then draw on my fieldwork in Pakistan to problematize the emancipatory reading of schooling by highlighting its affordances and limitations for girls from minority religious and low-income backgrounds.

CONVERGING ON THE GIRL

In the dominant discourse on girls' education, girls appear as ideal citizen-subjects who can contribute to their nations and families by taking personal responsibility for their welfare. This often means transforming themselves into workers, consumers, and entrepreneurs by acquiring an education. This promise of education is grounded in liberal humanist sensibilities that see schooling as one of the key practices that can equalize the playing field, give individuals the ability to enact freedom, increase their productivity, and enhance their competitiveness in the global market. In the context of the global South, where access to formal schooling, especially for girls, is limited in some areas, improving such access is posited as the solution to problems as wide-ranging as poverty, corruption, terrorism, and environmental degradation. Thus, a broad range of formal and informal actors and projects have emerged in recent decades that advocate for girls' education. It is this paradigm within which Malala, too, locates herself, as readers will recall from the first chapter. Furthermore, with the increasing strength of global norm-setting mechanisms[6]—such as the UN declarations and goals (MGDs and SDGs)—as well as the proliferation of nonprofit, philanthropic, and corporate campaigns—such as Nike Foundation's Girl Effect or USAID's Let Girls Learn—ideas around girls' education have attained a commonsense status.

The notion that girls' education can solve a wide range of social problems has found resonance in Pakistan as well. For instance, in October 2015, the daughter of the then prime minister of Pakistan, Maryam Nawaz Sharif, paid a visit to the first lady of the United States, Michelle Obama, to express support for the Let Girls Learn initiative. During this meeting, Maryam Nawaz made the commitment that Pakistan will double its GDP spending on education (from 2 percent to 4 percent) and in return Michelle Obama announced a contribution of $70 million toward Pakistani girls' education.[7] This aid contribution was in addition to previous commitments. The promises to increase budget allocations to education, however, were not new; in 2008, the government of Pakistan had already committed to spending 4 percent of its GDP on education, a goal which it had been unable to meet. Similarly, a large number of corporate, philanthropic, nonprofit organizations, and foundations—both foreign and local—are now found in Pakistan that articulate some of the same systems of reasoning in relation to girls' education. This includes movements such as Girl Effect, Girl Rising, and the Malala Fund, transnational organizations such as Plan International, World Vision, and Pakistan Coalition for Education (whose partners include the Open Society Foundation and Oxfam), and celebrities such as Madonna. Madonna, for instance, sold a painting to establish girls' schools in Pakistan and Afghanistan, claiming: "I cannot accept a world where women or girls are wounded, shot or killed for either going to school or teaching in girls' schools. We don't have time to be complacent. . . . I want to trade something valuable for something invaluable—Educating Girls!"[8]

Several scholars, however, have critiqued this "girling of development." While some interrogate the emancipatory promise of education that undergirds girls' education campaigns,[9] others highlight the production of a homogenous girl-subject and female exceptionalism.[10] Specifically, girls' education campaigns often posit girls in the global South as either heroines with extraordinary potential or as victims of poverty and patriarchal cultures to be freed by their counterparts in the global North.[11] These binary subject positions reduce the complexities of the lives of girls and have often been used to legitimize western interventions. This "turn to the girl" in development can be situated within the wider valorization of postfeminist subjectivities in the context of neoliberalism, which prioritizes individual autonomy, choice, and agency, and places the burden of improving one's life on individuals themselves. Girls who abide by the neoliberal scripts of individualization, consumerism, and entrepreneurial identity are therefore marked as successful.[12] However, both Anita Harris and Angela McRobbie direct attention to the racialized and classed character of this girlhood, noting that such life scripts are often available only to white, middle-class girls. They observe that in western contexts, girls who are unable to enact this vision of girlhood due to structural disadvantages—such as living in poverty or in neighborhoods rife with violence, crime, and drugs—are marked as "at-risk."[13] They are folded into an intricate apparatus of surveillance, which includes school personnel, psychologists, and social workers. Girls in the global South, on the other hand, who, due to structural disadvantages, may be out of school, marry early, or engage in domestic/agricultural work to support their families become the specter of failed girlhood. They are variously marked as tribal, backward, or traditional. Often religion and culture are blamed for their wretched conditions, and their poor conditions are depoliticized and ahistoricized. These girls, however, are not written off. It is assumed that through proper education they too can be molded into "successful" girls. Hence, this new interest in girls' education and empowerment brings with it a significant regulatory aspect. More crucially, this discourse depoliticizes women's issues rather than calling on women to understand and resist the structures that create the conditions of their marginalization in the first place.

Joining this body of critique, in this and the following chapters I provide evidence from Pakistan that points to the ways in which social class, state practices, and norms of respectability and religious morality, mediate the lives of girls. In doing so, I also trace the contours of ideal/failed girlhoods in Pakistan today. These chapters aspire to go beyond the trend of painting neoliberalism as a bogeyman that magically infects everything, and instead show how it works—how transnational discourses are renegotiated in local contexts; how students, parents, and teachers are not necessarily passive pawns of neoliberal domination but strategically push back against elements of transnational discourses, and also at times mobilize neoliberal rationalities to their own advantage.[14]

I draw on focus-group conversations with girls, teachers, and parents in South Pakistan to provide a glimpse into the ways in which the promise of education unfolds in their lives. Their accounts complicate the neat and tidy narrative of education as empowerment. The case study shows that while schooling has provided some avenues for girls to participate in public life, concerns around respectability and marriageability, often articulated as lack of safe working conditions, mean that only low-income girls engage in waged work. Furthermore, since schools in Pakistan privilege the teaching of the dominant, Sunni, interpretation of Islam, my participants who belonged to a minority interpretation of Islam, expressed concerns around the erasure of their identity. The role of schools in producing ideal religious subjects, thus, continues to be as central as it was in the early days of Pakistan. Before delving into the case study, I situate the current turn to the girl within the broader dynamics in the field of international development.

"PROMARKET DEVELOPMENT"

Colonial relations of power based on territorial conquests have morphed into modes of human relationality that reproduce the colonial project's unequal distribution of epistemic, material, and aesthetic resources through renewed forms of division of labor, accumulation of capital, and imposition of racial and gender hierarchies.[15] These renewed relations of domination advance the interests of global capital by transforming girls into cheap labor, consumers, and precarious entrepreneurs who willingly take on the burden of improving their own welfare without relying on the state. In other words, the construction of the ideal girl facilitates the withdrawal of the state via the empowerment of the individual. It hides the systemic practices that produce dispossession and displacement. It can, therefore, be read as a technique of neoliberal governmentality that puts the onus of solving social problems on the individual by acquiring appropriate knowledges and reshaping the self, rather than holding the state or global capital accountable.[16] Schooling, in this context, often gets reduced to producing workers who can function in the neoliberal social order.

The logics of transnational girls' education campaigns become meaningful against this convergence of the development regime with promarket practices.

Since World War II, institutions such as the World Bank and the International Monetary Fund (IMF), dominated by countries in the global North, in particular the United States, have played a critical role in framing and facilitating the economic development of newly independent nations in the global South. While having previously utilized Keynesian principles with its protectionist impulses, these institutions have shifted toward neoliberal logics since the 1970s. This shift, popularly known as the "Washington Consensus," proposes that privatization and deregulation of public assets and services is the best way to promote consumption, economic growth, and efficiency. It also advances understandings about human welfare and capacity in economic terms. The 1970s debt crisis in third world economies created an opportunity for the IMF to transform these principles into practice through its Structural Adjustment Programmes (SAP). These programs often called for decreasing public expenditure on social services as a precondition for loans, thereby reducing the capabilities of the recipient states to provide welfare to their populations. Governments in the region eager for aid and loan monies readily implemented SAPs. It became clear over time that these policies, instead of helping the poor, deepened poverty and increased the vulnerability of the poor. Indeed, prior protectionist policies had sheltered not only the elites in these countries but also the working classes. A major contribution of neoliberal projects, then, has been the transfer of wealth from subordinate to dominant classes and from poor to rich countries, as well as large-scale displacement of the poor.[17]

This ascendency of economic measures to determine human well-being was criticized by proponents of the human capabilities approach. First introduced by Amartya Sen and extended further by Martha Nussbaum, the approach posits that economic measures such as GDP and GNP are not sufficient to determine human development.[18] Instead, Sen noted that an individual's capability is determined by her ability to choose the particular functionings that she values. Enhancing an individual's agency and freedom, then, was critical for increasing her capability. Nussbaum extended Sen's theorizations by creating a list of ten "central human capabilities" that she deemed were necessary to pursue in order to achieve human development.[19] The capabilities approach has been welcomed by some scholars who had long argued for international educational development agendas to move beyond issues of access to include a consideration of social justice.[20] Other scholars, however, argue that this approach fails to account for the complex contexts of schooling.[21] Postcolonial feminists, for instance, have criticized the capabilities paradigm for erasing the social stratifications that constitute women's lives, its impetus toward universalization, and its construction of culture and religion in monolithic and antagonistic terms.[22] In my previous work, I too have attempted to expose the valorization of "choice" as the key element of the capabilities approach.[23] Yet, the human capability approach remains one of the dominant paradigms in the field of development, one that sits alongside theories of human capital—at times in agreement, at other times in opposition.

More recently, in response to mounting critique of the Washington Consensus, a revised consensus, often called the "Washington Consensus Plus" or the "New Washington Consensus," has emerged. While aid and loans to developing countries continue to be tied to particular conditions around public expenditure, notions such as "good governance," "freedom," "empowerment," and "gender equality" are now used to legitimize these prescriptions.[24] This new consensus is not a departure from market rationalities, but it is different in its ambition, as it endeavors to produce resilient market subjects for a globalized world and relies on micromarket transformations to compensate for macromarket failures.[25] The "New Washington Consensus" has authorized an environment where for-profit corporations and philanthropic foundations can legitimately enter the field of development, take on the task of providing social services that were previously viewed as the responsibilities of the nation-state, and use market tools and mechanisms to deliver them. Significantly, for-profit corporations are viewed as capable advisors that can increase the efficiency of the development enterprise by infusing best practices. Katharyne Mitchell and Matthew Sparke describe this convergence of development and market agendas as "pro-market development."[26] Girls have emerged as ideal sites for investment in order to achieve wide-ranging social *and* market goals. A brief example will clarify this convergence.

Consider the SPRING Initiative, a public-private partnership involving the USAID, the UK's Department for International Development, and the Nike Foundation that has been launched in Kenya, Rwanda, and Uganda, with plans for expansion to Pakistan.[27] Part of USAID's broad range of interventions for "gender equality and women's empowerment,"[28] this initiative aims to support "businesses whose products and services could transform the lives of adolescent girls." A cursory review of the program's rationales illuminates the economic logics that inform it. The program seeks to "accelerate the economic empowerment of girls . . . [and] will help businesses bring products to market which enable girls to learn, earn, invest and save." The initiative hopes to attract sponsors (established businesses from the West) who may be interested in mentoring entrepreneurs in the global South. It grounds its work in light of the fact that "right now, products and services are rarely designed for, marketed to, or distributed to the majority of the world's adolescent girls—they're a *massively underserved market*" (emphasis mine). Hence, to incite established businesses, SPRING provides opportunities for sponsors to "interact first-hand with SPRING enterprises, *learn about new markets and opportunities for innovative practices,* and directly engage employees and partners in our programme as mentors, coaches, and event speakers" (emphasis mine). Furthermore, to attract investors, it highlights "the rare opportunity to infuse capital into innovative, high-growth enterprises" and notes, "with your investment,

SPRING businesses can embrace one of the *greatest social opportunities of our time—adolescent girls—and deliver ROI while they're at it"* (emphasis mine).

Clearly, the SPRING Initiative articulates girls in the global South as primarily an untapped market (of labor and customers) to be harnessed by local entrepreneurs and established, western sponsors/investors alike. Such projects imagine an economically savvy and financially self-disciplined subject, and unleash processes of subjectivation that can be read as part of the "triple movement" of the New Washington Consensus, which "shores up global market practices and rationalities through local social projects that at once acknowledge and cover for market failure while simultaneously cultivating new market subjects."[29] Indeed, in the context of the 2008 financial crisis and the exhaustion of western markets, financial enterprises have had to aim elsewhere to remain profitable. The financial system has, thus, shifted to different "types of financial ecologies, those made up of less privileged individuals and households that are located more towards the margins of society."[30] A move toward African and Asian markets, consumers, and labor through initiatives such as SPRING, then, could be read as a critical practice of transnational capital that facilitates the transformation of girls into economic actors and enrolls them in the (new) global economy, all the while benefiting large corporations.

Such promarket development projects advance a particular kind of rationality or valuation of human life and social projects. Here, all aspects of life are reduced to economic logics. The projects thus also produce governing logics around what it means to be modern, valuable, and empowered. Within this landscape, education continues to be a key site of investment as it straddles "both equity—and productivity—conceptualizations of development, while limiting commitment to stronger redistributive measures that might conflict with neo-classical economic theories."[31] This is precisely what we observe in contemporary calls for girls' education, which highlight girls as potential sites of investment and link girls' education to economic growth. The World Bank's 2012 *World Development Report,* for instance, calls for investing in girls' education because it is "smart economics." In fact the World Bank, which initially did not have any mandates around education, is now ". . . the largest single international funder of education for development in low-income countries, and its technical and knowledge-based resources tower over those of other international institutions."[32]

Furthermore, promarket development approaches see women's empowerment as closely linked to women's access to education and the labor market. This logic presumes a direct correlation between women's economic independence and their quality of life *as women.*[33] There is, then, extensive focus on attaining gender parity in the realm of education and employment. These ideas persist in spite of studies that show that education can be empowering as well as constraining. For example, even in countries where gender parity in education has been achieved, gender equality remains elusive. Consider Arlie Hochschild and Anne Machung's study in the context of the United States, which shows that middle- and upper-class women continue to remain responsible for household and care work even as they hold paid jobs in the formal sector.[34] Likewise, professional women in India and Nepal end up taking additional responsibilities on the domestic front to exhibit their new educated selves.[35] In Pakistan, Ayesha Khurshid's ethnographic study with female teachers shows that educated women not only have to excel in their new public roles but also their traditional roles as homemakers and childcare providers in order to prove that they deserve educational opportunities.[36] Khurshid thus concludes that "this interplay between the traditional and new roles for educated women in the domestic sphere complicates the linear narrative of women's education that uses gender parity in public spheres as proxy for gender equality. Instead . . . gender equality is a complex process shaped by structural inequalities and cultural norms that determine the meaning and purpose of education in a specific context."[37]

Likewise, Willy Oppenheim also contests the epistemological basis of the widely popular assertion that girls' education leads to reduction in fertility rates or reduces early marriage. He contends that such chains of reasoning are often premised on the idea that education increases women's autonomy in the household, an assertion that is debatable and difficult to prove. On the contrary, he points to other structural changes due to the provision of schooling that alter the calculus for educated as well as uneducated parents. So, changes in fertility rate may have less to do with women's empowerment and more with structural limitations/possibilities.[38] In spite of this critique, gender parity approaches in girls' education remain dominant, and access to schooling persists as a paramount goal.

It is, therefore, not surprising that the government of Pakistan has also marked girls' access to schooling as a priority and sees girls through dominant framings of citizenship and future-labor. In fact, the very objective of education as outlined in the 2009 *National Education Policy* privileges the skills necessary for a neoliberal order and outlines the purpose of education as earning a living and preparing citizens:

> The objective of education is the development of a self-reliant individual, capable of analytical and original thinking, a responsible member of his community and, in the present era, a global citizen. . . . The other relevance of education is its ability to provide the graduates with an opportunity to earn a living. Education should be able to increase the earning potential of the individual who is literate; irrespective of the eventual vocation opted.[39]

The privatization of the education sector in Pakistan has not only introduced multiple new actors in the space, but has also facilitated the responsibilization of the citizen,[40] as the onus of education is transferred from the state to parents and communities. In the 2009 *National Education Policy*, the government, in conjunction with celebrating "public-private partnerships," devolved the responsibility for education from the federal to the provincial level, thus taking a further step back in providing social services to its citizens.

While the state hopes to attend to girls' education and points to the Gender Parity Index (GPI) to show the disadvantage that girls and women face across the educational spectrum,[41] its privileging of access and enrollment means that limited attention is paid to the quality of girls' education. Willy Oppenheim observes that the Pakistani policymakers' and researchers' focus on simply increasing girls' rates of enrollment and persistence in school distracts them from the fact that many of "Pakistan's educational gender gaps have shrunk dramatically over the past twenty years and thus risks missing the opportunity to explore the subtleties of this historic shift."[42] Likewise, we know very little about the ways in which ideas made common sense through the transnational discourse are taken up, modified, and resisted at the local level. Against this background, it is significant to explore girls' experiences of schooling in order to understand the opportunities as well precarities that schooling introduces in their lives. In other words, how is the empowerment and emancipation postulated by the transnational discourse on girls' education actually experienced by girls? Such an investigation also provides insights into emergent visions of girlhoods. With this objective, I conducted a qualitative study in Pakistan during 2015 with girls, parents, and teachers to examine their engagement with schooling. My hope was to explore how girls from minority religious and low-income backgrounds engaged with the enterprise of schooling.

SCHOOLING GIRLS: A CASE STUDY

I present key themes that emerged from twelve focus-group conversations with girls, parents, and teachers conducted in a small city in South Pakistan. In these conversations, I tried to understand the participants' experiences with formal schooling and the possibilities that schooling afforded them, as well as its limitations. I view this study as providing a peek into the complexities of schooling, particularly for those who are on the margins of society. First, I show that even as my participants—who were predominantly from lower-middle-class backgrounds—unanimously agreed to partake in the enterprise of schooling, they recognized that its purpose varied for people from different social classes. While the majority of my participants saw schooling as a pathway to "office jobs," which was a code for work deemed respectable for middle-class women, they noted that girls from upper-class backgrounds consumed schooling primarily to secure good marriage prospects. Next, even as my participants engaged in schooling to access middle-class privileges, they realized that it might fail them because "office jobs," too, are classed and accessible only to those who have the requisite social capital. As a result, they critiqued the kind of education that was provided in schools which left them with limited options for respectable work. They called instead for more *hunar*-based training to secure an alternate, respectable life-script in the informal economy. Finally, since my participants belonged to a minority Muslim community, they saw official school knowledges—which inscribed the Sunni interpretation of Islam—as threatening their identity and desired greater attention to Shii religious education.

What we observe then are themes similar to those that appeared in chapters 2 and 3—the links across education, respectability, and social class, and anxieties around religious identity formation—but now in relation to different concerns. Schooling is articulated both as a social practice *and* as a commodity. It can signal social-class status through the kinds of opportunities that it can create—access to "safe" professions and better marriage proposals—and has the ability to reshape girls into subjects who can attract such possibilities. However, it can also be experienced in problematic ways, especially by those who are already situated on the margins of society due to their social class, gender, and/or religious interpretation. Together, these themes disrupt the flat, celebratory stance toward schooling posited by the development regime. They also provide insights into the making of girl-subjects in Pakistan.

Focus-Group Site and Methods

I collected data in a minority community of Shia Muslims in South Pakistan. I selected the community and city for several reasons. First, I grew up in this town and have worked with the same community-based organizations for the past decade. During this time, I have volunteered as a teacher and teacher educator, and have helped to raise funds for housing rehabilitation after floods and for scholarships for ultrapoor children. I have also conducted research in this community, which has been published.[43] In other words, I bring to the study an intimate knowledge of the community, a commitment to enhancing its welfare, and an ethic of empathy. I recognize that my decade-long experience with this community influences my interpretation of the data. Second, this city was a good site for this study due to its location as a transition town between the rural areas of the province of Sindh and the nearby metropolitan city of Karachi. Often, people from the rural areas settle here first in the hopes of moving on to Karachi to find better work and/or educational opportunities. In recent years, the city has increasingly become a focus of investment from private corporations, having opened its first mall, Pizza Hut, and McDonald's. During the past decade, it has also seen the establishment of new curricular offerings—such as the British O- and A-levels system—previously only available in Karachi. While the community boasts some families who own land and may be constituted as elite or upper class, the majority reside in different multifamily complexes that can be mapped onto social class. The center, with high real estate prices, is occupied by the elite or upper middle class, and the periphery by middle-class and low-income families. The economic elite of the community as well as upper-middle-class families enroll their children in

English-medium schools to pursue the British curriculum (much like elsewhere in Pakistan). Community members live in close proximity to each other and attend a local community center every evening. I visited the community center each evening, explained my project to prospective participants, and met with those who signed up the following day for interviews. I recruited participants through snowball sampling. After the interviews, participants would often ask their friends to participate as well. The local community-based organization, whose offices I used for conducting the interviews, also facilitated some introductions. Since I am also a member of this transnational Muslim community, it made recruitment much easier than it would have been for an outsider.

Overall, I conducted a total of twelve focus-group conversations—four of these were with teachers, three with parents, and five with female students between the ages of thirteen and twenty-one. Each focus group had a minimum of three and a maximum of five participants. Two parent groups, however, ended up having two members each because some parents did not arrive at their designated time and ended up joining another group (hence, one parent group had five instead of the assigned three participants). I used open-ended questions, including: What does education (ta'alim) mean to you? What is the purpose of education? Where does education take place? What limitations (if any) does formal schooling have? What changes would you want to see in your own schooling? During the focus groups with parents, the questions were reframed to be about their female children. Not all questions were asked in all focus group conversations. The themes that I discuss below emerge from the interview transcripts. I undertook thematic coding in order to highlight recurring themes and patterns in the participants' narratives. In addition, I commenced the process of analysis simultaneously with data collection. That is, after a few focus groups I evaluated the data for emergent findings and recurring themes, on the basis of which I modified the questions for subsequent groups in order to probe particular topics further. For instance, some of the female students emphasized how pressures of schooling were leading to a deprioritization of religious knowledges. To explore this theme further, I decided to add focus groups composed of teachers from the local Religious Education Center (REC).[44] In these conversations I tried to explore teachers' own ideas about the need for religious education, the available spaces for such knowledges, and the difficulties their students were facing in accessing these knowledges. Thus, the exercise of data collection was a recursive process, which made the study a mobile, fluid project, amenable to taking new directions as and when needed.

The themes I present below are not representative of all Pakistani girls, parents, or teachers. Indeed, the minority religious positioning of my participants necessarily makes these themes specific. However, the interviews serve as clues toward broader problematics around gender and schooling, pointing to how social class mediates assumptions about ideal girlhood. These narratives also problematize the neoliberal celebration of individual autonomy, choice, and responsibility, which permeates current discourses on girls' education.

NADIA: A SCHOOLED GIRL

From a distance, Nadia (age seventeen) appears to be the ideal girl imagined by girls' education campaigns. She attends school regularly, obtains high grades, secured a scholarship from the U.S. Embassy to spend a year at an American high school, and has good facility with the English language. She is not interested in marriage right now, and wants to make money to secure material comforts for herself and her family. When asked to elaborate on her everyday routine, she explains that she attends school all day, followed by tutoring sessions and homework. She avoids social gatherings to ensure that she can get enough sleep. She willingly regulates her behavior, time, and social life in ways that produce the kind of ideal girl-citizen desired by the contemporary social and economic order. Nadia displays the "potential" of girls when they stay in school, and her subject position is desirable in terms of both social objectives and state planning.

A deeper conversation with Nadia, however, illuminates the range of social and economic precarities that schooling has introduced in her and her lower-middle-class family's life. Nadia repeatedly referred to education as a "burden" (using the English word). She explained that education is not only a drain on her, as she has to struggle with academics at school and attend several tutoring sessions, but also for her family, as they have to sacrifice basic necessities to ensure that they have enough money to send her and her siblings to private schools. Given the low quality of education in public schools, any family that seeks to reap the promise of upward mobility via education must partake in expensive private schooling. Nadia's family has to deal with severe financial difficulties, including having to organize care for a disabled child, save for college expenses, and bear the high cost of schooling. She, then, argued that education was a burden for an entire range of actors who were involved in facilitating the process: "Whether we have food, housing, or other basic necessities does not matter. Due to education we have to kill our other basic necessities." Nadia's tone was angry and frustrated. Nadia found schooling to be all-consuming, leaving her with limited additional spaces to engender a sense of social belonging: "We are always either at school or at tuitions. I have lost my identity. I am only someone who went to [name of school] and did her O levels. That is the only way people know me. But education does not decide everything. Background and origins are important too but they are forgotten."

The terms "background" and "origins" in this context refer to a sense of local provincial and Shia identity. The majority of my participants were Sindhi and in the context of decades of suppression of their ethnic identity, they have developed a narrative that seeks to recenter this identity. This is further compounded by the fact that these participants are from a Shia minority community which fears that without the constant labor of sustaining its identity, they may be overwhelmed by the majority. In addition to a lack of belonging outside the identity of "student" and the labor of schooling, Nadia pointed out in a dejected tone, "learning has lost its own purpose . . . I study for formality's sake, not for enjoyment or learning."

At the same time, Nadia observed that "education gives status," and that unless she attended an elite university she would not be able to obtain a good job or make a living. Nadia's equivalence of "status" with having a job and making a living signals that only when one has the latter can she be seen as a subject who has arrived, has made it, or is even an adult. This narrative points to the paradox, whereby in today's social order adult citizenship is no longer linked to age but to one's employment and dependency status.[45] To become a fully participating adult citizen of society, Nadia has to become economically independent. However, longer periods of education and training, a precarious job market, and reduced state support translate into future uncertainties for individuals like Nadia, who are unable to achieve adulthood.

I open with Nadia's story because it signals the complicated ways in which schooling is consumed and experienced by girls from low-middle-income backgrounds in Pakistan today. It shows how social class, future job prospects, lack of quality public school education, and desire for religious belonging, intersect to inform schooling experiences.

SCHOOLING AS PROPER CONSUMPTION

The majority of my participants were from low-middle-income backgrounds. This often meant that their fathers were the primary breadwinners, their mothers were homemakers, and that they were enrolled in mid- to low-tuition private schools. With rising inflation and a stagnant job market, this gendered division of labor is becoming increasingly untenable for low-middle-income families. Hence, across the board my participants expressed the desire for education because they expected to enter the labor force. They often described schooling as a "pathway" (Erum, age fifteen) or "ladder" (Kiran, age thirteen) toward "success" (Naila, age sixteen), which entailed "having a good standard of living," "having a good job," or "making money" (Kiran, Erum, Naila, respectively). There was consensus among these participants that in order to progress in life one had to follow a particular life-script that included going to school followed by university so that one could obtain an "office job" (white-collar job). For my participants "office job" was a stand-in for work that was secure and not menial; it is the type of work undertaken by educated and professional women, rather than the uneducated women who might be engaged in manual labor or who set up their own petty business enterprises. To be educated meant that one worked in an office. Such work was also legitimized by the broader community for single women; once married, however, girls whose husbands could provide often did not work in offices either. By avoiding work after marriage, women could also signal their social-class standing. Most of my participants, however, could not afford such luxury. They knew that regardless of their marital status, they would need to work in order to make ends meet. Sania (age twenty-one) explained that "education is for a job." She was adamant that it was important for girls to get an education so that they could support their families financially. Hence, education was seen as proper consumption for low-income girls—it was a commodity that they consumed today in order to reap its rewards in the future. Any deviation from this pathway—such as completion of only ten grades of schooling, opting for vocational or technical training, taking time off to care for family members, or taking a couple of years off to memorize the Quran[46]—was a source of anxiety because it would inevitably decrease the chances of obtaining a white-collar job. Sabiha (age sixteen) explained: "no degree, no job, no identity."

This perspective of education has created an atmosphere where acquisition of credentials is emphasized over education's potential for effecting social justice or democratic change. My participants, for instance, pointed to the increasing "credentialization of education" (Anita, age twenty-one), which produced a "business-like movement of life" (Nadia). Anita complained that "education has become a business. One now needs a master's or even a Ph.D. to get a decent job. We are unable to pursue our interests because it is difficult to convince ourselves and others to pursue disciplines that cannot be converted into money quickly."

Similarly, Ram Chand (a parent) noted that children see education as a pathway to *aasaish* (luxury) and have a "utilitarian and egocentric view of education," which is often "self-serving and oriented toward materialism and consumption." He further observed that with the transformation of schooling into a commodity, students are read as consumers and school-student or teacher-student relationships are viewed as transactions. He went on to describe these trends succinctly:

> These days education has become commercialized and students are clients. It is as if schools provide customer care. Schools now see children as customers, versus the caring role that a parental figure might have. Commercialization also means that schools need profits, so they give what the child wants. In the current market-driven, degree-oriented environment, students want high percentages [in public examinations] in order to get into highly sought-after professions, and schools try to provide that.

Likewise, Yasmeen, a parent and an assistant professor at a local college bemoaned, "education these days is a machine for earning money."

What Ram Chand, Yasmeen, Anita, and Nadia are pointing out is the neoliberalization of everyday life and education. The dominance of economic rationality has reduced all aspects of schooling to economic calculations. Paul Bylsma, an American scholar who has examined the evolution of the American higher-education system, observes that today, "the transactional nature of investing resources toward a diploma is emphasized over the transformational nature of learning toward the end of democratic deliberation and a community-based vision of flourishing and social prosperity.... The *telos* ... of higher education is in danger of being reduced to producing quantifiably successful graduates seeking to flourish in shallow and material terms."[47] Bylsma goes on to observe that the model citizen of today is imagined as someone who has the "ability to choose between universally sufficient and available options" and "will make the most rational and responsible decision for their own welfare. . . . The model citizen in the neoliberal state is active, entrepreneurial, rational, responsible, ultimately affluent, and thus morally superior."[48] This is exactly the sentiment that sixteen-year-old Sabiha expressed: "even if you are a bad human being you are everything if have a degree and high paying job." Consuming education to obtain a degree and to transform one's self into a productive worker, thus, appeared as the dominant rationale for pursuing schooling. It was not only a practice that was required of my participants due to their social class positioning, but also a pathway that was marked as the most logical and commonsensical for all youth.

My participants, however, noted that girls from upper-class backgrounds did not consume schooling in the same way. For them education conferred a form of respectability that opened doors to better marriage prospects. As Nabila noted, "Some girls believe in inserting 'Engineer' or 'Doctor' before their names so they can get good marriage proposals." Sanum (age twenty-one) also explained that "given the attention to education these days everyone wants an educated wife; the more educated you are, the better your marriage prospects." Since being a doctor was considered a high achievement for girls in this community, I noticed that several girls in my focus groups as well as beyond were pursuing the field of medicine. Their purpose for doing so, however, was not necessarily appreciated by Nabila and Sanum. Sanum, who was from a low-income family, for instance, had been struggling to complete her M.B.B.S. (medical degree) and anxiously wanted to start working. She complained: "many [girls] will just do M.B.B.S. and not do house jobs (residencies)." This, to her, appeared as an improper consumption of education because it limited the opportunities for those girls who genuinely needed to pursue the degree to obtain a means of earning a living. This critique, however, does not mean that girls from low-income backgrounds do not see education as a pathway toward marriageability. Indeed, Sanum noted: "Education is a requirement for a better life partner." She defined a successful girl as "one who gets a good life partner, has the ability to earn a living, and knows how to run her household." For girls from low-income backgrounds, this equates to what Saadia (age sixteen) termed as the "triple shift"—"women have triple shift—*ghar* [home], *bachay* [children], job."

In contrast, Maria (age fifteen), a girl from a relatively well-to-do middle-class background, did not see herself as being the primary wage earner in the future.

She wanted to have the proper qualifications to earn, "*if needed.*" More significant than waged work for Maria was the ability that education would bestow on her to manage her household effectively and educate her (female) children in an increasingly competitive environment: "Women are the primary caregivers. Boys can learn from outside but girls learn at home. Boys' nourishment can happen from outside." The trend of upper- and middle-class girls' pursuit of education for reasons other than joining the formal labor force has also been found in other settings in South Asia and the Middle East. For instance, while Jordan boasts high enrollment rates for both primary and secondary schooling, this has not been accompanied by lower birth rates and higher female workforce participation as typically envisioned by the development narrative. Fida Adely, in her ethnographic study of girls' educational experiences in Jordon, finds that highly educated middle-class women choose to stay at home.[49] The World Bank has termed this as a "gender paradox." However, Adely argues that these trends become intelligible when we take into account norms around marriageability, class, and respectability. Girls indeed value education, but for different reasons and toward different ends. Adely concludes that "the logic of the World Bank can be turned on its head . . . as people have appropriated the imperative of education for their own status concerns and needs, a reminder of the limits of the power of global development institutions."[50]

Likewise, Willy Oppenheim in his study in an agrarian village in Punjab, Pakistan, also found that parents valued education not only for the potential for girls to be able to secure jobs but also due to education's enabling girls to "make a house very well" and train children, as they are "responsible for many generations."[51] Oppenheim thus argues that the "social value of schooling can shift and diverge within a given community."[52] My participant, Maria, like Adely's middle-class participants, is neither the kind of subject envisioned by transnational girls' education discourse, nor the "consumer-worker" desired by the nation. Although she conforms to the neoliberal principles of self-interest and is driven by economic logics, these same principles lead her to consume education differently. She seeks to become a better mother and prepare her children for a competitive world. These practices also help her to signal her social class, as only upper-class women can afford to become full-time mothers. She lacks the desire and the financial drive to enter the labor force that both the neoliberal and national projects deem imperative.

These differences in how education is consumed are reminiscent of the purpose of education for *ashraf* girls, articulated at the turn of the twentieth century. Indeed, whereas Sharifun was urged by Muhammadi Begum to obtain an education so that she could engage in waged work available to struggling families, well-to-do girls were to acquire an education to manage their households and train their children. My focus-group participants engaged in a similar reasoning to some extent. Much like the *ashraf* women of the turn of the twentieth century, Maria consumed education to improve her domestic-management skills and secure good marriage prospects. Girls from low-middle-income backgrounds (the majority of my participants), however, saw schooling primarily as a pathway to waged work. What is different in the present moment, however, is the greater public discourse around the *necessity* for women to enter the workforce. Whereas, at the turn of the twentieth century, women avoided working for money until pressed to do so, in our own time it seemed an inevitable reality for most of my participants. The fact that they would need to work to make ends meet was not an idea that they had to be socialized into. They already believed that it was their *personal* responsibility to improve their lives without relying on the state.

This is perhaps also one of the reasons that not many of my participants connected education to citizenship; while education was seen as a practice that would enhance the self, it appeared to contribute nothing toward enhancing the development of the nation. This is a stark contrast to earlier discourses, whereby education was expected to transform young people into ideal Pakistani citizens. Recall Asaf Hussain's interviewees from chapter 3, who consistently drew connections between education and contribution to the new nation of Pakistan. I suspect that since the Pakistani state has been failing to provide basic services to its citizens, my participants have disciplined themselves into citizen-workers who are expected to strive to improve their own lot without guarantees from the state. Girls like Nadia then see their inability to secure a job as their personal failing.

So, there are different but overlapping patterns of how schooling is consumed. In my case study, for upper-middle-class girls, schooling provided potential rewards in the form of marriage proposals as well as the "option" of entering the formal workforce if needed. For low-income participants, while schooling had similar social meanings, it was first and foremost a means to access future waged work, although they experienced intense scrutiny and precarity in the process. It is this latter group that put forth a critique of schooling for failing to deliver on its promise of prosperity and erasing particular identitarian knowledges.

CONTESTING SCHOOL KNOWLEDGES

School knowledge can be theorized as all aspects that students learn in school whether intentional or unintentional. These knowledges provide a glimpse into the kinds of discursive possibilities that are available for students to (re)make themselves. I present two critiques of school knowledges that emerged during the focus groups. In this section, I discuss how participants critiqued the exclusion of skills-based training from official school curricula, which limited their possibilities for becoming economically independent; and in the next section, I explain how they noted that in privileging particular moral regimes, schools erased knowledges about religious minorities—in their case, Shia Muslims. This evidence should be read in light of how schooling has evolved in postindependence Pakistan (and also India). Krishna Kumar argues that one of the key consequences of colonial education policies has been the disconnect between school knowledges and everyday knowledge.[53] And, in the context of Pakistan, we might consider teachings of Islam to be a part of the latter.

While participants saw schooling as a pathway to white-collar jobs, they also recognized that "there were no guarantees" (Fazila, age seventeen). Fazila added, "After all, how many doctors and engineers does a nation need? Who will do the rest of the work?" Likewise, Sanum questioned: "If people do not choose those [blue-collar jobs] then the nation loses. Who will fulfill the small roles?" It was clear that my participants understood the classed nature of "office jobs." Such jobs often went to those who had the requisite cultural and social capital. This led us into conversations around the devaluation of *hunar* (skills) in society and the decline of apprenticeship systems due to the privileging of particular knowledges in formal schooling. For example, participants noted that vocational or crafts-based education was looked down upon and available only in nonmainstream educative spaces such as technical boards or informal apprenticeship arrangements. These spaces of learning and forms of knowledges were assumed to be reserved for *unparh loag* (the uneducated people). As Gulnaz (age thirteen) elaborated, "we live in a two-tracked society—those who have 'education' and those who have *hunar*; the latter are often deemed to be *unparh* [uneducated]."

At the same time, many participants recognized that having a *hunar*—especially one that could be monetized—is useful in today's context where schooling is failing to deliver on its promise of jobs that provide financial security. They identified tailoring, fashion designing, beautician, mobile technology repair, electronics repair, computer hardware maintenance, and plumbing as some economic domains where jobs were plentiful but from which "educated" people stayed away. Participants explained that learning such skills is considered "low status" because "education" entails progressing through the chain of school, college, and university, and ending with an "office job." They cited the example of many people whom they knew personally who worked as tailors, blacksmiths, and plumbers and made a better income than many "educated" people with master's degrees.[54] Laila (mathematics and science teacher), for instance, gave specific examples of many children she knew at her brother's apprenticeship arrangement who were brighter than her own students in school. Asma (mathematics teacher) also provided similar examples. Both of these teachers taught in schools that catered to children from low-income families, and argued that while official school knowledges were deemed more worthy of study, *hunar* would in fact be more useful for their students and prevent economic hardship.

The participants' concerns around unemployment seem to stem from their personal experience of "educated" family members being unable to secure adequate employment, as I have noted in my previous work with this community.[55] This rings especially true in the case of women in Pakistan. According to data available in 2014–15, unemployment rates for women in urban areas is nearly 20 percent, with female labor force participation only around 10 percent.[56] With over 18 percent of the urban population below the poverty line,[57] and nearly 39 percent estimated to be vulnerable to poverty,[58] a low labor-force participation likely indicates that most women are stuck working in the informal sector. In fact, many women in the community where I conducted the study made an income by running home-based beauty parlors, boutiques, and producing handicrafts (such as *rallis*, quilts). Such home-based, contingent work often does not provide the labor protections of full-time work, as Anita Weiss's work with women in home-based cottage industries in the Walled City of Lahore during the late 1980s illustrates.[59] These women had to often rely on middle-men for raw materials and for bringing products to the market, which decreased their ability to negotiate better rates for their work. Even in the 1980s, however, Weiss noted the significant lack of technical schools for girls where they could learn industry-related skills.[60]

When all else fails, girls from low-income backgrounds often end up in factories. Although only a very small percentage of girls whom I interviewed would fall in this category, manual labor in factories was not outside the scope of their imaginations, since many knew others who indeed worked in a nearby factory. While factory jobs are valorized by girls' education advocates like Nicholas Kristof, who in his *New York Times* article "Two Cheers for Sweatshops,"[61] praises factory jobs as a pathway to address poverty, factories in Pakistan are notorious for exploiting workers. This was clearly visible in the May 2017 protests of the apparel brand Khaadi in Pakistan. Khaadi's employees have detailed their mistreatment—from long working days and low wages to lack of job security and resistance to unionization. Their cries are met by a government that has been unwilling to enforce labor laws. With the global focus on women's participation in the labor force, it would seem logical that state and nonstate actors would seek to improve the status of women working in the formal economy through higher wages, better living conditions, opportunities to enhance skills, and provision of insurance. However, that has not been the case in Pakistan. Implementing labor protections is not in the interest of global capital and the neoliberal state. Nike, the global leader of Girl Effect, for instance, closed its factories in South Korea when women started organizing for better wages.[62]

My participants' desire for *hunar* can be read, then, as an effort to devise ways to access income security in an environment where schooling is not fulfilling its promise of economic independence. In fact, a 2014 "World of Work" report by the International Labour Organization argued that it is the quality of work, and not work in itself, that can alleviate poverty. The report noted that half of the workers in developing countries are twice as likely to be trapped in a "vicious circle of low-productivity employment, poor remuneration and limited ability to invest in their families' health and education, which in turn reduces the likelihood that current and subsequent generations will be able to move up the productivity and income ladders."[63] When properly supported, women can even thrive in male-dominated professions that require specialized skills. Consider the Aga Khan Cultural

Services' Women Social Enterprise (recently renamed CIQAM) project, in the village of Altit in Hunza. The project trains poor and marginalized women in professions dominated by men, such as carpentry, furniture making, and woodworking. Entrance in these male-dominated professions translates into better incomes for these women than would otherwise be possible in feminized professions of handicrafts or through factory work. Projects like these, however, are rare and require not only initial capital but extensive work in the community to create an authorizing environment for women to work. Such projects call for development interventions and vocational training that are long-term and participatory. They also call into question the types of knowledges and skills centered in formal schooling, pointing toward a broadening of the definition of what it means to be educated.

My participants' calls for learning concrete skills were hence aimed at securing alternate ways for survival and decreasing their dependence on men. Instead of opting out of schooling, they called for modifying it in ways that they thought would fulfill their needs and give them viable life-scripts. These insights show that girls in Pakistan actively engage with school knowledges and understand the ways in which partaking in particular learning opportunities can increase or decrease their chances of a "good life."

RELIGION, IDENTITY, AND MORAL INSTRUCTION

Moral instruction of young people remains a crucial objective of schools. That is precisely why in both chapters 2 and 3 we observed extensive debate about English language/literature, dress codes, and the teaching of Christianity in schools. These debates have continued to the present, but with a sectarian tinge. The state of Pakistan has drawn on the institution of schooling to produce proper "Muslims" and "Pakistanis." It has sought to do this by introducing elements of Muslim morality in schools through courses such as *Islamyat* and Pakistan Studies, appointments of public school teachers, and dress codes. Indeed, the *National Education Policy* published in 2009 recognizes the "importance of Islamic values" and emphasizes the "need for developing Pakistani children as proud Pakistani citizens having strong faith in religion and religious teachings as well as the cultural values and traditions of the Pakistani society."[64]

Girls' dress codes continue to be a site of tension in these debates. In October 2017, for instance, a public university, the International Islamic University of Islamabad, issued a circular warning that women not conforming to its dress code will be punished. The dress code was defined as: "Shalwar Qameez with at least knee-length shirt, dress should not be see-through, deep necks strictly prohibited, sleeveless shirts are not allowed, trousers are allowed only with long shirts, skinny jeans, tights and capris are not allowed, dupatta or scarf is compulsory with all dresses, make-up and heavy jewellery [*sic*] are not allowed, and high heels are also not allowed."[65] Even at private educational institutions girls are disciplined around what they can and cannot wear. Earlier in October 2017, a female faculty member at the Institute of Business Management (IoBM) in Karachi was reprimanded by a security guard over what she was wearing. The faculty member's Facebook post about this incident went viral. It noted: "Today, I was rudely stopped at the [IoBM] gate by a weird man who said he was the security head, and told that I wasn't 'following the dress code'. . . . Ladies, please help me understand, how I am a security threat?"[66] The post included a photo of this faculty member wearing a white shirt and a long scarf over pants.

Anxiety over women's dress is just one example of how the state as well as other societal institutions and individuals advance their particularized assumptions about public piety and morality. These contestations often spill over into the realm of curriculum as well, as I will describe later. Significantly, these debates now take on an explicit sectarian tinge. Since state-sponsored interpretation of Islam in Pakistan has been Sunni, it marginalizes minority interpretations of the faith. The community where I worked has faced persecution and threats of excommunication in the past. It has, therefore, developed a strong sense of identity as a minority, and engages in boundary-making practices, such as living in gated neighborhoods and establishing strong social-welfare institutions to meet the needs of its members. Furthermore, it has developed evening religious education services, where young members of the community learn about their interpretation of Islam. At the Religious Education Center, classes are held every weekday evening for an hour, on topics such as Shia theology, Muslim history, and prayers.

While I was conducting focus groups, one of the key anxieties that emerged was around the religious formation of girls and the religious identity of the community. Some female participants complained about the lack of time, and consequently interest, to attend REC classes. Sidra (age sixteen) observed that, "we prioritize rational knowledges of school and think religious teachings of REC teachers are stagnant." Similarly, Nadia commented that in the contemporary environment, where money reigns supreme, REC is devalued because attendance is free: "I have a nonserious attitude toward REC. We have no time. We pay for secular education and don't pay for REC." I, therefore, decided to include additional focus groups with REC teachers to explore this theme further. In this section, I provide a glimpse into my conversations with the teachers around the need for religious knowledges (read: Shia theology and moral instruction). Teachers' narratives become intelligible when we situate them within the national project of producing "Muslim" (read: Sunni) subjects through schooling.

REC teachers explained that "*mazhab* [religion] is an integral part [of life] and it is important for young people to follow religion" (Naureen, REC teacher). For them knowledge of religion was essential for producing an ethical subject. They were, therefore, concerned about the lack of attendance at RECs. They worried that schools did not expose students to the kind of behaviors, knowledges, and sensibilities that their interpretation of Islam espoused. They also believed that religious education was crucial for students to be able to articulate their identity in a hostile environment. This was an implicit reference to Sunni domination in Pakistan. Rashida, a veteran teacher of eighteen years, bemoaned that students and parents alike ignored religious knowledge acquisition due to the "overwhelming pressures of secular schools." Since students spent the majority of their time in schools, at tuitions, or doing homework, they had little time left for REC classes. The teachers believed that this was a problem given that community members are often asked to explain their interpretation of Islam. Rashida observed that, "there is much misconception in the population about us [Shia Muslims], and children need the REC for resolution." Rashida's narrative suggests that she was anxious about her minority interpretation of Islam being made invisible in and through school knowledges, and feared erasure of her community's identity.

Significantly, in the context of Pakistan, where the national identity is intricately linked to Islam, being the "wrong" kind of Muslim can bring out the wrath of the populace as well as the state. The persecution and discrimination of members of the Ahmadiyya community in Pakistan is a case in point. Members of this community were first persecuted in 1953 during the Lahore riots (led by Islamist parties, including Jamaat-e-Islami),[67] followed by another massive persecution effort launched by Islamist parties in 1974, which led to the government of Pakistan passing a constitutional amendment declaring members of the community as *kafirs* (unbelievers). In 1984, another amendment was made which restricted the community from calling itself "Muslim." On May 28, 2010, approximately ninety members of the Ahmadiyya community were killed during attacks on two mosques; and, as I write this chapter in October 2017, three members have been sentenced to death on blasphemy charges. This time the flames of violence have been stoked by the son-in-law of the former Pakistani prime minister Nawaz Sharif, perhaps in a bid to distract attention from an ongoing investigation into the family's corruption. In the context of these examples, and everyday sectarian violence against Shia groups as well, the community where I conducted research has remained very cautious. Members realized that schools played a critical role in erasing their subject positions, and hence emphasized that children of the community participate in the REC.

Their fears around erasure are not unique. Consider the controversies in relation to textbooks which shed light on the political stakes of school curricula. Textbooks in Pakistan are prepared under the guidance of and approved by the Central/National Curriculum Wing of the Ministry of Education. They are published, distributed, and marketed by the four Provincial Textbook Boards in their respective jurisdictions. In 2014, the political party Jamaat-e-Islami in the Khyber-Pakhtunkhwa province demanded that chapters on Muslim personalities that had been removed by the previous provincial government in 2006 be reinstated, and that "all secular, un-Islamic chapters be removed."[68] It asked for the addition of eighteen Quranic verses to the ninth-grade chemistry book and for replacing "Good morning" with "Assalam-o-alaikum" in first-grade textbooks.[69] Their request also included the removal of what they deemed to be inappropriate images, specifically pictures of schoolgirls with their heads uncovered. The Tehrik-e-Insaaf (political party)–led government acquiesced to their demands. This was criticized by others as giving in to extremist interpretations of Islam. Between 2000 and 2005, the northern areas of Pakistan had been engulfed in another textbook-related controversy when the state introduced new, overtly Sunni textbooks. The local Shia population agitated for a more balanced curriculum. The events culminated in violent confrontations during 2004–5. These controversies show how contestation over school knowledges is also a contestation over identity and belonging. As anthropologist Nosheen Ali, writing about this incident, notes:

> The right to have representation of Shia identity in school textbooks was seen by Shia protestors . . . as a mode for securing recognition and cultural reproduction. . . . Through the idiom of religion, the Shia subjects of the Northern Areas were also articulating a political demand for legitimate, substantive inclusion in a polity that has historically denied them even the most basic citizenship rights. . . . Hence, asserting religious difference and getting it politically recognized in official arenas such as education becomes a potential, and perhaps the only viable way to achieve similarity and equal treatment as citizens of the Islamic Republic of Pakistan.[70]

It is against this background that I interpret Rashida's comments about misconceptions about her community and the desire that young women and men engage with religious knowledges. She saw schools as potentially erasing already precarious knowledges about minority communities in Pakistan. These fears also compelled other teachers to advocate for greater space for Shia religious knowledges. As Hina (REC teacher) said, "we should maintain balance between *din* [spiritual] and *duniya* [material]; secular education only focuses on *duniya*." However, teachers did not seek to replace "secular" schools with RECs. Instead, for them the REC provided an additional space for learning. Unlike the mainstream madrasas in Pakistan, which are often compelled by the state to define their "usefulness," and have become a site of constant intervention and reform, RECs are not viewed as threats because they do not seek to substitute for public schooling.

At this point it is also crucial to note the slippage between religious/Shia knowledges and moral instruction that often happened during focus-group conversations. Teachers emphasized that "religious knowledge" (*dini ilm*) was important in order to engender a distinctly Shia identity, and believed that such an identity would shape the public and private conduct of young people in different ways when compared to school knowledges. For example, our conversations about REC often veered toward the increasing pressures of social media, the incitement to display intimate details about one's life for public consumption, the collapse of the joint family system, and the increasing isolation of young men. All of these were areas that the teachers believed could be addressed through proper moral instruction, a task that secular schools were not adept at. Teachers also noted that parents, too, were ill-equipped to address such issues, since they were often engrossed in their own difficult lives, just barely surviving. So, they considered the RECs and their own profession of pastoral care/teaching as ideally placed to address the needs of young men and women.

BECOMING EDUCATED GIRLS

The transnational discourse on girls' education positions girls in the global South as being on the precipice of failure if not saved by education. Education is expected to help delay marriage and childbearing, prepare girls to enter the workforce, and so propel them onto paths of success and prosperity. This system of reasoning articulates girls as agents who can take personal responsibility for their development, secure rights, and gain economic empowerment; and schooling appears as the primary social project that can unfold this progress and emancipation. However, when we actually consider the realities of girls (as glimpsed in the narratives of the participants), we see that schooling is at times experienced in problematic ways. Social class often mediates experiences of schooling. The calls for self-making embedded in the current articulation of girls' education produce different possibilities and limitations for girls, especially those from disadvantaged backgrounds. Since my focus-group participants belonged to socioeconomic classes that had just begun to access the privileges of the middle class, they found themselves simultaneously enticed by the promises of upward mobility that neoliberal visions of schooling offered and constrained by the absence of the economic and social scaffolding necessary for girls to emerge successfully out of schools. Nadia's case demonstrates this aptly—she identified the deep economic and social investment required by her family to ensure access to good schooling and how these sacrifices produced additional precarities for her. Likewise, girls from lowmiddle-class backgrounds often called for a rethinking of school knowledges, so that they could eventually become economically independent. We also saw how schooling appeared to be problematic for religious minorities, as they grappled with the implications of moral instruction in schools dominated by Sunni ideologies. Since schools are seen as being ill-equipped to provide moral instruction, nonformal educative spaces (such as the RECs and the home, as the next chapter will show) have emerged as the ideal sites for engendering an ethical subjectivity. This move recenters the patriarchal family as well as religious leaders, assigning them the authority to regulate youth.

The case study centered in this chapter reveals how concerns around respectability, religious formation, and orientation to waged work continue to inform conceptualizations of ideal girlhood. The specificities of social class and religious orientation in particular signal that it is impossible to imagine homogenized girlsubjects. Furthermore, the evidence in this chapter, as well as the progress made in Pakistan to close the gender gap in education, suggests that at least in the urban areas, education for girls is viewed as an important endeavor. While parents engage in different evaluations around what type and how much education to give to girls, and girls consume schooling for different purposes, there is plenty of evidence to suggest that their education is not taboo. According to a 2009 Pew survey, 87 percent of Pakistanis believe that education is equally important for boys and girls.[71]

This background helps us make sense of the backlash against Malala in Pakistan. The backlash, I argue, has less to do with Pakistanis' discomfort with girls' education and more to do with what Malala represents in relation to Pakistan and Muslims. Given Malala's prominent stature these days, and the unfortunate abundance of Pakistan "experts" or prowomen journalists—such as Nicholas Kristof—who draw on Malala to articulate reductive ideas about Pakistan, before closing the chapter I will briefly analyze Malala's uptake in the discursive regime of girls' education.

Returning to Malala

Malala, the idea, tells a particular story about Islam and the people of Pakistan. She is represented as the girl who defied the cultural logics operative in Pakistan, and who now embodies a transnational, secular modernity exemplified by her emphasis on the autonomous self, enactment of choice, advocacy for freedom, and arguments for gender equality.[72] Instead of being a symbol of the courage of Muslims and Pakistanis to stand up against local forms of violence, Malala is shown to be an exception. Through extensive media coverage and uptake of her image by international organizations, she is individualized in her courage and successful performance of empowerment. She is presented as succeeding against all odds, as a heroine or, as Chelsea Clinton in *Time* magazine calls her, the "*champion* for girls everywhere."[73] She is made into an exception by practices such as celebrating "Malala Day," receiving the Nobel Peace Prize, and book deals. Even the title of her book, *I Am Malala: The Girl Who Stood Up for Education and Was Shot by the Taliban,* centers on her person, emphasizing her uniqueness.

To create Malala as an exception entails individualizing and abstracting her from the local environment and cultures, and connecting her positive attributes to another source, such as her formal education, desire for success, and ambition. Her courage, then, is not read as grounded in Pashtun cultural practices that valorize social justice. Instead, she is positioned as a singular force *against* local customs and cultural elements. Malala's transnational uptake, then, sustains assumptions that transform all Pakistani, Muslim men into terrorists, and all Muslim women into victims or potential victims. Malala is distanced from other Muslim girls. She is made to simultaneously stand in for, represent, and symbolize the oppressed Muslim girls, and positioned as the empowered girl who is not one of them. The idea of Malala denies other Muslim girls similar forms of empowered subjectivities. It sustains the façade of Islam as an oppressive religion, position-ing interventions—such as universal education of girls, empowerment projects, or even drone attacks—as necessary or even ethically imperative.

However, reading *I Am Malala* against the grain highlights Malala's radical specificity as a Muslim and as a Pakistani.[74] In this book, we come face to face with vibrant cultures and societies, an abundance of strong-willed women, and kind, thoughtful men. The text reveals aspects of the Pushtun culture and its people: we learn about their hospitality,[75] their oral traditions of poetry,[76] their love for knowl-edge,[77] the imperatives for kindness,[78] and the beauty and precarity of mountain societies.[79] There are incidences when the religion of Islam emerges as a source of generosity and peace. For instance, the only charities that stayed behind to help local people after the earthquake in 2005 were local Muslim charities.[80]

In *I Am Malala,* we encounter women who shatter the trope of the victim-ized Muslim woman awaiting a savior. From Malala's namesake, the Malalai of Maiwand, who fought the British,[81] and her great-grandmother, who "walked forty miles alone over mountains" in order to appeal for the release of her son,[82] to the women of Spal Bandi "who had great freedom and were not hidden away,"[83] we find evidence of women's tenacity within socioeconomic and political constraints. These glimpses into the lives of Muslim women add complexity to, and work against, the narrative that reduces freedom to "resistance" against local practices. It would be simplistic to read these actions axiomatically as moments of women's empowerment and agency; however, they do signal the possibility of differently constituted lives where empowerment and agency may or may not look the same as that proposed by western liberal feminists. Here, women seem to be working to establish their rights within local frameworks, and against domestic and global patriarchies.

We also come across a wide range of kind, thoughtful, and intelligent Muslim men who work for the betterment of their communities, including contesting the advances of the local Taliban-inspired militants. Figures such as Malala's father, Ziauddin Yousafzai (an activist); Jehan Yousafzai (Zaiuddin's cousin, who brought a gift upon Malala's birth);[84] Uncle Dada (a conscientious teacher);[85] Nasir Pacha (a stranger who helped Ziauddin complete his college education);[86] Akbar Khan (Ziauddin's mentor);[87] Usman Bhai Jan (the beloved school-bus driver);[88] and Dr. Javid (the Pakistani-British doctor who arranged Malala's hospitalization in the United Kingdom),[89] all strike at the heart of the ahistoricized and decontextualized figure of the violent, brown, Muslim man. The key Taliban characters in the book, Fazlullah, Sufi Mohammad, and the mufti who tried to close Ziauddin's school, are viewed as anomalies, and their actions are contested by local men and women alike. Indeed, the challenge to Fazlullah comes from within the community—the Pushtuns called their assembly of elders to oppose him,[90] and those who viewed him favorably earlier retracted their support when his initiatives did not align with their sensibilities.[91] Challenges to Fazlullah's militancy were also featured prominently in the local media.⁹² *I Am Malala* is, then, a radically specific story, one which gets erased as all the specificity is removed in western media discourses and Malala is transformed into a caricatured, first-oppressed, now-empowered girl.

The contestation around Malala in Pakistan, thus, represents the struggle for the meaning of Pakistan and Muslim; it is less about girls' education or any protest against the education of girls. It also signifies a struggle against certain meanings imposed or implied by volunteers, donors, and aid agencies of the global North. Evidence in this chapter clearly shows a remarkable desire for education in Pakistan. That education remains a classed enterprise and does not afford possibilities for all is a key issue at stake. This issue, however, is sidelined in aid and development discourses. Rather, what is highlighted is a false assumption around Pakistanis' and Muslims' animosity toward education, and Malala's image is often taken up in the service of that ideological project.

5

Akbari and Asghari Reappear

As the previous chapter showed, mass schooling in Pakistan has become one of the most dominant societal institutions for the reproduction of the next generation of citizen-subjects. Schools have taken over some of the key roles around the nurturing and instruction of young people that were previously reserved for the family and religious authorities. This has led to contestations around appropriate training of young people and the reassertion of the role of the home and/or alternate educative institutions in the cultural and ethical formation of the child. Education, thus, has transformed into a densely contested field with multiple actors—the state, the family, religious institutions, as well as mass media—seeking to define ideal subjectivities and proper relationships that young people must have to the state, home, waged work, the opposite sex, and religion. These relationships are important because they are the means in and through which economic and cultural privileges are reproduced and new ones accessed, and identities reinforced and remade. Against this background, in the current chapter I explore televised visualities, which prescribe and prohibit particular forms of femininity.

As forms of "public pedagogies,"[1] cultural productions such as television teach viewers about certain possible subjectivities, while simultaneously reproducing and resisting others. In the immediate aftermath of Pakistan's political independence, television programming was closely tied to nationalistic interests. However, the wider availability of television sets and the entrance of numerous private television networks in recent decades has enabled diverse programming. Television today forms one of the most accessible and influential discursive spaces that mediates social imaginaries. Hence, I see a television production as yet another kind of "text" in a genealogy that functions as an "actant" within a social system. While a plurality of voices in television means that there is a simultaneous reproduction and subversion of relations of power, television as a technology and cultural text is closely tied to urban and middle-class sensibilities in the context of Pakistan. The writers and producers of television shows, as well as owners of television networks, often come primarily from middle-class, urban backgrounds, and have exposure to transnational issues, which influences the representational practices of television. Hence, in the context of this book, which is attempting to explore distinctly middle-class tensions around the construction of the ideal girlhood, television is an apt medium to analyze. Furthermore, even with the entry of private networks, the state continues to harness television—by influencing it through advertisement dollars as well as through censorship practices—for its national integration and development goals. Television, thus, plays a complex role in social reproduction and critique.

Specifically, I have selected two recent televised shows that are based on Nazir Ahmed's popular novel *Mirat-ul-uroos* (The Bride's Mirror), which as we saw earlier was first published in 1869. Attending to the reproduction of *Mirat-ul-uroos* with its representation of ideal versus failed femininities facilitates a tracing of the kinds of lives that are authorized/normalized in contemporary Pakistan as well as the ones that are marked as deficient. It also helps to explicate the role of the family, religious ideologies, and school in crafting girlhoods. I will argue that through these representational practices television not only inculcates middle-class mores that reproduce the patrilineal family but also demarcates the home as the site for moral instruction (*tarbiyat*) and schools as places where education (*talim*) linked to waged work takes place.

ADAPTATIONS OF *MIRAT-UL-UROOS*

In *Mirat-ul-uroos* Nazir Ahmed explicated desired and failed *sharif* femininities through the contrasting figures of Akbari and Asghari. While the older sister, Akbari, personified recklessness, petulance, and greed, the younger sister, Asghari, was shown to be intelligent and thoughtful. It is Asghari's intentional privileging of the welfare of the patriarchal family that gains her the respect of not only her male relations but also her neighbors. She later starts a home-based school where other *sharif* families send their daughters so that they can emulate her. As mentioned earlier, Nazir Ahmed's book was picked up by the Department of Public Instruction, awarded a prize, and circulated to public schools. What is remarkable, however, is that the text has not lost its potency; it remains in circulation even today in India and Pakistan. Many girls receive this text as a gift at the time of their wedding, which signals its broad appeal. Furthermore, the binary subject positions represented by Asghari and Akbari have come to inform everyday lexicon. Consider an opinion piece published in 2013 in the Pakistani newspaper the *Express Tribune,* entitled, "Seeing Each Other in Black and White."[2] In the article, the author criticizes the tendency of Pakistanis to see everything "in black and white," naming it as the "Akbari and Asghari mentality" and the "Akbari/ Asghari lens." Akbari and Asghari, thus, continue to be relevant frames of legibility in the context of Pakistan today. In fact, *Mirat-ul-uroos* has been adapted for Pakistani television at least three times in the recent past: during the 1990s for the Pakistan Television Network, in 2011 for HUM TV, and in 2012 for Geo TV. In this chapter, I examine the representational practices of the HUM TV and Geo TV productions.

The Hum TV production *Akbari Asghari* (2011) is based on *Mirat-ul-uroos,* but rewritten as a comedy by the novelist Faiza Iftikhar.[3] Here, the protagonists—Akbari (also known as Becky) and Asghari (also known as Sara)—grow up in England and return to their family's village in Punjab, Pakistan, to marry their cousins, Akbar and Asghar, to whom they were betrothed when young. The comedy centers on the sisters' struggle to find a sense of belonging in the new environment. The 2012 Geo TV production of *Mirat-ul-uroos,* on the other hand, retains the original title.[4] This production revolves around Akbari's granddaughters, Aiza and Aima, who get married to Asghari's grandsons, Hammad and Hashim. Aiza, raised by Akbari, mirrors some of her values, while Aima reflects a thoughtfulness and maturity that is reminiscent of Asghari (even though she was not raised by her). These systematicities in characters help the viewers to readily assimilate Aiza, Aima, Becky, and Sara into familiar binary frames of desired/failed female subjects.

In both the Hum TV and Geo TV productions there are intense negotiations around performances of ideal femininities, which are linked to prevailing anxieties and aspirations around middle-classness. For instance, in the Geo TV production, through the characters of Aima and Aiza, we learn about economic pressures linked to rising inflation, unemployment (particularly of men), and the high cost of English-medium education.[5] Such pressures impinge upon the ability of Pakistani middle-class families to reproduce themselves culturally, as is evident by the discussion of extensive dowries for girls, living in a joint-patrilineal family arrangement, and tensions around women's entrance into waged work. The Geo TV production, then, teaches its viewers about habits and behaviors that are necessary for sustaining and reproducing middle-classness. It calls upon its viewers, particularly Pakistani middle-class women, to reinvent themselves in specific ways if they wish to continue to enjoy middle-class privileges and the familial harmony that accompanies such stable economic grounding.

The HUM TV production also explores economic precarities but does so through the theme of transnational migration. Here, middle-class identity is expressed through cultural mores and linguistic affiliations. To assert authenticity, many characters attempt to speak in Punjabi and Urdu, as well as English to varying degrees, which signals their comfort with, or aspirations for, middle-class social norms. Becky and Sara's family in England is shown to be working-class, which creates pressures for the sisters to find waged work, a practice that is read as a compulsion. Thus, both television shows give a glimpse into the local, national, and transnational forces that are shaping possible subject positions for women (and men) in Pakistan and the diaspora.

The fact that the two television shows are based on a nineteenth-century text shows how the present is neither a continuation nor a radical rupture from the past—rather, the relationship across gender, education, social class, the patriarchal family, and the nation continues to modulate in different ways. Women and girls continue to emerge as key players in reproducing middle-classness economically as well as culturally, and the ideal, educated woman is one who can perform this role adeptly.

THE ECONOMIC AND CULTURAL REPRODUCTION OF THE MIDDLE CLASS

One of the key framing themes in *Mirat-ul-uroos* (2012) is the economic precarity of middle-class families, and the role educated women are to perform to preserve familial economic and cultural status. The contrasting figures of Aima and Aiza symbolize modes of being that can either reproduce or threaten middle-classness. In this context, social class is theorized not simply as an economic position but also as a set of cultural mores, which include consumption habits, orientation toward waged work, and relations with the opposite sex and servants. In taking up these topics, *Mirat-ul-uroos* (2012) prescribes feminine performances crucial for the preservation of both economic *and* cultural middle-class status. Significantly, moral instruction, which takes place in the context of the home rather than the school, is elevated as the essential social practice that can transform girls into ideal subjects. In other words, it is the home where girls/women learn about appropriate social roles.

Mirat-ul-uroos (2012) revolves around Aiza's decision to leave the joint family and establish a separate household, disconnecting her husband (Hammad) from his family at a time when they relied heavily on his income. Aiza and Hammad eventually regret their decision when their marriage falls apart due to Aiza's extravagant consumption habits and Hammad's extramarital affair. In contrast, Aima provides valuable counsel to her underemployed husband (Hashim), takes up waged work (tutoring students) occasionally to relieve the family's financial burdens, and through careful financial planning helps her in-laws repay their debts. She also secures a proposal for her divorced sister-in-law and tutors her brother-in-law when he is on the brink of failing high school examinations. Whereas Aiza is self-centered, spendthrift, desires material possessions, and eventually leaves the joint-family, Aima is pragmatic, frugal, adept at homemaking (managing a budget, cooking, and sewing) and strengthens the joint-family unit. These portrayals of femininities neatly align with Nazir Ahmed's characterization of Akbari and

Asghari; a commitment toward familial harmony and loyalty to the patrilineal family thus appears as an ideal orientation for women.

The drama establishes Aima's and Aiza's contrasting womanhoods through a broad range of techniques. Aiza, for instance, is shown to pay too much attention to new styles of clothing, shoes, and makeup—which creates financial pressures for her parents and, later, her husband. She often appears in heavy makeup, wearing heels and designer clothes that do not call for a *dupatta* (a form of long scarf normally worn over a *shalwar kameez* by women in Pakistan as a sign of piety/modesty). In contrast, Aima appears in *shalwar kameez, dupatta,* and slippers. Aiza's hair is dyed and styled in short layers, whereas Aima's retains its original color and is worn in simple styles, such as a low ponytail. We also often do not find Aima in heavy makeup—in fact, it sometimes appears as if the makeup artists intentionally try to create a pale look by deliberately lightening her lips! These visuals signal that being too engrossed in one's physical appearance, which often also entails spending extravagant amounts of money, is not ideal for middle-class women. Such practices are also linked with notions of middle-class respectability, where dressing modestly is a way to secure one's honor and not invite the male gaze. In fact, in the final episode, when Aiza reforms her ways, she also undergoes a physical transformation: she is shown to wear a *dupatta,* her hair is not heavily styled, and she wears minimal makeup. This transformation delineates the kind of reinvention that the drama calls on its female viewers to undertake.

There are many additional critiques of women's consumption habits which outline the practices that are at odds with the reproduction of the patrilineal middle-class family. For instance, early on, when Aiza and her grandmother (Akbari) decide to move in with Nasir (Akbari's son and Aiza's/Aima's father), their carefree use of electricity becomes a point of contention in the household. Aiza's mother—Amna—advises her daughter to be careful in her use of electricity, since "Pakistan is undergoing an energy crisis and the higher electricity bill will also put the household over the monthly budget." Aiza, as expected, scoffs at her mother's advice. Her spendthrift and carefree attitude becomes more problematic when she asks her parents to celebrate her wedding with Hammad with *dhoom dhaam* (elaborate festivities). The family does not have much savings, so considers selling a plot of land that they had acquired as a form of investment for retirement. Matters come to a head when Aiza demands a car in her dowry, which again puts pressure on their already overstretched finances. The elaborate wedding celebrations also cause Hammad's family to draw loans.

Aima, in contrast, refuses to demand a dowry even when her husband taunts her for not bringing as large a dowry as her sister. She critiques not only large wedding celebrations and dowry practices, but also the crucial role that women can play in breaking this cycle. Indeed, extravagant weddings that compel middle-class families to take on debt have become a norm in Pakistan in recent years. Many have argued that such celebrations not only create undue pressures for families but also lead to public nuisance and promote exhibitionism, which is contrary to the ethics of Islam. Consequently, the government of Pakistan has advanced multiple legislations to regulate wedding celebrations. In 2003, the Punjab Marriage Functions Act, also known as the Prohibition of Ostentatious Displays and Wasteful Expenses, established a rule that permits only one dish at wedding parties. As with other laws in Pakistan, this law has been slow to take effect—in fact, in the Geo TV production, there is a discussion around how helpful it would be if everyone followed this rule.

An interesting point to note, in this regard, is that while Aima's younger brother, Farhan, also refuses to ask for a dowry, his approach is represented quite differently. Farhan uses the language of religion (noting that these practices are un-Islamic) to legitimize his stance. In contrast, Aima's preferences appear to be an effect of her concern for her parents. In other words, Aima wants to avoid a large wedding and extensive dowry because she is a conscientious daughter, whereas Farhan arrives at this decision as a thinking, rational man. Hence, women's critique of social norms is accepted, even praised, only when it is framed within the context of enhancing the welfare of the patriarchal family. Indeed, Farhan, too, could have adopted this stance against dowry out of a sense of responsibility as a conscientious son; however, that is not the case. He is portrayed as someone who arrives at this choice after careful and rigorous reflection on Muslim teachings. Aima's decisions, like Asghari's in Nazir Ahmed's text, are linked to her subject position as a daughter, wife, and, later, mother. In fact, Aiza who prioritizes her personal desires, interests, and ambitions is actively portrayed as a failed subject in *Mirat-ul-uroos* (2012). Women are called upon to reshape themselves for the reproduction, and financial and social survival, of the patrilineal family. This logic is also at play in the two sisters' stance on waged work.

After completing her master's degree, Aima decides not to work: "I thought about it but decided against it. Thought I might as well relax."[6] However, when her parents struggle financially after investing their savings on Aiza's lavish wedding, Aima decides to get a job. The following exchange between Aima and her father signals the specific conditions under which it is acceptable for middle-class women to work outside the home. It also highlights how *talim* (education) is understood in the contemporary Pakistani context:

Aima (to her father, Nasir): What's the use of getting all this education [*talim*] and then wasting it by sleeping and watching TV at home all the time? I was thinking about working until I get married; that way there will be some savings.

Nasir: What will do you with the savings?

Aima: What all girls do: collect items for a dowry.

Nasir: There is no need for you to prepare your own dowry. *Beta* [child], I'm alive. My situation is not such that I can't provide a dowry for you.

> *Aima:* I know. But I don't want to be a burden on you like Aiza. *Abba* [Dad], you gave me an education [*talim*] so that I can be independent. So now I want to take advantage of that education.
>
> *Nasir:* You are a fool.

As discussed in the previous chapter, here too we find substantial connections between education and waged work. Aima offers to work because she believes that this will enable her to contribute to the family income, specifically to prepare her own dowry. However, she only offers to do so when her family is undergoing financial constraints. Readers will recall from the previous chapter that upper-middle-class participants in my focus groups also wanted to acquire an education because it would enable them to earn an income if needed. Likewise, the two occasions when Aima chooses to work are linked with financial hardship (first her father's and later her in-laws'). As soon as her financial circumstances improve, she quits work and articulates a gendered division of labor that places the responsibility of providing for the family on men.

Let me illustrate this further. Aima convinces her father and secures a job that pays her quite well—Rs. (Rupees) 70,000 compared to the Rs. 50,000 that her future husband, Hashim, would make. However, she constantly complains about having to work hard all day long (*khuwari*), and yearns for the day when Hashim gets a job so that they can get married and she can "at least get rid of the job."[7] However, Hashim is quite pleased with Aima's job:

> *Hashim (to Aima):* It's excellent that you started working. After getting so much education [*talim*] it's not good to waste it. And I like working women; I don't like typical housewives—they just gain weight sitting at home, that's all.
>
> *Aima:* Don't worry, when I become a housewife, I will not gain weight.
>
> *Hashim:* What do you mean?
>
> *Aima:* I mean that after marriage, I don't plan to work.
>
> *Hashim:* Why?
>
> *Aima:* I don't want to take on two responsibilities. Husband, house, kids are a big responsibility. And so I cannot take on the additional trouble of a job.
>
> *Hashim:* What's the trouble with a job? There are many girls who work after marriage and manage their homes too. How do they manage?
>
> *Aima:* Everyone is different; they may be able to manage both but I cannot. I cannot be that hard-working [*mehnat-kasht*].
>
> *Hashim (scoffing):* Then be ready for all the household management to fall on you. You won't be able to have the luxury that Aiza *bhabi* [a term of endearment for a brother's sister] has.

> *Aima:* I am not in the mood to live luxuriously [*ayashi*]. I want to
> fulfill my responsibilities but by staying inside the home; outside
> responsibilities are yours.

The explanation that Aima provides for not wanting to work is not framed as a contestation of the double burden placed on women. Instead, she trivializes the struggle as one of personal preference—"Everyone is different"—and then responsibilizes women: if you are indeed a *mehnat-kasht* (hard-working) woman you can do both. It is this simultaneous opening and closing of subject positions in Aima's narrative that is instructive for how the patriarchal family provides space for women to engage in men's worlds while also regulating it. In other words, Aima's character shows that if there is no financial need, then middle-class women need not engage in waged work that requires them to leave the home. Such narratives preserve men's control over public spaces and women's bodies and labor. Women's labor then is available for exploitation in the service of the family.

We should also notice that it is Hashim (the lazy, underemployed husband) and not Hammad (the older, responsible brother) who advocates women's work. Hammad, the good son/husband, in fact discourages his wife from working outside the home. In other words, a good provider is one who creates the conditions for women to not leave the security of the home. This rhetoric further constrains the possibilities for women's work, especially for those women who do not have a choice in this regard. When ideal representations of femininity mark waged work as *optional* (as Aima said, you do it because you want to work hard) or *temporary* (you do it for a limited time when you need to), it becomes easier to dismiss the real struggles of low-income women in the formal and informal economies. Such narratives facilitate the withdrawal of the state from its responsibilities toward women. Women who are forced to work due to economic necessity are then often demeaned and find themselves in exploitative relationships and unsafe working environments. And, since the workspaces are male-dominated and unsafe, women who can afford to stay out of the workforce do so. Thus, a vicious cycle ensues that equates waged work with low-income familial status, inviting women's exploitation and in turn keeping women out.

Eventually when Hashim gets a job and the two get married, Aima quits her job. Coincidentally, Hashim soon gets into a fight at his company and quits his job as well. Unemployed, he tries to convince Aima to get back her old job or start working elsewhere. She adamantly refuses; she wants Hashim to fulfill his responsibility of providing for her: "In difficult times it is not necessary for a woman to work. It is important for her to support her man. I will help you find work but I will not take over your responsibility."[8] On another occasion when Hashim cajoles her about getting a job, she notes, "I am your responsibility; you are not my responsibility."[9] While there is an undercurrent that women should step into the workforce when their families are in dire circumstances, it is not acceptable to step in for reckless and lazy men, like Hashim. Here, the educated, *samajhdar* (intelligent) woman sticks to her predefined gender roles, compelling her husband to find a job. Later, when Hammad stops providing financial support to his parents and Hashim's income is inadequate to run the household, forcing her retired father-in-law (Wajahat) and young sister-in-law to begin thinking about getting jobs, Aima volunteers to start working again as a part-time tutor.

Aiza's character is often deployed as a stylistic devise to lend credence to Aima's views. For instance, it is only after hearing that her sister is making Rs. 70,000 that Aiza thinks that she, too, should have worked after completing her master's degree. She is mesmerized by Aima's salary and mentions it repeatedly, which makes her appear greedy and jealous. This in turn calls on viewers to dismiss her interest in professional work as yet another frivolity. Aiza is again discredited later on when she expresses her desire to work after having children:

Aiza (to her husband, Hammad): I made a mistake. After studying so much, I should have started a job like Aima. . . . I wasted time. I should have worked too. After our child is born, I will work then.

    Hammad: Why do you need to work, especially after our child is born? It will just be a drain on you [*khuwari*].

    Aiza: There are many people at home to take care of the child. And if needed I can get daycare services. But I want to work for sure since I get bored sitting at home.

    Hammad: Then why don't you help out at home? That will make Mom happy too.

    Aiza: A job is a job. Any servant can do domestic chores for only four thousand rupees.

    Hammad: If a household is left for servants to manage then it does not remain a home.

In this conversation, Aiza clearly appears as the unreasonable one. First she wants to work because she is captivated by her sister's salary. Then she is ready to pass on the responsibilities of raising her child to her in-laws or daycare services, and when her husband tries to reason with her, she mocks him. While Aiza's arguments around working to establish a sense of self may be valid, they are framed as unreasonable since they involve displacing her responsibilities for her children onto others.

I see *Mirat-ul-uroos* (2012) as reflecting distinctly middle-class anxieties related to women's entrance in male-dominated working environments. These anxieties have to do in large part with workplaces being unsafe for women, and less about men's conservative/disempowering stances. Hashim, for instance, constantly cajoled Aima to work and "make use of her education." And while not welcomed wholeheartedly, neither Aima's father nor her in-laws stop her from working. Indeed, economic anxieties appear to be moving both men and women from adamantly refusing women's entrance into the workforce to a more tentative stance. However, *Mirat-ul-uroos* (2012) also displays the tension that pervades this social class as it struggles to reproduce its economic base while holding on to real and imagined cultural practices that middle-classness affords—such as maintaining a household with one male earner. It is precisely due to this tension that *Mirat-ul-uroos* (2012) fails to capitalize on its platform. Rather than calling for safer working conditions and higher incomes for women, it articulates nostalgia for a time when middle-classness could be reproduced without women's entrance into the workforce and, hence, valorizes a division of labor along gender lines.

Relatedly, *Mirat-ul-uroos* (2012) identifies specific cultural and social practices through which middle-classness can be reproduced. Readers will recall that in Nazir Ahmed's version, Akbari freely socialized with women from lower social classes (the *hajjan*), and suffered later, when the *hajjan* robbed her. Likewise, in *Mirat-ul-uroos* (2012), Aima and Aiza's contrasting views on appropriate social relations with men as well as those from lower-income classes demonstrate the type of interactions that are deemed (in)appropriate for the reproduction of middle-classness. One scene in particular illustrates these dynamics vividly. In it, Aiza and Aima are chatting in Aiza's bedroom, with Aima lying carefree on the bed without her *dupatta*. In that moment, their young male servant, Guddu (who is Aiza's servant and has come from Karachi to live with her in Lahore), enters the room without knocking. This startles Aima, who scolds Guddu: "You have to knock before entering any room. In fact, just hand us things at the threshold of the room." She gives him the example of her own servant (Sharfoo) who is not permitted to enter the bedrooms. When Guddu leaves, the following conversation ensues between the sisters:

> Aiza: I asked him to bring me *chai* [tea]. He came in to give me *chai*.
>
> Aima: Yes, but *ammi* and *abba* do not like it when *mard mulazim* [male servants] enter the bedroom. And that too without knocking!
>
> Aiza: Excuse me [*Aiza uses English here*]. Mard? Mard mulazim? He has been with us since he was eight years old. He is barely fourteen or fifteen years old now.
>
> Aima: Aiza, boys become very mature by the time they are fourteen or fifteen. And as I said, *ammi* and *abba* do not like when *mard mulazim* enter the bedroom.
>
> Aiza: Why?
>
> Aima: Sharfoo has been with us for years; but he only remains in the kitchen and the lounge.
>
> Aiza: This is very strange. It means that you don't trust your servants.
>
> Aima: It's not about trust; it is about household etiquette [*ghar kay tarikay*].
>
> Aiza (scoffing): It's a very strange etiquette.

Here, we not only observe Aima's views on gender relations, where she deems it inappropriate for men who are not *mahram* (unmarriageable kin) to enter women's private spaces, but also how it intersects with social class. Whereas Aima seeks to keep a social and physical distance between herself and those who work for her, Aiza consciously crosses these boundaries. On one occasion, when Aiza is watching a movie with Guddu, she is severely reprimanded by her mother. As proof that such an attitude toward servants is correct, we later learn that Guddu steals money from the household and runs away. The older servant, Sharfoo, who is earlier portrayed as exemplary, is also found stealing clothes, jewelry, and other items for his daughter's wedding. Hence, both servants eventually turn out to be untrustworthy, legitimizing the caution that Aima and her parents had toward them.

This storyline proposes that middle-class boundaries need to be constantly monitored for encroachment from lower classes. And it is women's caution (or recklessness) that is crucial in the cultural reproduction of social class. This is also the case when it comes to socializing with those who are above one's social class. Aiza, for instance, seeks to socialize with upper-class folk so that she can afford more opportunities to her son. To do so, she hosts expensive parties and buys designer clothes, and is tentatively successful in these efforts when she secures her son's admission to the Lahore Grammar School—a school accessed predominantly by the country's wealthy elite. Her husband, however, critiques her extensive socialization with the wealthy, noting that they cannot sustain it financially. Eventually, Aiza's aspirations for moving up the social ladder are squashed when her husband becomes fed up and is unwilling to fund her social habits any longer. The underlying message here is that women are responsible for managing relations up the social ladder as well as down.

Aiza and Aima's characters signal the kinds of consumption patterns, orientation to waged work, and gender relations desired to reproduce the middle class economically and culturally. Middle-classness, thus, is more than financial standing; it is, as Purnima Mankekar describes, "a *moral* virtue, a structure of feeling, the habitation of safe space that distinguishe[s] one from less fortunate (less worthy) Others, and therefore a vantage point on the world."[10] Such virtue cannot be taught at schools. The differences shown between Aiza and Aima are not due to their *talim* (education)—both sisters completed their master's degrees. The difference lies in their *tarbiyat* (upbringing and nurturing), of which education in schools/universities is only one element. The broad concept of *tarbiyat* includes moral instruction that takes place at home, in which both immediate and extended family members participate. This instruction is often also influenced by religious principles. I therefore theorize *tarbiyat* as a discourse of governance that prescribes the kinds of subjectivities needed for the reproduction of the patrilineal family.

While what constitutes proper *tarbiyat*—like education—changes across the different moments considered in this book, it remains a discursive space through which individuals and social groups are able to critique competing discourses that seek to effect different youth subjectivities. This is clearly visible in *Mirat-ul-uroos* (2012), as well as *Akbari Asghari* (2011), discussed below. School- or university-based education (*talim*) is seen as meaningful only in relation to accessing waged work, and not beyond it. Indeed, phrases such as "taking advantage of education," "education is an investment," or "using education" appear throughout *Mirat-ul-roos* (2012) to signify education's primary purpose. In contrast, the home is elevated as the ideal didactic space where young people learn proper dispositions as subjects of the family, the Muslim *ummah*, and the nation. This, readers will recall, was not always the case. Especially at the turn of the twentieth century, and less so during the first decade after the political independence of Pakistan, writers of *Ismat, Khatun,* and *Tehzib* did not view *tarbiyat* and *talim* as completely unconnected. Terms such as *talim wa tarbiyat* (education and upbringing/nurturing) abound in the archives. It is only against the emerging threat from English schools and the expansion of mass schooling that *talim* and *tarbiyat* fragment along different tracks and spaces. Aiza's and Aima's characters illustrate the completion of this process; while schools continue to partake in ethical training of youth, it is the home that is elevated as the primary site for the ethical formation of young people, which includes class sensibilities. In other words, the patrilineal family is the ideological site for *tarbiyat*.

COMPLICATED FEMININITIES

While *Mirat-ul-uroos* (2012) features contrasting performances as foils to elucidate ideal girl/womanhood, HUM TV's production *Akbari Asghari* (2011) portrays the diverse subject positions available to women, and so performs a subversive function in some ways. It takes several other bold departures from the original text as well. The sisters, Akbari/Becky and Asghari/Sara, grow up in England and are to be married to their uncle's sons, Akbar and Asghar, who live in a rural village in the province of Punjab in Pakistan. The different contexts of their upbringing (*tarbiyat*) appear as one of the central themes through which questions of what it means to be an "eastern girl" and "Muslim" are examined, which in turn are linked to concerns about the reproduction of middle-class respectability. However, in this version, the female characters are no longer entirely good or bad; rather, they are shown to be complex subjects who negotiate their personal desires with familial and societal expectations. Furthermore, while Becky and Sara remain the protagonists, additional female characters are carefully developed and given an extended storyline to show the diversity of women in Pakistan, as well as their varying concerns and investments. What we end up with, then, are figures who evade neat categorizations of good/bad or eastern/western. Readers should keep in mind that *Akbari Asghari* (2011) is a comedy production, which enables the writers and producers to exaggerate the characters and storylines for the purposes of entertainment and social critique. That the show utilizes tired, caricatured portraits of village people to elicit a comedic effect will be discussed later as well.

In *Akbari Asghari* (2011), Akbari/Becky takes up the subject position of *achi beti* (good daughter) actively, while manipulating others into doing what she actually desires. Asghari/Sara, on the other hand, is frank and honest. She speaks whatever is on her mind, without fearing the consequences. Hence, Sara is seen by others to be harsh and is reprimanded by her parents for being selfish. For instance, on one occasion when Becky is late returning home after visiting her boyfriend, rather than letting her parents know, she manipulates Sara (who is also late returning home) into leaving the room without providing any explanation to her parents: "I will take care of it." When Sara leaves, Becky tells her parents that she was actually out looking for Sara. In this way, Becky hides her own faults while appearing to be a concerned sister. Her duplicitous personality is seen on myriad other occasions as well, especially when she tries to create chaos at her in-laws. She lies to her parents about her in-laws' mistreatment of her, hoping that they will ask her to break off relations with them and return to England. She fabricates stories about family members in relation to each other, creating distrust in the extended family. To be deceptive, superficial, and manipulative, hence, are marked as undesirable traits in women. The writer, Faiza Iftikhar, however, does not stop there. Rather than letting audiences deem Becky as an unsalvageable subject, Iftikhar uses the technique of internal dialogue to show that Becky is not oblivious to these tensions. There are several instances where we see her engage in a monologue, grappling with the imperatives of being the daughter that her parents imagine her to be while also hoping to do that which she desires. On multiple occasions, she admits that she is agreeable and polite because she does not want to hurt her parents, and because she desires praise—"I need praise and compliments; that's my addiction." These insights into Becky's personal struggles get audiences to empathize with her, resisting her reduction to a failed subject.

Likewise, Sara does not neatly fit the characterizations of Asghari as set out in Nazir Ahmed's *Mirat-ul-uroos*. While she is honest and caring, her parents criticize her forthright personality. Unlike Nazir Ahmed's Asghari, Sara consistently prioritizes personal desires and ambitions. For instance, to her parents' dismay, she initially refuses to marry Asghar. On another occasion, she dances at her sister's wedding in front of men—an action that brings shame to her family. She is also seen to socialize with female servants. Furthermore, she raises questions around public piety, eventually showing that a local religious figure was actually a charlatan. Hence, questioning sedimented class boundaries that have divided the Pakistani society, and exposing the hypocrisy of those who hide their greed behind religion, come across as courageous acts, as they are linked to a character whom viewers understand to be a "good girl."

That said, there are certain boundaries that Sara does not cross. Unlike Becky, who has a Catholic boyfriend, Sara resists the advances of her Hindu friend Raj, and in doing so articulates that some differences are indeed insurmountable. Whereas in *Mirat-ul-uroos* (2012), Aima thought that class differences could not be overcome, in *Akbari Asghari* (2011) Sara views religious differences in the same vein. Yet, when Akbar criticizes Sara for wanting to wish her Hindu friend on the occasion of Diwali, she contests his reductive understanding of religion. I will examine questions around religion and gender in detail later; for now, I want to point out the ways in which both Becky and Sara are complex, evading essentialized depictions as either good or bad. Viewers, then, are left with tentative assumptions about what kinds of performances are constituted as ideal, as both characters display the fluidity and tension that characterize women's everyday lives.

The fact that Becky's and Sara's characters are not one-dimensional is not a coincidence. In an interview, Iftikhar explains her desire to portray characters that break away from the binaries of good/bad: "[Television] channels just want heroines who make people shed tears. There is a trend nowadays to portray women in binaries—either very good or very bad, very intelligent or totally stupid, completely innocent or totally devious."[11] Discussing Nazir Ahmed's *Mirat-ul-uroos,* Iftikhar complains that Akbari was always shown negatively because she was lazy and did not cook or sew as well as her sister: "Mothers and wives aren't the only women in the world. Many women are single or without children, so are they all bad women? . . . Should all women like Akbari just die off and only those like Asghari be heroines? Every home has an Akbari. . . . It doesn't mean that they can't excel in other things if they can't cook!"[12] So Iftikhar notes her intention to create more complex characters: "It is easy to write about realistic characters. They are all around you." In addition to Becky and Sara, Iftikhar develops a broad range of additional female characters that provide insight into the multiple contexts in which women find themselves, and how they negotiate patriarchal norms. Through these intricate portrayals audiences come face to face with subjects who can be marked as neither ideal nor failed, but as fluid and in-the-making.

Consider the character of Bayji (also known as Baybay), Becky and Sara's aunt. She often appears next to the patriarch, her brother Chaudhry KFC, and given her age has secured respect among both male and female members of the extended family. Her story of personal tragedy highlights the tension women experience as they make a life within patriarchal systems. It was on her wedding day, after the signing of the *nikkah* (Muslim marriage contract), that her husband's family insulted her *veer* (older brother, Chaudhry KFC) in front of the entire *baradari* (community). Her brother asked her if she would let this insult stand. He gave her two options: to stand by him and not leave with her husband (that is, to postpone the ceremony of *rukhsati,* when the married woman officially departs with her husband), knowing that her husband will likely acknowledge his mistake and return to take her home; or leave with the people who insulted and dishonored him. Bayji decides to side with her brother, who, after all, had been her primary source of support after the death of their parents. Now, decades later, Bayji is still awaiting her husband's return (who eventually marries someone else). Throughout the drama, Bayji is often seen talking to her husband's photograph. At one moment in particular, she makes an astute observation while crying: "I neither thrived nor was destroyed. I didn't know that this was a fight between men, and not between a brother and a husband. In this fight between two men, I was left in limbo."[13] Bayji's story provides insights into how relationships between men and women unfold in localized contexts. She prioritized loyalty to her brother over her desires for personal happiness in an environment where women's practices are intimately tied to familial honor. While her choices can be read as reinscribing patriarchy, it is significant to note that choices are always mediated by structural conditions. In this case, in spite of her wishes, Bayji chooses her brother's honor over her personal happiness. When Sara later criticizes her grandfather for not resolving his fight with Bayji's husband, he becomes aware of his mistake and makes amends. *Akbari Asghari* (2011), then, portrays complex gender relations, which are mediated by a range of factors, including assumptions about honor and a delicate balance between self and familial interests.

The characters of Becky, Sara, and Bayji shed light on the multiple contexts within which women move and the kinds of subject positions that are available to them. Rather than hold women exclusively responsible for their actions, *Akbari Asghari* (2011) shows how women's actions are an effect of a range of factors, which include histories, social commitments, loyalty, and responsibility. Women, thus, engage in what Deniz Kandiyoti has described as the "patriarchal bargain" wherein they "strategize within a set of concrete constraints."[14] This assemblage of complicated female characters also gives insights into the pressures that Pakistanis and heritage-Pakistanis face as they forge new ways of balancing individual and familial interests. The desire for an ideal femininity is thus questioned and even suspended in *Akbari Asghari* (2011).

Even with this diversity of female subject positions, women in *Akbari Asghari* (2011) are only legible within the context of a patriarchal family, and it is the practice of marriage that marks one as a complete, fulfilled woman. This is clearly apparent in the final episode, which shows Chaudhry KFC resolving his differences with Bayji's husband (whose second wife has passed away) and leading her to *rukhsati*. Even though Bayji's character is forceful and powerful (she is, after all, the matriarch), and has a central place in the comedic production itself, she is ultimately represented as unfulfilled until she finds her true home—the husband's household. Happiness and fulfillment for women are staunchly situated within the institution of the patriarchal family. This is precisely the belief that was reflected by my focus-group participants; they, too, engaged in schooling in order to improve their marriage prospects and hence find a home they could call their own. Parent-participants in my study similarly wanted to educate their daughters as a way to secure better marriage proposals and to prepare them to become adept wives. The institutions of marriage and the patrilineal family, hence, remain central in *Akbari Asghari* (2011), even as it seeks to contest reductive portrayals of women as good/bad.

WHAT DOES IT MEAN TO BE EDUCATED?

In *Akbari Asghari* (2011), as in *Mirat-ul-uroos* (2012), we find a close link between women's performances of an educated subjectivity and the reproduction of middle-classness. We learn this through the character of Batool (Sara's and Becky's aunt), whose attempts at "appearing educated" through the consumption of expensive products and speaking broken English, make her a laughing stock. In contrast, Sara performs an educated subjectivity by calling out the hypocrisy of traditional customs and practices that marginalize women and might harm the patrilineal family. To be educated, then, is to be willing to simultaneously critique the ways in which local patriarchies constrain women *and* advance the welfare of the patriarchal family. It is a complicated balancing act that women must perform.

Batool, like her brothers, was raised in the village but marries into a family in Sialkot, a midsized city in Punjab. To mark herself as urban and educated, she constantly reminds everyone that she is from the "city" and tries to distance herself from her relatives who still live in the village. Her efforts to claim an urban/city status are criticized by her sister-in-law, who sneers that "after all, she is only in Sialkot (and not Lahore or other larger cities in Punjab)." There are myriad other ways in which Batool attempts to claim a middle-class, educated, urban subjectivity. She speaks in Punjabi but tries to include words in English at every possible opportunity, including transforming the words to fit Urdu sentence structures. She constantly asks her daughter (whom she refers to as "dotter") to translate Punjabi words into English. When her daughter resists the constant pestering, she reveals that she does so in order to appear educated vis-à-vis her brother's wife who has a bachelor's degree and lives in England. Batool consumes goods—expensive clothes, jewelry, and make up—to assert her nonrural status. She prefers to wear a sari, which, in this context, is perceived as a nonindigenous, cosmopolitan article of clothing. Her gaudy dress and mixing of languages elicits a comedic effect; however, it also illuminates how middle-classness in contemporary Pakistan is equated with the ability to speak in the English language, live in urban areas, and consume specific goods. Indeed, to speak in English is taken to be the ultimate marker of modernity (and hence, social difference), much as the writers of *Ismat* feared during the 1950s. It is through the practice of this language that the urban/rural divide is established. However, given the caricatured portrayal of Batool, *Akbari Asghari* (2011) calls on its audience to rethink its assumptions about middle-classness and "education." It offers Sara as an ideal educated, discerning, middle-class subject.

Sara tries to reform the customs and practices in the village that marginalize women. Her critique of her grandfather's neglect of his sister is an example of how educated, middle-class, and even foreign value systems (which are named as "liberal") can help reshape the customs of the village. On another occasion, Sara again appears as the voice of reason and stands up against patriarchal, duplicitous customs. This time she is running around in the fields having fun with some friends when Akbar passes by and reprimands her, because such actions "create a bad *mahol* [environment] in the village." He further notes that women should not engage with *khas wo aam* (special and ordinary) people in the same way. These boundary-making logics are often employed to restrict women's movement and create spaces of segregation. Akbar concludes: "Women have their limits." To this, Sara retorts: "What kind of limits are these that women cannot go around and enjoy as they desire? This is what makes the village's *mahol* bad? What about when women work day and night in the sun, in the rain, all day, in the fields? That doesn't create bad *mahol*? When this village's women, like men, can work hard in the fields all day and that does not create a difference in the *mahol,* then women can also go around and enjoy themselves as they desire." Sara, then, highlights the double standards at play that restrict women's mobility in some situations while encouraging it in others to exploit their labor.

Another instance of a similar critique of women's exploitation takes place when Sara chooses to dance with a professional dancer who has been invited to perform at Becky's wedding. Her entire family is ashamed, and her grandfather says, "*Sharif* girls do not dance with a street woman / professional dancer [*bazari aurat*]." While all men are shown to thoroughly enjoy the dance, it is only when their own female relative (Sara) partakes in it that they see it as an unwelcome consumption of women's bodies, calling the professional dancer *gand* (dirt). Sara picks up on this hypocrisy and asks: "Then why did you bring the *gand* (dirt) home? If she is a *buri aurat* (bad woman), why did you invite her to celebrate a happy occasion?" Sara's character highlights the hollowness of the family's claims to respectability and the politics of surveillance in relation to "honorable" women's bodies. That it takes a woman who has been educated in the West to critique and reform her family's attitude is a storyline that reinscribes the logic that only western values and education produce a sense of awakening. This, however, does not detract from the explicit social critiques that *Akbari Asghari* (2011) sets forth, as well as the positive valuation of those women who are forthright and speak their minds, willing to interrogate duplicitous attitudes and cross class boundaries. Sara's criticisms, however, are only tolerable because they further the purity of the patrilineal family (for instance, by calling on men to not seek pleasures with professional dancers), as well as due to her conformity with the prescribed ideals of a good Muslim subject (she refuses to consider Raj's proposals).

THE TRIUMPH OF A MUTED RELIGIOSITY

Discourses on ideal educated subjects have always been linked with discourses on ideal performances of religiosity. From the efforts of the Muslim reformers at the turn of the twentieth century to codify Islam, to present-day tensions around school curricula in Pakistan, religion has been invoked to articulate ideal female subjecthood. Given the role of religion in opening up as well as closing spaces for women, *Akbari Aghari* (2011) emerges as an interesting text that interrogates what it means to be a Muslim. Female characters—especially Sara—contest the ways in which religiously and/or culturally inspired discourses constrain women's mobility.

Readers will recall that the endeavor to reform women at the turn of the twentieth century was connected with clarifying what it meant to be a Muslim. Women's customs and practices were subjected to reform in order to demarcate an authentically Muslim identity, one that could be distinguished from the Hindu identity. In Nazir Ahmed's text, the figure of the *hajjan* (a woman who had recently returned from completing religious pilgrimage in Mecca) is revealed to be a charlatan, as the text sets out to caution its readers about those people who instrumentalize religion to prey upon innocent people. There is also an implicit effort to carve out and bolster the authority of the predominantly male *ulama* (religious scholars), who were being made increasingly irrelevant with the rise of colonial institutions. Authority was to be vested in the *ulama* and not the uneducated masses, and *sharif* women were called upon to become discerning consumers of religion. *Akbari Asghari* (2011) takes up religion in similar ways, elaborating on how some religious personalities are to be viewed with suspicion. The educated, discerning subject is able to detect religious charlatans from true believers.

The most evident way in which religion and religious practices are invoked in *Akbari Asghari* (2011) is through the character of Akbar. Akbar keeps a beard, is always seen in a prayer *topi* (cap), and often carries a *tasbeeh* (rosary). Instead of speaking in Punjabi like the rest of his extended family, he converses in Urdu with a healthy smattering of Arabic phrases and words. He dislikes dance, excessive celebrations at weddings, and prefers that women observe strict *purdah*. He keeps close company of a *pir/murshid* (religious guide), who is despised by other members of his family because they believe him to be a charlatan (which he, in fact, eventually turns out to be). Akbar's family mocks his appearance and social attitudes—on several occasions he is pejoratively called a "mullah" and his grandfather wonders how someone who is educated in the city would choose to return to the village to teach kids. Upon seeing him for the first time, Sara and Becky's parents go into shock wondering how this "Taliban will get past UK security officers." They worry that Akbar's comportment may bring suspicion upon the entire family in the United Kingdom. Likewise, when Akbar goes to the train station to pick up Asghari—who does not know what he looks like—she gets scared and imagines him to be a "Taliban." Recalling that incident later she notes, "I was really afraid and thought to myself that maybe he is from Al-Qaeda and wants to take revenge of America or London on me." These instances cast excessive displays of religiosity as unwelcome and unnecessary. Even Akbar's mother finds his religiosity unacceptable. On one occasion, after convincing his mother to see his *pir*'s daughter as a potential wife for him, the following conversation about *purdah* ensues when they arrive at the *pir*'s house:

> *Akbar:* *Ammi* [mother] wear the *chadar* [shawl].
>
> *Shaheen:* I am wearing it. It is not locked up in a box.
>
> *Akbar:* I mean, *Ammi*, wear it properly. Cover your head [his mother's head is covered with a *dupatta*—scarf—not the shawl]. You don't know. At the *pir*'s household, everyone observes strict *purdah*. I don't want them to see you and then . . .
>
> *Shaheen (raising her voice):* Listen up! I am here to see the girl and not show myself off to your *pir*.

As noted earlier, the *pir* turns out to be fake—he dupes people into giving him money and is a pervert (he hits on Asghari)—which is yet another indication that true religiosity does not need overt displays and those who emphasize public performances of piety may in fact be impostors.

The kind of religiosity that the drama advances is one that informs one's values. For instance, when Raj expresses his love for Sara, she notes that their religious differences are insurmountable: "Even though I am not very religious, I cannot marry someone whose roots are different." This way of engaging with religion restricts it to a set of orientations and values, disconnecting it from active practice. In other words, Sara symbolizes a category of Muslimness where one does not have to engage in *purdah* or the rituals of regular prayer and fasting and can still be Muslim. This is clearly in contrast to the version of religion that Akbar—and by proxy many Pakistanis—practice. However, *Akbari Asghari* (2011) rejects such enactments of religiosity. "Mullah Akbar," then, in many ways resembles the *purdah-nashin* from Asaf Hussain's text who were considered misfits due to their excessive religiosity. Today, it is the likes of Akbar—young, educated men, whose practice of religion calls for a serious commitment to prayer, fasting, and following the *sunnah* of the Prophet (by keeping a beard, for instance)—who appear to be in misalignment with the project of modernity. They are seen as outside the pale of recognition of ideal masculinity and are quickly named as "Taliban"—a term that signals extremist tendencies. Ideal performances of religion, according to *Akbari Asghari* (2011), entail keeping religion private; religion is to inform ethical formation and not public performances.

At the same time, while making fun of Akbar, *Akbari Asghari* (2011) also contests the reduction of religious people like him to "Taliban" and fundamentalists. Consider the following conversation between Becky and Sara, when Sara first learns that Becky will be marrying Asghar and not Akbar. Sara wonders why Becky rejected Akbar:

> *Becky:* I think you have not seen Akbar closely.
>
> *Sara:* I have met him. He is a little strange; his points of view and his thoughts are very different from us. But Becky, it is not necessary that those who are different are bad.

Becky: You just want to oppose Mom and Dad regardless of whether or not you have any logic. And, how would I have been happy with a *maulvi* [religious leader]?

Sara: Why? Can't the wives of *maulvi*s be happy?

Becky: By the way, why are you taking his [Akbar's] side? You only say *namaz* [prayer] once a year, that too in Ramadan.

Sara (in a mocking tone): And since you say *namaz* regularly, why do you dislike him?

Becky: Hello. I limit religion to myself, to my person [*zaat*]. And Akbar? Fundamentalists like Akbar try to impose their views on others. Even though you are so liberal, you are asking me to be with someone like Akbar.

Sara: I am a liberal, which is why I am giving into logic. The people who have Islamic views and that's the aim of their life, they are seen as fundamentalist; and the people who oppose Islamic views and that's their aim, are they not fundamentalist? You know my friend, Shushma, she is a brahmin Hindu; Sandy is Catholic, and Jacob is Jewish. These are all dear friends of mine. They are not bad. Then why do you dislike Akbar so much?

In this dense exchange, Sara tries to recover the category of religious (including practices of religiosity that include public embodied performances) from fundamentalists and the Taliban by proposing that those who take religion seriously—like those from other religious traditions—are not necessarily bad. She assigns this logical approach to her liberalism. In other words, to be liberal is to not blindly write off all religious people.

That *Akbari Asghari* (2011) takes up the theme of "good" versus "bad" Muslim is an effect of the broader surveillance of Muslims globally,[15] and the consistent articulation of Islam as a political category rather than as a religious system of beliefs. Muslims are racialized and pitted against presumably western, rational, enlightened subjects. In public discourse today, Muslims often appear as backward, entangled in premodern sensibilities, and longing for a golden age of the past. Often, culture and religion are blamed for the mistreatment of women in the global South, as well as seen as causes of acts of terrorism and violence. Against this background, there has also been an effort to mark some Muslims as "good" and others as "bad." Muslims, too, are participating in defining this good/bad binary and the exchange between Becky and Sara is an example of that process. There is, hence, a simultaneous mocking of some categories of "religious"—those who are extremists, Taliban, fundamentalist, or charlatans (like the *pir*)—and an effort to reclaim religion from dominant meanings that reduce it to a political ideology by signaling it to be a site of faith. That this is done through women's narratives is not surprising; just as women are to play a crucial role in the reproduction of the middle-class patriarchal family, they must play a similarly important role in amplifying the correct image of Islam and forms of religiosity.

Relatedly, there is a class component to these representations of religiosity as well. As noted earlier, members of the urban elite dominate the television industry in Pakistan, and television programs are produced for the consumption of both urban and rural populations. While there is an increasing trend in Pakistan where both men and women are adopting a more overtly religious identity through the uptake of clothing items such as the burka, keeping a beard, and learning the Arabic language, this trend is predominantly found in middle-income and low-income social classes. Hence, one way to understand Akbar's mocking (and tentative recovery) in *Akbari Asghari* (2011) and the downfall of the *pir,* as well as the eventual triumph of a more muted religiosity, is to interpret this as a distinctly elite, urban view of the ideal place of religion in public life.

This chapter has focused on the changing landscape in Pakistan, where economic precarities, pressures of transnational migrations, flows of capital and ideas, as well as demands for gender segregation and maintenance of social-class boundaries form the context within which different subject positions for women and girls become available. Since schools have become the most prominent didactic space, I read the television shows discussed in this chapter as reasserting the role of the home in providing moral instruction and ideal representations of gendered subjectivities. Both *Mirat-ul-uroos* (2012) and *Akbari Asghari* (2011) outline the performances—consumption habits, relations with members of the opposite sex as well as other social classes, orientation to waged work, and engagement with the patriarchal family—that can help secure the economic and cultural reproduction of middle-classness. These shows call on women to monitor their desires and reshape themselves into ideal daughters, wives, domestic managers, and religious practitioners. In doing so, they reinstall the patriarchal family as the regulator of women's morality. At the same time, television also affords the possibility to critique social norms. *Akbari Asghari* (2011), therefore, sets out to resist women's reduction to ideal/failed subjects, and lays out multiple possible life-scripts for women. In doing so, it rejects the caricatured portrayals of educated feminine subjectivities, pointing to the complex relationships at the nexus of which women have to make decisions. As public pedagogies, then, these television shows provide insights into the contested making of ideal female subjects in Pakistan.

Tracing Storylines

This book has explored multiple invocations of educated woman- and girlhoods to argue that discourses on women's and girls' education are often deeply entangled in class, familial, nationalist, and hetero-patriarchal interests. Be it the British colonizers and Muslim social reformers at the turn of the twentieth century, the Pakistani state during the 1950s, or transnational corporations and nongovernmental entities today, a broad range of social actors have participated in articulating ideal performances for women and girls. These articulations often signal anxieties about, and hopes for, distinctive social orders where women and girls are expected to play particular roles, ranging from taking charge of domestic happiness, overseeing the nurturing of future citizens, laboring to advance the economic growth of the nation, maintaining gendered spaces, and reproducing social-class positioning by means of their aesthetics, public piety, and labor participation or withdrawal. The result is a range of subject positions for women—some of which are marked as desirable and others as failed. These include *sharif beti, sughar beti, purdah-nasheen,* teddy girl, ultramodern girl, modern girl, *buri aurat, bazari aurat,* student, and empowered girl, among others. As I trace these subject positions, I have elaborated on how they open up as well as close possibilities for women and girls.

I attend to the diverse appearances of the educated female subject in cultural archives, not in order to identify its evolution, but to isolate the different scenes where she engages in different roles.[1] In some instances, such as at the turn of the twentieth century, we see the ideal educated woman as rearticulating the respectable status of *ashraf* Muslims through her practices in the domestic sphere. During the 1950s, she enables a fuller articulation of what it means to be Pakistani and Muslim by standing in contrast to women who perform excessive piety (the *purdah-nasheen*) as well as women who are enamored of the West (the ultramodern girls). During this time, she also clarifies what it means to a "modern" subject through her consumption and labor practices. In the contemporary moment, she highlights for us how boundaries of social class are forged in and through women's labor-force participation and marriage. As an upper-middle-class woman, she values education in order to increase her marriageability and shows a clear preference for the home where she can nurture the next generation. Her low-middle-class counterpart, however, values education to enter the workforce but seeks to identify professional spaces that might preserve a semblance of middle-class respectability. They both attempt to preserve their class status by distancing themselves from poor and lower-class women who must engage in menial labor, as well as the wasteful ultrarich. In forging these diverse woman-girl-subjects, the question of education seems to always be about the kind of orientation that women and girls are to have in relation to themselves, their families, waged work, and the nation.

Significantly, across the three periods we observe a repetition of discourses with *difference*. As Gilles Deleuze notes, "to repeat is to behave in a certain manner, but in relation to something unique or singular which has no equal or equivalent."[2] For instance, notions of respectability emerge across all moments taken up in this book but signify different kinds of relationships between women and capital, women and the nation-state, and women and the patriarchal family. This translates into different possibilities and limitations for women and girls. Likewise, while education is invoked across all three moments, the institutions and actors that the discourse authorizes are quite different. In this concluding chapter, then, I tease out such themes and view them as overlapping storylines. I trace shifts and patterns across the three moments taken up in this book with the hope of signaling the systems of power within which these stories take shape. Indeed, a genealogy does not tell one grand story, rather it traces overlapping storylines.

TRANSMUTATIONS OF RESPECTABILITY

One of the enduring themes in this book is in relation to respectability (*sharafat*). Women's practices seem to be a key discursive space through which respectability is expressed. This book, however, shows that concerns about respectability are often closely linked with efforts to forge a class identity. In other words, social class is often expressed and consolidated through expressions of *sharafat*, which are in turn conveyed through women's practices. This includes women's performances of piety, domestic management, movements/mobility, as well as consumption patterns. Respectability, then, is a name given to a collection of performances that signal class status. Education appears as both a social project that can direct women toward desired performances, and a commodity (such as English-medium educa-tion in contemporary Pakistan) whose consumption signals class status. Thus, one of the storylines in this book relates to the endurance of class concerns, which manifest themselves through the idiom of respectability.

At the turn of the twentieth century, calls for Muslim women's education were intricately linked with the shifting social, economic, and political landscape of Muslims in South Asia. Under the Mughal rule, privilege in the form of access to resources, administrative positions, and stipends accrued to *ashraf* Muslims, a social category that included the descendants of Arab, Persian, Turkic, and Afghan ethnicities. Others who earned their living through scholarship and erudition were also part of this social class. Being a member of this social class signaled one's noble and respectable status. However, by the turn of the twentieth century, with the administration securely under the British, the privileges that members of this class enjoyed were on the decline, and *ashraf* Muslims of North India and Punjab had to adjust their economic and social lives to the new regime. Respectability could no longer be asserted on the basis of one's familial background or ethnicity, as the nobility no longer enjoyed control of resources and labor. This opened up the space for the assertion of new forms of respectability.

One such effort entailed dissociating respectability from ethnicity and attaching it to social practices and aesthetics, such as domestic management, proper Muslim rituals, and elementary reading and writing skills. Such characteristics made *shara-fat* accessible to social groups, such as merchants and traders, who previously had been excluded from this category. Similarly, the opportunity to be a part of the British bureaucracy and gain economic prosperity also created the possibility for class elevation for the professionalizing social groups. Women emerged as a means in and through which this new definition of respectability was forged. They were to be educated in specific ways so that they would display the right kinds of cultural dispositions and behaviors that would be constituted as respectable. Education thus allowed for the cultural reproduction of the new *ashraf* social class.

It would, however, be naïve to assume that this transformation was uniform. In fact, in chapter 2, I have traced the diverse views about what constituted *sharif* womanhood and girlhood and the role of education in cultivating these subjects. While some social reformers called on women to reform their religious practices by avoiding superstitious customs and becoming experts at house management and childrearing, others envisioned a role for women as generators of income and began to imagine women as individuated selves. The different orientation toward waged work is a reflection of the economic anxieties experienced by some mem-bers of the *ashraf* social class. Thus, the content and spaces for women's education came under intense scrutiny as different segments articulated their own visions for the kinds of transformations that education should bring about in women in order to display *sharafat*. Evidence from novels as well as women's magazines shows that women, too, participated actively in these conversations and were as equally varied in their opinions as men.

For the new *ashraf* women, *khana-dari* (household management) emerged as a domain where they could enact a distinctly educated version of themselves. Readers will recall Muhammadi Begum's texts *Sharif beti* and *Hayat-e-Ashraf,* both of which provide excruciating details of how young girls and women are to reshape themselves into ideal wives, mothers, and domestic managers. However, there was also a recognition of the tough economic times that lay ahead for Muslims. The texts called on women to acquire skills that could be monetized during times of difficulty. This included *hunar* such as sewing, as well as the possibility of setting up *maktabs* (small, informal schools) at home. Indeed, *Sughar beti* illuminates what such a life in economic precarity might look like. Here, a *sharif* family undergoes severe financial constraints and the daughter has to take up the task of making an income, while keeping true to the norms of her social class, in particular maintaining *purdah.* Bibi Ashraf's story is yet another example of a woman who figures out a way to survive financially while adamantly reproducing norms of gender segregation and preserving her family's claims to *sharafat.* These novels signal the emergent ties between familial respectability and women's practices.

In the early decades after the political independence of Pakistan, the state became yet another entity that framed respectable womanhood/girlhood. From the perspective of the state, the ideal educated woman/girl was one who contributed to the nation's modernization and development project, either through participation as labor or as a scientifically inclined mother, nurturing the next generation of citizen-subjects. Since, during this period, questions about what constituted a "Pakistani" citizen were closely linked with the role of Islam, women's religious practices came under intense scrutiny as well. Excessive performances of religiosity, particularly those that kept women away from the workforce or the nation's new industries and consumer products, were looked down upon. Likewise, westward orientation, too, was deemed inappropriate. In short, the ideal educated female subject was one who engaged with the institution of religion in ways that did not hinder the homogenizing and modernizing project of the Pakistani state. What is crucial to note is that this educated female subject is also a classed subject; access to education, consumer products, and professional jobs was often only available to members of upper and middle social classes.

The close links across education, respectability, and social class continue to the present. Participants in my focus groups from low-middle-class families aspired to reach middle-class status. They went to school in order to obtain "office jobs"—a code for jobs that were deemed acceptable for middle-class women. This often included jobs as teachers, program officers, secretaries, and so on. The assumption was that women can shield themselves from sexual harassment in these contexts; an assumption that often proved to be incorrect. Any other job—manual labor, in particular—would automatically mark the girls as belonging to lower socioeconomic strata. In contrast, participants from upper-middle-class backgrounds wanted to acquire an education primarily to prepare for their future roles as wives and mothers and to enhance their marriageability. They were willing to work only during financially precarious times. For members of this social class, working outside the home was a definite marker of a decrease in familial status, and hence a threat to respectability. This reasoning is visible in *Mirat-ul-uroos* (2012), where Aima has to work in order to provide temporary respite to male members of her household, but she insists on quitting her job as soon as her husband is able to obtain one. When Aiza wants to work for personal pleasure and fulfillment, her husband does not support her, noting that her primary responsibility is to her home. Upper-middle-class families thus signal their status and respectability through the lack of women's need to enter the workforce. Alternately, women who do enter the public sphere signal non-elite status, which makes them susceptible to harassment and exploitation. The public space in Pakistan thus continues to be marked as masculine, and respectability politics limit a possible transformation of the space in favor of women.

THE EXPANSION OF MODERN SCHOOLING

This book traces how the institution of the modern school, with its systems of learning, bureaucratic administration, and examinations, gradually becomes the hegemonic institution for educating young people. The expansion of modern schooling has displaced the multiple community-centered educative spaces that were prevalent in colonial India during the nineteenth and early twentieth centuries. Education of *ashraf* women during that time, for instance, included the study of seminal Arabic and Persian texts, reading and writing skills, learning of *hunar* such as sewing and cooking, as well training in ethics. The home was viewed as the primary pedagogical site, where multiple actors, such as mothers, fathers, *ustani*s, and *maulvi*s, performed the duties of educating the young. Writers in women's periodicals often used the phrase *talim wa tarbiya* (education and nurturing) to denote these wide-ranging purposes of education. These educative arrangements were no doubt meant to reproduce the privilege of the *ashraf* social classes. Familiarity with Persian and Arabic texts, for instance, signaled the non-Indian origins of the *ashraf* families. The British model of schooling disrupted some of these social functions of education and replaced them with new hierarchies. It was now English schooling that would confer upward mobility through access to British administrative apparatus and exposure to Victorian norms.

By the 1950s, the school, rather than the familial home, emerged as the primary site for education and moral instruction, leading to intense debates around curriculum, language policies, and dress codes. These debates were not only about changing social-class dynamics but also, crucially, about who would have the authority to engage in the ethical and moral instruction of young women (and men). Hence, the debates were often framed in terms of the fear of Christian proselytizing in English schools.

With the global entrenchment of the modern school as the primary social institution for the education of the young, debates around *where* girls should be educated are becoming largely irrelevant. The current concerns in the field of international development are around getting girls *into* schools; there is little to no discussion about the sort of learning that is offered in schools, nor an investigation into alternative, viable models for education. However, this does not mean other social institutions, such as the family and the religious community, have given up their claims over molding the young generation. Instead, there continues to be a robust discussion about the moral instruction of youth in postcolonial contexts such as Pakistan. These contestations are visible in the periodic tensions around curricular choices and language of instruction that have erupted in recent years, the development of parallel formal and informal tracks of schooling such as the madrasas, as well as the continued use of *ustanis* and *maulvis* for the teaching of the Quran at home. As shown in chapters 4 and 5 of this book, schools are marked as being useful only for credentialization and obtaining jobs. Through the discourse on *tarbiyat* (upbringing and nurturing), the home is recentered as the ideal environment for moral instruction. This entails engendering ideal dispositions in young people, including educating them in ethics and religion (as was depicted in both the HUM and Geo TV productions). In the process, mothers continue to be considered as ideally placed to produce future citizens. Such a womanhood, as should be clear by now, can only be performed by upper-middle-class women who can rely on the incomes of their male relations. Thus, the recentering of the home as the site for moral instruction also props up particular conceptualizations of mothering, which call on women to depend on men, and in the process, strengthen male domination.

FROM MUSLIM WOMAN/GIRL TO MUSLIM GIRL

Whereas during much of the nineteenth century it is the composite figure of the Muslim woman/girl who is to be civilized, rescued, and educated, this figure gets disaggregated over time into the figures of the Muslim woman and the Muslim girl, with the latter rising to dominance as the ideal site for reform and rescue by the turn of the twenty-first century. This shift from an all-encompassing Muslim feminine figure to the Muslim girl / Muslim woman takes shape in the context of the rise of mass schooling as well as the peculiar preoccupation of the international development and aid regime with the figure of the girl, as explained in chapter 4. In tracing this shift, I show how gender categories are (re)made and how they function across multiple discursive fields. Understanding the construction of gender categories and their impact is crucial because the figures of the Muslim woman and Muslim girl are increasingly invoked not only within the development and aid regime but also in foreign policy discourses, particularly in relation to countering violent extremism (CVE). We, therefore, have to sharpen our analytics to understand how these categories are being used, what kinds of affective histories and collective assumptions they draw on, and how their current deployment is closely tied to these affects.

The rise of the girl is an effect of a number of related trends, some of which I discussed in chapters 1 and 4, such as the ascendency of human capital theories, which see "girls" as untapped labor. However, there are additional shifts in relation to conceptualizations of Muslim women that are at play when it comes to the attention focused on Muslim girls. First, over the last few decades, feminist scholars have launched a robust critique of the trope of the "oppressed brown woman." This includes a number of ethnographic studies that illuminate the complex lives of Muslim women, including their agentic negotiations with local forms of patriarchy, as well as a critique of political and military interventions in Muslim-majority nations. The works of scholars such as Lila Abu-Lughod (Egypt), Saba Mahmood (Egypt), Fida Adely (Jordon), Ayesha Khurshid (Pakistan), and Lara Deeb (Lebanon), among others, are examples of such interventions. This scholarship is accompanied by a rise in Muslim women's organizations that deploy non-Eurocentric idioms to call for justice and empowerment. This includes women drawing on the Quran and Muslim legal traditions to call for reforms in their societies. Together, these trends cast doubts about Muslim women's apparent silent status.

Second, the figure of the "Muslim woman" is increasingly being cast as suspect, making way for the "Muslim girl" to emerge as a competitor for the salvific rhetoric previously associated with Muslim women. While stories about Muslim women's complicity with "terrorists" have always circulated—such as during the Algerian revolution—it is only recently that Muslim women are being portrayed as embodying the same type of "threat" that Muslim men have represented for a long time. Consider the media coverage of Chechen Muslim women's actions during the Chechen-Russian conflict in the 1990s. Sara Struckman observes that Muslim women were primarily characterized as passive victims.[3] However, when they started to participate in suicide bombings their articulation moved to vengeful actors—"Black Widows." Later, when it was found that women did not act simply to avenge the death of male relations, it was believed that they were coerced by Islamic extremists who drugged or raped them on video and, hence, compelled them to carry out attacks against their will. Such explanations obfuscated these women's political agency to fight for Chechen independence. More recently, however, with the rise of Daesh globally, women's agency in enacting antistate and antiwestern attacks has been more centrally recognized. Earlier, in 2008, we learned about Samina Malik, from the United Kingdom, who called herself the "lyrical terrorist," writing poetry about beheadings. In 2010, Roshonara Choudhry stabbed a British MP, explaining that she did so because he had voted to send British troops to Iraq. There is, then, a steady portrayal of Muslim women as new suspects and a new threat.

The ascendency of the figure of the "female jihadist" is a case in point. The term is often used to describe Muslim women who have launched attacks in western contexts, most recently in California (December 2015) and Paris (November 2015). The female jihadist is viewed as abject and dangerous, an intimate threat. Consider the case of Tashfeen Malik, who along with her husband, Syed Rizwan Farook, opened fire during a party and training session at the Inland Regional Center in San Bernardino County, California, killing fourteen people and wounding twenty-four others. In the aftermath of the event, extensive interest emerged in Tashfeen's education and background—as the headline in Reuters noted: "Female attacker stands out in California mass shooting."[4] There was interest in finding out what had transformed her from a "happy bride to [a] shooter."[5] Exclusive feature articles that attempted to piece together her life in the United States as well as abroad, particularly in Pakistan and Saudi Arabia, appeared in major newspapers. For instance, the *New York Times* featured an article entitled "Tashfeen Malik, San Bernardino Suspect, Attended Conservative Religious School in Pakistan,"[6] which explored potential connections that Tashfeen may have had with an educational institute, Al-Huda Center, in Multan. Drawing connections between religiosity and violence, the article notes: "critics in Pakistan have long accused Al Huda, which urges women to cover their faces and study the Quran, of spreading a more conservative strain of Islam. But it has never been directly linked to jihadist violence. Still, confirmation that Ms. Malik had studied with the group offers a new clue to her disposition in the years before she left Pakistan for the United States."[7] Clearly, her education in Pakistan and upbringing in Saudi Arabia were seen as pivotal moments in transforming her into a "jihadi." Tashfeen has also been portrayed as an autonomous subject, an articulation that has normally not been afforded to Muslim women. Speaking of Tashfeen, a *New York Times* article posits that, "the threat is coming from a more independent, feminist type of jihadist, who sees herself as acting similarly to a man." Her marking as a "feminist" points to her autonomy.

The framing of Muslim women as suspect is also visible in public-policy discourses in western societies. It is most perceptible in the debate over hijabs, *niqabs*, burkinis, and burkas. From Australian parliamentarians asking burka-wearing women to sit in glassed enclosures in 2014 and the French burkini ban of 2016 to the 2017 ban on the *niqab* in Austria, Muslim women are increasingly seen as a threat to/in public spaces in the West. Shakira Hussein situates this suspicion of Muslim women in a longer trajectory of suspicion of Muslims, where concerns over halal food certification, construction of minarets, and demographic changes to Muslim populations are often linked to, and interpreted as, the imposition of sharia law.[8] As a collectivity, then, Muslims have become a hidden enemy, and Muslim women who were earlier spared such characterization, are no longer immune to it. This trend is producing what Hussein calls (drawing on Mahmood Mamdani) the "Good Muslim Woman / Bad Muslim Woman" binary, where the latter joins extremists on the battlefields while the former keeps Muslim men in check, nurturing them to become docile, patriotic citizens, and even government informants.

Against this background, the figure of the Muslim girl as a subject in-the-making, has emerged as an ideal site for training and protection not only for the international development regime but also for the nation-state. This young Muslim girl, if properly educated, can be transformed into the "Good Muslim Woman." Thus, in addition to an economic logic that seeks to shape girls into labor, consumers, and entrepreneurs, there is an ideological and political logic attached to girls' education as well. Indeed, it is argued that Muslim girls can be valuable to countering violent extremism (CVE) in their own societies. Muslim girls are now being called upon to produce counternarratives (particularly online) to resist the propaganda of terrorist organizations. An example of this is the Kofi Anan Foundation's recent Extremely Together campaign,[9] which brings together ten young activists from countries such as Syria, Somalia, Nigeria, Pakistan, the United Kingdom, and the Philippines. The foundation sees its work as "creating a generation of young activists . . . [as] adept at fighting hate speech online as the extremists are at spreading it."[10] Such programs construct young people as the bulwark against violent extremism.

The treatment of Naureen Leghari in Pakistan is yet another example of how the state deploys itself as the caretaker of girls and how young people are increasingly positioned as being responsible for addressing violent extremism. Leghari, a nineteen-year-old married woman was arrested after a police encounter in Lahore. It is reported that she was radicalized, had traveled to Syria to join Daesh, and had returned to Lahore to join her husband and the militant network.[11] On April 15, 2017, she was arrested during a raid. What is interesting, however, is the way in which this episode unfolded. Even though she was guilty of being a member of a militant network, she was released. Her culpability was erased through references to her as a student, *larki* (girl), *beti* (daughter), *bachi* (girl-child), and *quam ki bachi* (nation's girl-child). During a press briefing held in April 2017 by Inter-Services Public Relations, which is the media wing of the Pakistan Armed Forces, the director general, before playing her confession video, introduced her as "our own girl-child, the nation's girl-child [*hamari apni bachi hai, quam ki bachi hai*]." After the video, he noted, "The reason for showing you this video confession is that these children are our children. The youth surge is our strength."[12] Later, in another press briefing in May 2017, the director general used familial language to mark Leghari as the nation's daughter (*beti*), and installed the army as the caretaker of the nation and its inhabitants:

> We recovered Naureen Leghari from Lahore. She is a nineteen-year-old girl. We also showed an interview with her on media. Naureen Leghari was on her way to becoming a terrorist. She was not a terrorist. She was incited . . . her immature/young [*kam-umar*] brain was . . . she was brain-washed, which was not right. . . . And, we saved her in time. . . . Now, if she was my daughter or your daughter [*beti*], and if we

save her from being used per the design of terrorists . . . then should we punish her like a terrorist? Or should we give her a chance to go out and tell our other young generation about how she was instigated . . . and how she was used wrongly . . . parents should be aware, institutions [need] to be aware and we [should] use her in our society for correction. We shouldn't punish her. Let me tell you more. In Swat, when radicalization and extremism was underway, Taliban had also taken young children there and brainwashed them. We took many of those children later on when they were free (after the military had rescued them). If we send them to jail then afterward will they become good citizens or will they work against Pakistan? We sent them to a deradicalization center, we brainwashed them positively, told them about being Pakistani [*Pakistaniyat*] and today, after three to four years, they are good citizens, they earn for their parents, go to school, go to colleges, and contribute to Pakistan. So with regards to Naureen, I would like to say [the same] . . . to tell our male and female children [*bachay aur bachiyan*] about threats they face, how her brain was damaged.[13]

Even though there was evidence that Leghari received training to use weapons, and she explained in text messages to her brother that she had "migrated to the land of Khilafah [caliphate],"[14] she was viewed as an immature girl, not really in control of her actions. Her gender, biological age, and status as a student were emphasized by the army to transform her from an agentic subject to a tool used by terrorists. She, therefore, deserved protection and not punishment.

This example shows how the figure of the Muslim girl has become a productive site, functioning across multiple discursive networks and authorizing a range of entities and discourses. However, the rise of the figure of the Muslim girl does not mean that tropes about Muslim women's oppression and silence have lost their potency. To the contrary, they continue to have robust political function, in *specific* moments. Muslim women's oppression and assumptions around Muslim men's violence continue to be utilized to establish the superiority of western civilization, and mark Muslims as having a unique propensity to both engage in violence and tolerate harm done to female bodies (as we have seen in President Trump's 2017 executive orders banning Muslims). What is different now is the availability of diverse Muslim feminine figures through which multiple political ideologies are advanced.

MUSLIM WOMEN'S ACTIVISM

To disturb present-day certainties about Muslim women of the past as silent victims of patriarchy/Islam/Muslim men, I have engaged with an archive that paints a different picture. While I draw on women's magazines such as *Ismat, Khatun,* and *Tehzib-e-Niswan* to explore the debates about education at that time, I also read these writings as autobiographical and argue that they give us a glimpse into women's lives. In fact, if we consider the range of writings that appeared at the turn of the twentieth century, from these magazines and novels to travel narratives, reformist texts, cookbooks, and manuals for childcare, housekeeping, and personal hygiene, we get a markedly different picture of Indian Muslim women when compared to their dominant representation as secluded and silent. Indeed, as feminist scholars Leigh Gilmore and Elizabeth Marshall note, women of color have used the autobiographical genre to talk back to the constructions that mark them as permanently vulnerable,[15] and hence such texts are "an important and yet under-theorized area of feminist resistance."[16] In these texts, women emerge as thoughtful, engaged, and politically active, even as they struggle within the constraints imposed by patriarchal structures.

Consider Muhammadi Begum and Wahid Jahan, both of whom belie the dominant image of Muslim women of the past. Muhammadi Begum was literate and had a thriving writing and editing career; Wahid Jahan was an author and an adept administrator who ran a women's Normal school and then a hostel. Likewise, Bibi Ashraf strategized her own education and went on to become a teacher in an English school.[17] In the pages of women's magazines, we find evidence of women who are active and engaged in their political and social milieu—women took up the roles of editors, teachers, writers, fundraisers, and political workers. Indeed, being the official journal of the All India Muhammadan Education Conference, *Khatun* is teeming with such evidence. The second issue of *Khatun*, published in 1906, provides details of the ladies conference that was organized in Aligarh on December 28, 1905, by Mrs. Mushtaq, the daughter of Nasr-al-Baqir, Miss Nasir-uddin Haider, and Mrs. Raza Allah. The conference was attended by forty *bibiyan* (*sharif* women), none of whom were from Aligarh, which meant that they had to travel to the conference. During the conference, Zahra Bint Faizi was named the first president. Elsewhere, in *Tehzib-e-Niswan,* we learn about the "Tehzibi Fund," to which women regularly sent monetary contributions that were used as prize money for girls to encourage them to go to school in Lahore.[18] Women were also engaged in the reform movements and were not shy about sharing their discontent with male leadership. In the 1907 issue of *Khatun*,[19] for instance, A. W. J. Begum, from Delhi, wrote:

> I have heard a lot of noise about the fact that the quest for knowledge has not reached Muslim women, and that they are not interested in education in any way. People make speeches at meetings and write articles in newspapers. . . . But if you ask them what they have done to spread knowledge among women . . . the answer is simply nothing. Everyone says that our *gari* [vehicle] will reach its destination, but no one seems to be willing to hitch it to an engine, or a horse, or even a bullock, and then everyone regrets that the cart is still sitting in one place. If this keeps up, we will never get anywhere.[20]

There is also a sense of solidarity among women, which is apparent in the letters they wrote to each other, sharing personal information and seeking advice. The phrases *Tehzibi behnain* (Tehzibi sisters) and *Ismati behnain* also attest to that.

What we have here is evidence of elite Muslim women's active engagement in securing reforms for themselves even as the limits of such activism were defined by men. Muslim women were, indeed, speaking—in the periodicals and didactic novels, at rallies, and during meetings of political associations.

While the periodicals give us insights into women's lives, it is only the *ashraf* women whose lives we can learn about through them. Poor and illiterate women did not write in the periodicals. When poor women do make an appearance in the periodicals or didactic novels, it is often as caricatures. Figures such as *mama*, who appeared in Muhammadi Begum's writings, or the *hajjan* in Nazir Ahmed's work, belonged to the working class. They are portrayed as helpful and skillful but also clever and conniving. *Ashraf* women were, thus, directed to maintain their distance from them. There are, however, hints of how working-class women were more effective at managing their employers' affairs given their greater exposure. Since they were not restricted to the *zenana* like their *ashraf* counterparts, these women had greater mobility and exposure to the opposite sex. This often meant that they were adept at tasks such as negotiating loans and interest rates, managing domestic budgets, and maintaining social relations (as both *mama* and *hajjan* appear to do). Thus, reading the periodicals and didactic novels against the grain can be an effective strategy to learn about some aspects of the lives of poor women at the turn of the twentieth century. However, such a project will always be limited in scope.

During the political movement for Pakistan, a large number of women were mobilized. This included not only elite women but also middle-class women who joined the Muslim League, which actively courted women to support its activities. Jinnah, for instance, noted that "no nation [could] make progress without the co-operation of its women. If Muslim women support their men as they did in the days of the Prophet of Islam, we should soon realise our goal."[21] Sarah Ansari observes that Jinnah's involvement in the passage of the Shariat Application Act of 1937 (which targeted the customary laws that deprived women of their inheritance rights in relation to immovable property), and the Muslim Dissolution of Marriage Act of 1939 signaled to women that the Muslim League would offer a nation where their conditions would improve.[22] During the civil disobedience movement of 1946–47, therefore, women took to the streets, participated in public protests and picket lines, hoisted flags on British buildings and got arrested. Fourteen-year-old Fatima Sughra climbed up the gate of the Secretariat Building in Lahore, removed the Union Jack, and replaced it with a *duptta*.[23] On April 3, 1947, fifteen hundred Pathan women from the North Western Frontier Province protested publicly.[24] The nationalist movement, hence, radically changed the parameters of women's participation—women could cast off the veil, talk to strange men, protest on streets, endure tear gas and batons, go to jail, and fight for political seats. Even though men set the terms of women's involvement in this struggle, it is noteworthy that women came out in large numbers to participate in the endeavor.

After the establishment of Pakistan, while the state again asked women to participate in the development of the nation, this participation was circumscribed by assumptions about their naturalized (gendered) abilities. The primary activist projects that were deemed appropriate for women at that time concentrated on "social work"—addressing the needs of the refugees who had migrated from India, the homeless, widows, and children. This extended women's responsibilities in the public without seriously threatening the status quo. That said, women from elite families continued to fight for political rights—the first legislature of Pakistan, for instance, had two women representatives. In 1948, when the Shariat bill, which recognized women's right to inherit property, was removed from the agenda of the Assembly, women legislators took up the cause with the Muslim League Women's Committee, and effectively protested to get it reinstated. Hence, women pushed on the political fronts where they could. Upper-middle-class women also formed organizations such as the All Pakistan Women's Association and Women's Action Forum, which organized for women's rights and stood up against military rule.

In rereading women and girls of the past as political agents, I do not intend to minimize their suffering or erase the class dynamics of this activism. Indeed, this book has been a story about how women and girls are constrained not only by colonial logics and state practices but also by respectability and class politics. Yet, this subjection is never absolute. Muslim girls and women have found ways within patriarchal and capitalist constraints to secure spaces to breath. Such an understanding of women's lives offers ways for scholars and practitioners alike to move away from interpreting Muslim women's lives in absolute terms—as either always-oppressed or free, always-silent or empowered. Instead, they point to how different social forces regulate the lives of women as well as how women who suffer, resist, strategize, withdraw, and overcome, are crucial players in such stories. Furthermore, such readings make it possible to hold accountable forces that are both external as well as internal to Muslim societies that shape women's lives. In other words, it becomes possible to critique colonial and now imperial and corporate feminism's exploitation of Muslim women, while *simultaneously* calling attention to the debilitating effects of local forms of patriarchy and state practices that constrain them.

ONLY MIDDLES . . .

Foucauldian genealogies do not have beginnings or ends; thus, this book will also not provide any neat conclusions. Rather, I have traced overlapping storylines and move between the past and the present to signal that we are very much in the middle of stories—stories about the preservation of class privileges, of changing norms of respectability, of exploitation of women's labor, of fluid gender categories, and of activism and political agency. These stories are ongoing as gender and education continue to be powerful discursive fields that regulate the lives of both men and women. Our task, therefore, is to constantly subject naturalized categories and social projects to an interrogation as they crystalize particular power-knowledge relations.

This book, I hope, has accomplished at least a couple of objectives. First, it should give pause to practitioners and advocates of girls' education, particularly those from western contexts embedded within the aid-industrial complex. It calls on them to avoid abstracting girls and their education from broader concerns related to social class, domestic and foreign politics, and missionary impulses of international development. Significantly, it problematizes education's emancipatory promise by showing how schooling can reinscribe old hierarchies and/or produce new ones. Hence, any effort towards girls' education must account for the entrenched and systemic subjugation of girls and women across multiple social spaces. Otherwise, schooling and its attendant rewards of participation in the labor force only add additional burdens to the lives of girls.

The second objective is to amplify women's resilience and political agency, while highlighting how women's actions have always been severely constrained. Be it limited access to literacy and capital for publishing during the turn of the twentieth century, or the systematic discrimination by the state and the formal and informal attempts to demarcate women's domains today, women have exercised choice and empowerment within contexts that limit their possibilities. The political stake of this book, then, is to rally allies who are interested in empowering girls to not focus simply on education and waged labor, but to also critically analyze the underlying conditions of women's subjection—a move away from the service-delivery model and toward a more politicized feminism.

Finally, I hope that this book will pique the interest of researchers in engaging in deeper studies of Muslim masculinities. With the extensive focus on Muslim women and girls within aid and development regimes, there is limited engagement with the representations of Muslim men or complex enactments of masculinities. As this book has shown, particular spatialities are marked as masculine and the masculinizing impulses of the state are often expressed through the infantilization of adult women. Tracing masculinities, masculinizing practices, masculine posturings, and representations of Muslim men thus appears to be a worthy endeavor for future research.

NOTES

CHAPTER 1. GIRLS' EDUCATION AS A UNIFYING DISCOURSE

1. In dominant discourses the specificities and histories of groups such as the Taliban, Boko Haram, or more recently also al-Shabab, are erased and what emerges are broad generalizations about Muslim men, Islam, and Muslim cultures as inhospitable to women and girls.

2. For an exception see Dan Murphy, "'Boko Haram' Doesn't Really Mean 'Western Education Is a Sin,'" *Christian Science Monitor,* May 6, 2014.

3. Nicholas Kristof, "What's So Scary about Smart Girls?" *New York Times,* May 10, 2014.

4. Joe Hemba, "Nigerian Islamists Kill 59 Pupils in Boarding School Attack," Reuters, February 26, 2014; Lanre Ola, "Boko Haram Abduct Dozens of Boys in Northeast Nigeria— Witnesses," Reuters, August 15, 2014; Aminu Abubakar, "Boko Haram kidnaps 30 in northeast Nigeria," CNN Online, October 28, 2014.

5. Quoted in Eliana Dockterman, "After Boko Haram: Hillary Clinton Promises Education for 14 Million Girls," *Time,* September 24, 2014.

6. Gordon Brown, "Girl Power," Project Syndicate, June 15, 2014, www.project-syndicate. org/commentary/gordon-brown-highlights-girls--emerging-leadership-in-the-struggle-to-secure-their-rights?barrier=accessreg (accessed February 20, 2018); and see Gordon Brown, "Malala: Everyone's Daughter in the Flight for Girls' Education," *New Perspectives Quarterly* 30, no. 1 (2013): 59–60.

7. In discussing the production of news, Stuart Hall argues that in order to allow audiences to make sense of random events, newsmen often bring audiences back to horizons of that which they recognize: "an event only 'makes sense' if it can be located within a range of known social and cultural identifications" (p. 54). Hall goes on to note that this "means, in essence, referring unusual and unexpected events to the 'maps of meaning' which already form the basis of our cultural knowledge, into which the social world is already 'mapped'" (54).

For more see Stuart Hall, *the Crisis: Mugging, the State, and Law and Order* (London: Macmillan, 1978).

8. The graphic is available at http://educategirls.ngo/pdf/GirlEffect_Smarter-Economics-Investing-in-Girls.pdf (accessed October 15, 2017). I did not have permission from *Girl Effect* to reproduce it in the book.

9. Emily Canal, "How Shiza Shahid and the Malala Fund Are Championing for Girls' Rights," *Forbes*, September 18, 2014.

10. Ibid.

11. These introductory sections were first included in Shenila Khoja-Moolji, "Suturing Together Girls and Education: An Investigation into the Social (Re)Production of Girls' Education as a Hegemonic Ideology," *Journal of Diaspora, Indigenous, and Minority Education* 9, no. 2 (2015): 87–107, and have been reproduced with permission.

12. Edward Said, *Orientalism* (New York: Vintage Books, 1978).

13. Neferti Tadiar, "Empire," *Social Text* 27, no. 3 (2009): 112.

14. Laura Bush, "A Nation Challenged: The First Lady; Mrs. Bush Cites Women's Plight under Taliban," *New York Times*, November 18, 2001.

15. Haideh Moghissi, *Feminism and Islamic Fundamentalism: The Limits of Postmodern Analysis* (London: Zed Books, 1999).

16. Steve Turnham, "Donald Trump to Father of Fallen Soldier: 'I've Made a Lot of Sacrifices,'" ABC News, June 30, 2016, http://abcnews.go.com/Politics/donald-trump-father-fallen-soldier-ive-made-lot/story?id=41015051 (accessed February 20, 2018).

17. The White House, "Executive Order Protecting the Nation from Foreign Terrorist Entry into the United States," Official of the Press Secretary, March 6, 2017, www.whitehouse.gov/the-press-office/2017/03/06/executive-order-protecting-nation-foreign-terrorist-entry-united-states (accessed January 24, 2018).

18. Nicholas Kristof, "Meet Sultana, the Taliban's Worst Fear," *New York Times*, June 4, 2016.

19. For a deeper analysis of Kristof's writings see Lila Abu-Lughod, *Do Muslim Women Need Saving?* (Cambridge, MA: Harvard University Press, 2013).

20. The term *zenana* refers to women's quarters, which were often not accessible to outsiders, particularly men. Since elite women preferred not to leave the *zenana,* female Christian missionaries started educational projects whereby they visited the *zenanas* themselves to teach women.

21. Ban Ki-moon, "Female Energy, Talent, Strength Represent Humankind's Most Valuable Untapped Resource, Secretary-General Says in Message for International Women's Day," United Nations, March 2, 2012, www.un.org/press/en/2012/sgsm14140.doc.htm (accessed January 24, 2018).

22. See www.girlup.org.

23. Elizabeth Adams St. Pierre, "Deleuzian Concepts for Education: The Subject Undone," *Educational Philosophy and Theory* 36, no. 3 (2004): 283–96.

24. Michel Foucault, *History of Sexuality, Vol. I: An Introduction,* trans. Robert Hurley (New York: Vintage Books, 1978), 49; and Chris Weedon, *Feminist Practice and Poststructuralist Theory,* 2nd ed. (Boston: Blackwell, 1997).

25. Michel Foucault, *Discipline and Punish: The Birth of the Prison,* trans. Alan Sheridan (New York: Vintage Books, 1977), 200.

26. Judith Butler, *Gender Trouble* (New York: Routledge, 1990), 5.

27. See Sandra Harding, "The Instability of the Analytical Categories of Feminist Theory," *Signs* 11, no. 4 (Summer 1986): 645–64; R. W. Connell, *Gender and Power* (Stanford, CA: Stanford University Press, 1987); Chandra Mohanty, "Under Western Eyes: Feminist Scholarship and Colonial Discourses," *Feminist Review* 30 (1988): 61–88.

28. Tim Allender, *Learning Femininity in Colonial India, 1820–1932* (Manchester: Manchester University Press, 2016), 11.

29. See chapter 6 of this book.

30. Judith Butler, *Bodies That Matter: On the Discursive Limits of "Sex"* (New York: Routledge, 1993), 7.

31. For more, see Shenila Khoja-Moolji, "Suturing Together Girls and Education: An Investigation into the Social (Re)Production of Girls' Education as a Hegemonic Ideology," *Journal of Diaspora, Indigenous, and Minority Education* 9, no. 2 (2015): 87–107.

32. Ruby Lal, *Coming of Age in Nineteenth-Century India: The Girl-Child and the Art of Playfulness* (New York: Cambridge University Press, 2013).

33. For more see Maureen Porter, "Making Gender Matter: Paradigms for Equality, Equity, and Excellence," in *Policy Debates in Comparative, International, and Development Education,* ed. John N. Hawkins and W. James Jacob (New York: Palgrave Macmillan, 2011), 131–54.

34. In May 2017 there were headlines that the new administration under Donald Trump will end Let Girls Learn. However, it was later denied by the White House and the program still seems to be functioning.

35. While during the 1990s and 2000s microfinance was touted as a "magic bullet" to address women's empowerment, tentative findings around its effects as well as strong critiques by feminists, have further strengthened the belief in the girl as the ideal "change agent" today. For more see Naila Kabeer, "Is Microfinance a 'Magic Bullet' for Women's Empowerment? Analysis of Findings from South Asia," *Economic and Political Weekly* 40, nos. 44–45 (2005): 4709–18; Christine Keating, Claire Rasmussen, and Pooja Rishi, "The Rationality of Empowerment: Microcredit, Accumulation by Dispossession, and the Gendered Economy," *Signs* 36, no. 1 (2010): 153–76.

36. For more see Anita Harris, *All about the Girl: Culture, Power, and Identity* (New York: Routledge, 2004); Marnina Gonick, *Between Femininities: Ambivalence, Identity and the Education of Girls* (Albany: State University of New York Press, 2003); Angela McRobbie, "Top Girls? Young Women and the Post-Feminist Sexual Contract," *Cultural Studies* 21, nos. 4–5 (2007): 718–37; Jessica Ringrose, *Postfeminist Education? Girls and the Sexual Politics of Schooling*/London: Routledge, 2013).

37. As cited in Tahera Aftab, "Women's Education, Zenana Instruction, and the American Missions in Northern India, Later 19th C," *Pakistan Journal of American Studies* 5, no 1 (1987): 104.

38. Allender, *Learning Femininity,* 6.

39. Ibid., 2.

40. Ibid., 6.

41. Jane Haggis, "White Women and Colonialism: Towards a Non-Recuperative History," In *Gender and Imperialism,* ed. Clare Midgley (Oxford: St. Martin's Press, 1998), 59.

42. For more see Antoinette Burton, *Burdens of History: British Feminists, Indian Women, and Imperial Culture, 1865–1915* (Chapel Hill: University of North Carolina, 1994).

43. For more see, Clare Midgley, *Feminism and Empire* (London: Routledge, 2007), 1.

44. Ibid.

45. Aftab, "Women's Education," 120.

46. Indian historian Faisal Devji has observed that the notion of a "Muslim community" or *quam* was an emergent sociological phenomenon at this time. Sutured to religious identity as well as ethnicity, and later used as a stand in for "nation," the term has an evolving history. However, it signals the effort by some Muslim groups to shape themselves as a collectivity. In this book, I use it to point to "religious or national community" as it is often deployed in the archives that I have studied to point to a group identity based on either religion or nation. For more see Stephen M. Lyon, "Power and Patronage in Pakistan," Ph.D. diss., University of Kent, 2002; and see Faisal Devji, "India in the Muslim Imagination: Cartography and Landscape in 19th Century Urdu Literature," *South Asia Multidisciplinary Academic Journal* 10 (2014): 1–17.

47. Michel Foucault, "Governmentality," in *Michel Foucault: Power*, ed. J. D. Faubion (New York: New Press, 2000), 201–22

48. Michel Foucault, "The Ethics of the Concern of the Self as a Practice of Freedom," in *Ethics: Subjectivity and Truth*, ed. Paul Rainbow (New York: Penguin Books, 1984), 300.

49. See Thomas Popkewitz, *Struggling for the Soul: The Politics of Schooling and the Construction of the Teacher* (New York: Teachers College Press, Columbia University, 1998); and Ian Hunter, *Rethinking the School: Subjectivity, Bureaucracy, Criticism* (New York: St. Martin's Press, 1994).

50. John Willinsky, *Learning to Divide the World: Education at Empire's End* (Minneapolis: University of Minnesota Press, 1998).

51. Bill Ashcroft, Gareth Griffiths, and Helen Tiffin, eds., *The Post-Colonial Studies Reader* (New York: Routledge, 1995), 426.

52. Edward Said, *Reflections on Exile* (Cambridge, MA: Harvard University Press, 2000), 392.

53. Suresh Ghosh, "English in Taste, in Opinions, in Words and Intellect: Indoctrinating the Indian through Textbook, Curriculum, and Education," in *The Imperial Curriculum: Racial Images and Education in the British Colonial Experience*, ed. J. A. Mangan (London: Routledge, 1993), 175–94.

54. As cited in Gauri Viswanathan, "The Beginnings of English Literary Study in British India," *Oxford Literary Review* 9, nos. 1–2 (1987): 2–26; 13.

55. Margrit Pernau, *Ashraf into Middle Classes: Muslims in Nineteenth-Century Delhi* (Oxford: Oxford University Press, 2013), 110.

56. Nishant Batsha, "The Uneducated: Education and the Mediation of Muslim Identity in the British Raj, 1858–1882," unpublished undergraduate thesis, Department of History, Columbia University, 2010.

57. Henry Harington Thomas, *The Late Rebellion in India and Our Future Policy* (London: W. Kent,1858), 5.

58. Ibid., 22.

59. Partha Chatterjee, *The Black Hole of Empire: History of a Global Practice of Power* (Princeton, NJ: Princeton University Press, 2012).

60. Thomas, *Late Rebellion in India*, 24.

61. Krishna Kumar, *Politics of Education in Colonial India* (London: Routledge, 2014). For more see Mary Ann Chacko, "Schooling as Counter-Socialization: Krishna Kumar's Contributions to Curriculum," in *Curriculum Studies in India,* ed. William Pinar (New York: Palgrave Macmillan, 2015), 65–81.

62. Allender, *Learning Femininity,* 31.

63. Kate Eichhorn, *The Archival Turn in Feminism* (Philadelphia: Temple University Press, 2014), 9.

64. Gilles Deleuze and Felix Guattari. *A Thousand Plateaus: Capitalism and Schizophrenia,* trans. Brain Massumi (Minneapolis: University of Minnesota Press, 1987).

65. Michel Foucault, *Language, Counter-Memory, Practice,* trans. Donald Bouchard and Sherry Simon (Ithaca, NY: Cornell University Press, 1977), 137–38.

66. Michel Foucault, s.v. "*Foucault,*" in *Dictionnaire des philosophes* (1984), 942–44, available at https://foucault.info/doc/foucault/biography-html (accessed February 20, 2018).

67. Foucault, *Language, Counter-Memory, Practice,* 140.

68. Larry Shiner, "Reading Foucault: Anti-Method and the Genealogy of Power-Knowledge," *History and Theory* 21, no. 3 (1982): 382–98.

69. Akhil Gupta, "Blurred Boundaries: The Discourse of Corruption, the Culture of Politics, and the Imagined State," *American Ethnologist* 22, no. 2 (1995), 385.

70. Exceptions include Gail Minault, *Secluded Scholars: Women's Education and Muslim Social Reform in Colonial India* (New York: Oxford University Press, 1998); Lal, *Coming of Age*; Geraldine Forbes, "Education for Women," in *Women and Social Reform in Modern India: A Reader,* ed. Sumit Sarkar and Tanika Sarkar (Bloomington: Indiana University Press, 2008), 58–77.

71. Lee Quinby, *Genealogy and Literature* (Minneapolis: University of Minnesota Press), 1995.

72. Cleo H. Cherryholmes, "Reading Research," *Journal of Curriculum Studies* 25, no. 1 (1993): 3.

73. Ibid., 5.

74. Sylvia Vatuk, "*Hamara Daur-I Hayat*: An Indian Muslim Women Writes Her Life," in *Telling Lives in India: Biography, Autobiography, and Life History,* ed. David Arnold and Stuart H. Blackburn (Bloomington: Indiana University Press, 2004), 149.

75. Wendy Hesford, *Spectacular Rhetorics: Human Rights Visions, Recognitions, Feminisms* (Durham, NC: Duke University Press, 2011), 11.

76. Tahera Aftab, *Inscribing South Asian Muslim Women: An Annotated Bibliography and Research Guide* (Leiden, Netherlands: Brill, 2008), 389.

77. Pierre Bourdieu, *Distinction: A Social Critique of the Judgment of Taste,* trans. Richard Nice (Cambridge, MA: Harvard University Press, 1984).

78. Jane Kenway et al., *Class Choreographies: Elite Schools and Globalization* (London: Palgrave, 2017), 5.

79. Ibid., 6.

80. I draw on a sociological and anthropological definition of social class in this book. There are, however, several studies that highlight middle class as an economic phenomenon. For instance, utilizing survey data and national accounts, Homi Kharas of the Brookings Institute notes that in contemporary Pakistan about one-third of Pakistanis (specifically 27

percent of the population) would be constituted as middle class. He notes that by 2030 this number may rise to 66 percent of the population. See Kharas, "Pakistan's Emerging Middle Class: Lessons from a Country in Transition," Urban Institute, October 31, 2017, www.urban. org/events/pakistans-emerging-middle-class-lessons-country-transition (accessed January 24, 2018).

81. Joan Scott, "Gender: A Useful Category of Historical Analysis," *American Historical Review* 91, no. 5 (1986): 1053–75.

82. Ibid.

83. Azra Asghar Ali, *The Emergence of Feminism among Indian Muslim Women, 1920–1947* (Karachi: Oxford University Press, 2000).

CHAPTER 2. FORGING *SHARIF* SUBJECTS

1. *Ismat* 6, no. 3 (1906).

2. Imtiaz Ahmad, "The Ashraf-Ajlaf Dichotomy in Muslim Social Structure in India," *The Indian Economic and Social History* 3, no. 3 (1966): 268–78.

3. Margrit Pernau, *Ashraf into Middle Classes: Muslims in Nineteenth-Century Delhi* (Oxford: Oxford University Press, 2013), uses this phrase, drawing on Gail Minault, *Secluded Scholars: Women's Education and Muslim Social Reform in Colonial India* (New York: Oxford University Press, 1998), 5.

4. Pernau, *Ashraf into Middle Classes,* uses this phrase drawing on Minault, *Secluded Scholars,* 266.

5. Faisal Devji, "Gender and the Politics of Space: The Movement for Women's Reform in Muslim India, 1857–1900," *South Asia* 14, no. 1 (1991): 141–53.

6. Ibid.

7. For more see Fatima Mernissi, *The Veil and the Male Elite: A Feminist Interpretation of Women's Rights in Islam* (Reading, MA: Addison-Wesley Publishing, 1991).

8. In "Beyond the Nation? Or Within?" *Social Text* 16, no. 3 (1998): 57–69, Partha Chatterjee also makes a similar observation in the context of colonial Bengal. He notes that Indian social worlds could be divided into two domains—material and spiritual. The British clearly surpassed their Indian counterparts in the material domain and, hence, western knowledges had to be studied and replicated. However, the spiritual—which embodied the essential Indian cultural identity—had to be preserved. It was often women's practices that came to mark this spiritual domain.

9. Pernau, *Ashraf into Middle Classes,* 256.

10. Ibid., 128.

11. Ibid., 142; and Christina Oesterheld, "Islam in Contemporary South Asia: Urdu and Muslim Women," *Oriente Moderno,* n.s., 23, no. 84 (2004): 217–43.

12. *Khatun* 1 (1906).

13. This term often means the study of English language as well as literary and scientific texts selected by the colonial administration. English schools often refer to schools established by the colonial administration.

14. For instance, on March 7, 1835, Lord Bentick in a resolution supporting Macaulay's famous Minutes noted that all funds appropriated for education "would be best employed

on English education alone" as cited in Alan Peshkin, "Education, the Muslim Elite, and the Creation of Pakistan," *Comparative Education Review* 6, no. 2 (1962): 152–59.

15. Margrit Pernau has identified earlier texts such as the *Risala-e adab-e nikah* by Abdul Wadir (n.d.), *Talim un nisa* by Karim ud Din (published in 1848), and *Tuhfa uz zujain* by Nawab Qutb ud Din (written in 1851).

16. Pernau, *Ashraf into Middle Classes*, 357; the book is still in circulation in India and Pakistan today, and has inspired at least three different television productions in Pakistan.

17. Discussions about women's education were taking place in other geographical contexts as well. For various efforts for women's education and emancipation in Egypt see Omina Shakry, "Schooled Mothers and Structured Play: Child Rearing in Turn-of-the-Century Egypt," in *Remaking Women: Feminism and modernity in the Middle East*, ed. Lila Abu-Lughod (Princeton, NJ: Princeton University Press, 1998), 3–27; for efforts in the United States, see Nancy Lesko, *Act Your Age! A Cultural Construction of Adolescence* (New York: Routledge, 2012); and Jane Roland Martin, *Reclaiming a Conversation: The Ideal of the Educated Woman* (New York: Palgrave Macmillan, 1985); and for efforts in Iran see Afsaneh Najmabadi, "Crafting an Educated Housewife in Iran," in *Remaking Women*, ed. Lila Abu-Lughod (Princeton, NJ: Princeton University Press, 1998), 91–125.

18. Minault, *Secluded Scholars*, 18.

19. As cited in ibid., 81.

20. Quoted in ibid., 18.

21. Sir Syed (1871), as cited in Reza Pirbhai, "Pakistan and the Political Awakening of the Muslim 'New Woman,' 1937–1947," *HAWWA: Journal of the Women of the Middle East and the Islamic World* 12 (2014): 9.

22. Ibid.

23. Pernau, *Ashraf into Middle Classes*, 363.

24. Syed Shamsuddin ibn Miansaheb Qadri, *Risala talim-niswan* (Mumbai: University of Bombay, 1895), 3.

25. Ibid., 15.

26. Ibid., 16.

27. Ibid., 26–27.

28. See Benjamin Lindsey, *The Companionate Marriage* (New York: Boni & Liveright, 1927), for additional information on the early twentieth century concept of companionate marriage.

29. Qadri, *Risala talim-niswan*, 25.

30. Mumtaz Ali, *Huquq-e-niswan* (Lahore: Punjab Publishers, 1898), 43.

31. Ibid., 44.

32. Ibid., 56.

33. For more on the Aga Khan's views on women's education see, Shenila Khoja-Moolji, "Redefining Muslim Women: Aga Khan III's Reforms for Women's Education," *South Asia Graduate Research Journal* 20, no. 1 (2011): 69–95.

34. Aga Khan, *India in Transition: A Study in Political Evolution* (New York: G. Putnam, 1918), 354.

35. Ibid., 258.

36. As cited in Qayyum Malick, *His Royal Highness Prince Aga Khan: Guide, Philosopher, and Friend of the Islamic world* (Karachi: Ismailia Association for Pakistan, 1969), 211.

37. Minault, *Secluded Scholars,* 220–21. Elsewhere, I have also considered the influence that emerging feminist movements in Britain, Egypt, and America had on the Aga Khan's views; see Khoja-Moolji, "Redefining Muslim Women."

38. I conducted focus group conversations with members of this Shia Muslim community (chapter 4). The current imam is Aga Khan III's grandson, His Highness Prince Karim Aga Khan IV.

39. As cited in A. K. Adatia and N. Q. King, "Some East African Firmans of H. H. Aga Khan III," *Journal of Religion in Africa* 2, no. 2 (1969): 187.

40. Aga Khan, *Message to the World of Islam* (Karachi: Ismailia Association of Pakistan, 1977).

41. Aga Khan, *The Memoirs of Aga Khan: World Enough and Time* (New York: Simon and Schuster, 1954), 27.

42. See Ali, *Huquq-e-niswan,* 60–70.

43. Quoted in K. K. Aziz, ed., *Aga Khan III: Selected Speeches and Writings of Sir Sultan Muhammad Shah,* 2 vols. (London: Kegan Paul International, 1997), 646.

44. Pernau, *Ashraf into Middle Classes,* 273.

45. Muhammad Qasim Zaman, *Ashraf Ali Thanawi: Islam in Modern South Asia* (Oxford: Oneworld Publications, 2008), 70.

46. Oesterheld, "Islam in Contemporary South Asia."

47. Zaman. *Ashraf Ali Thanawi,* 70.

48. Mahua Sarkar, *Visible Histories, Disappearing Women: Producing Muslim Womanhood in Late Colonial Bengal* (Durham, NC: Duke University Press, 2008).

49. Padma Anagol. "Agency, Periodisation, and Change in the Gender and Women's History of Colonial India," *Gender and History* 20, no. 3 (2008): 603–27; Padma Anagol, "Feminist Inheritances and Foremothers: The Beginnings of Feminism in Modern India," *Women's History Review* 19, no. 4 (2010): 523–46.

50. Anagol, "Agency, Periodisation, and Change," 619.

51. Tapan Ray-Chaudhuri and Geraldine Forbes, *The Memoirs of Dr. Haimabati Sen: From Child Widow to Lady Doctor* (New Delhi: Roli Books, 2000).

52. Tanika Sarkar, *Words to Win: The Making of Amar Jiban; A Modern Autobiography* (Delhi: Kali for Women, 1999).

53. Elora Shehabuddin, "Gender and the Figure of the 'Moderate Muslim,'" in *The Question of Gender: Joan W. Scott's Critical Feminism,* ed. Judith Butler and Elizabeth Weed (Bloomington: Indiana University Press, 2011), 102–42.

54. Mahua Sarkar, "Muslim Women and the Politics of (In)Visibility in Late Colonial Bengal," *Journal of Historical Sociology* 14, no. 2 (2001): 226–50; Mahua Sarkar, *Visible Histories, Disappearing Women: Producing Muslim Womanhood in Late Colonial Bengal* (Durham, NC: Duke University Press, 2008).

55. Sarkar, "Muslim Women and the Politics of (In)visibility," 227.

56. Marilyn Booth, *May Her Likes Be Multiplied: Biography and Gender Politics in Egypt* (Berkeley: University of California Press, 2001).

57. Ibid., xvii.

58. Beth Baron, *The Women's Awakening in Egypt: Culture, Society, and the Press* (New Haven, CT: Yale University Press, 1994).

59. Gail Minault, "Women's Magazines in Urdu as Sources for Muslim Social History," *Indian Journal for Gender Studies* 5, no. 2 (1998): 203.

60. Ibid., 201.

61. Ibid., 202.

62. Pernau estimates that, by 1911, half to a third writers were female: Pernau, *Ashraf into Middle Classes*, 372. Specifically, 1910 (vol. 4, nos. 4–6), 1911 (vol. 1, no. 1; vol. 6, nos. 1–6), and 1919 (vol. 23, no. 5).

63. Shaista Suhrawardy, in *A Critical Survey of the Development of the Urdu Novel and Short Story* (London: Longmans Green, 1945), notes that the novel was actually written in 1902.

64. Minault, *Secluded Scholars*.

65. Ibid.

66. Established in 1886 by the Muslim education reformer Sir Syed, the purpose of the conference (earlier known as All India Muhammadan Education Congress) was to create opportunities for Muslims to acquire higher education. Topics under discussion ranged from curriculum and religious education to women's education and reading materials. Shaikh Abdullah was appointed as the secretary of women's education section in 1902; the women's section of the conference had been established in 1896.

67. *Khatun* 3, nos. 1–2 (1906).

68. Ibid. This phrase should be understood in the context of the widespread belief that women's religious practices had become corrupt due to lack of engagement with *ilm* (knowledge) or the correct knowledges of Islam. Hence, the call for improving women's religious practices is simultaneously an effort to also define correct or proper Muslim practices (for more see Muhammad Qasim Zaman, "Religious Education and the Rhetoric of Reform: The Madrasa in British India and Pakistan," *Comparative Study of Society and History* 41, no. 2 [1999]: 294–323).

69. *Khatun* 3, nos. 1–2 (1906).

70. *Khatun* 3, nos. 1, 3 (1906),—and continued thereafter.

71. For example, the 1906 issues of *Khatun* feature a serialized story entitled "Mrs. Halburtun's Difficulties: *Eik Shaadi* (One Marriage)." Other series issues appear around discussion of key Muslim female figures such as Bibi Khatija, Bibi Fatima, and Bibi Ayesha (all in *Khatun* 3, nos. 1–5 [1906]).

72. Minault, "Women's Magazines."

73. See *Ismat* 3, no. 4 (1910).

74. *Ismat* 6, no. 2 (1911): 1.

75. *Ismat* 6, no. 3 (1911): 58.

76. Ibid., 58.

77. *Ismat* 6, no. 2 (1911): 53.

78. *Ismat* 6, no. 4 (1911): 43–48.

79. Ibid., 60.

80. Muhammadi Begum, *Sughar beti*, 2.

81. Ibid.

82. Ibid., 68–69.

83. Ibid., 16.

84. Ibid., 18.

85. Ibid.

86. Ibid., 28.

87. Ibid., 51.

88. Ibid., 55.

89. Ibid., 108.

90. Ibid., 106.

91. These articles were published in *Tehzib-e-Niswan* in 1899, in two installments, on March 23 and 30.

92. Muhammadi Begum, *Hayat-e-Ashraf,* 5.

93. Ibid.

94. Ibid.

95. Ibid., 7.

96. Ibid., 8.

97. Ibid., 11.

98. See ibid., 12.

99. Ibid., 13.

100. Ibid., 14.

101. Ibid., 16.

102. Ibid.

103. Ibid., 18.

104. Ibid., 19–20.

105. Ibid., 22, 25.

106. Ibid., 37.

107. Ibid., 35.

108. Ibid., 48.

109. Ruby Lal, *Coming of Age in Nineteenth-Century India: The Girl-Child and the Art of Playfulness* (New York: Cambridge University Press, 2013), 127.

110. Begum, *Hayat-e-Ashraf,* 28.

111. Ibid.

112. Ibid., 29.

113. Ibid., 11.

114. Angma Jhala, *Courtly Indian Women in Late Imperial India* (London: Pickering & Chatto, 2008).

115. Barbara Ramusack, *The Indian Princes and Their States* (Cambridge: Cambridge University Press, 2004), 108.

116. Najmabadi, "Crafting an Educated Housewife"; and Afsaneh Najmabadi, "Veiled Discourse-Unveiled Bodies," *Feminist Studies* 19, no. 3 (1993): 487–518.

117. Abu-Lughod, ed., *Remaking Women,* 259.

118. *Khatun* 3, nos. 1, 4 (1906).

119. Reproduced in ibid., no. 1.

120. Ibid.

121. As cited in Anwar Shaheen, "Patriarchal Education and Print Journalism: Their Emancipating Impact on Muslim Women of India during 1869–1908," *Pakistan Journal of History and Culture* 30, no. 2 (2009): 20.

122. *Khatun* 3, no. 1 (1905).

123. See issues from *Khatun* (1906).

124. See ibid.

125. Speech by Sikander Jahan Begum, *Khatun* 3, nos. 1, 12 (1906).

126. Shaheen, "Patriarchal Education."

127. *Katun* 3, nos. 3–4 (1906).

128. Shaikh Abdullah, ibid., 175.

129. Sanjay Seth, *Subject Lessons: The Western Education of Colonial India* (Durham, NC: Duke University Press, 2007).

130. Lal, *Coming of Age.*

CHAPTER 3. DESIRABLE AND FAILED CITIZEN-SUBJECTS

1. Specific *Ismat* issues explored are: 1948 (vol. 81, nos. 1–6); 1949 (vol. 82, nos. 1–6; vol. 83, no. 1); 1951 (vol. 87, no. 3); 1952 (vol. 88, no. 6; vol. 89, no. 4); 1954 (vol. 92, nos. 2–3, 5–6); 1954 (vol. 93, nos. 1–6); 1955 (vol. 94, nos. 1, 6; vol. 95, nos. 1–4, 6); 1956 (vol. 97, nos. 2–6); 1957 (vol. 98, nos. 1–6; vol. 99, nos. 1–6); 1958 (vol. 100, nos. 1–6; vol. 101, nos. 1–6); 1959 (vol. 102, nos. 2–6; vol. 103, nos. 1–6); 1961 (vol. 106, nos. 1–6; vol. 107, nos. 1–6); 1962 (vol. 108, nos. 1–6; vol. 109, nos. 1, 3–4, 6); 1963 (vol. 110, nos. 3, 6).

2. There is gap in *Tehzib*'s publication between August 9, 1947, and January 3, 1948. The editor in the January 3, 1948 issue notes that the region's events constrained publication. He further notes that the press where Tehzib (based in Lahore) was published as well as the paper industry owners were all Hindus and after partition left for India. The paper products were taken over by the government for its own use and the excess was not provided to businesses. The editor then complains about the lack of access to paper products.

3. While the scope of this book directs me to focus on women's magazines, it is significant to note the rise of All India Progressive Writers Association during the 1930s, which then split into All Pakistan Progressive Writers Association (APPWA), an organization whose anticolonial and socialist ideas were crucial to the cultural legitimacy of Pakistan and whose writers, as Saadia Toor (*The State of Islam: Culture and Cold War Politics in Pakistan* [New York: Pluto Press, 2011]) notes, were systematically marginalized after the creation of the nation by the establishment. These writers wrote in magazines such as *Savera, Naqush, Sang-i Meel,* and *Adab-i Latif,* which are not examined in this book but require further engagement.

4. For more see Faisal Devji, "India in the Muslim Imagination: Cartography and Landscape in 19th Century Urdu Literature," *South Asia Multidisciplinary Academic Journal* 10 (2014): 1–17.

5. Ayesha Jalal, *Self and Sovereignty: Individual and Community in South Asian Islam since 1850* (New York: Routledge, 2002).

6. Toor, *State of Islam,* 14.

7. As cited in ibid., 9.

8. Government of Pakistan, *The Constituent Assembly of Pakistan Debates: Official Report of the Fifth Session of the Constituent Assembly of Pakistan* (Karachi: Government of Pakistan, 1949), 101–2.

9. Toor, *State of Islam.*

10. Lubna Sunawar and Tatiana Coutto, "U.S. Pakistan Relations during the Cold War," *Journal of International Relations, Peace Studies, and Development* 1, no. 1 (2015): 1–11; Robert McMahon, *The Cold War on the Periphery: The United States, India, and Pakistan* (New York: Columbia University Press, 1994).

11. Sunawar and Coutto, "U.S. Pakistan Relations during the Cold War," 4.

12. Robert Wirsing, "Precarious Partnership: Pakistan's Response to U.S. Security Policies," *Asian Affairs and American Review* 30, no. 2 (2003): 70.

13. Toor, *State of Islam*, 86.

14. Kaiser Bengali, *History of Educational Policy Making and Planning in Pakistan*, Working Paper Series 40 (Islamabad: Sustainable Development Policy Institute, 1999).

15. Ayaz Naseem, *Education and Gendered Citizenship in Pakistan* (New York: Palgrave Macmillan, 2010), 41.

16. As cited in Bengali, *History of Educational Policy*, 1–2.

17. As cited in Sumaira Noreen, "Dynamics of Secondary Curriculum Organisation in Pakistan: An Historical Perspective from 1947 to 1970," Ph.D. diss. (Department of History, University of London, 2014), 133.

18. As cited in Afridi Arbab, "A Comparative Study of the Disparity between Urban-Rural Education at Elementary Level in NWFP and Development of an Action Plan (2010–2015)," doctoral thesis (Allama Iqbal Open University, Islamabad, 2007), 20–22.

19. As cited in Noreen, "Dynamics of Secondary Curriculum," 137.

20. As cited in Bengali, *History of Educational Policy*, 3.

21. Draft of the first five-year plan, 1955–60, 834, cited in ibid., 174.

22. Government of Pakistan, *Commission on National Education* (Karachi: Government of Pakistan, 1959), 115.

23. Ibid., 92.

24. As cited in Rubina Saigol, *Becoming a Modern Nation: Educational Discourse in the Early Years of Ayub Khan (1958–64),* (Islamabad: Council of Social Sciences, 2003), 2.

25. Habibullah Siddiqui, *Education in Sind Past and Present* (Sindh, Pakistan: University of Sindh Press, 1987), 316.

26. Noreen, "Dynamics of Secondary Curriculum."

27. Israt Husain, "The Role of Politics in Pakistan's Economy," *Journal of International Affairs* 63, no. 1 (2009): 1–18.

28. Naseem, *Education and Gendered Citizenship*, 41.

29. Shahid Siddiqui, *Education Policies in Pakistan: Politics, Projections, and Practices* (Karachi: Oxford University Press, 2016), 8.

30. Markus Daechsel, *Islamabad and the Politics of International Development in Pakistan* (Cambridge, MA: Cambridge University Press, 2015); George Grant, "The Ford Foundation Program in Pakistan," *Annals of the American Academy of Political and Social Science* 323 (1959): 150–59.

31. As cited in Bengali, *History of Educational Policy*, 5.

32. *Ismat* 107, no. 6 (1961).

33. As cited in Saigol, *Becoming a Modern Nation*, 31.

34. As cited in ibid., 32.

35. Franc Shor and Jean Shor, "At World's End in Hunza: This Strange Shangri-La near the Himalayas Has Few Laws or Taxes and No Army; Bridegrooms Take Mother on the Honeymoon," *National Geographic*, October 1953, 485.

36. For more see Catherine Lutz and Jane Collins, "The Photograph as an Intersection of Gazes: The Example of *National Geographic*," *Visual Anthropology Review* 7, no. 1 1993.

37. Such imaginations about this part of Pakistan have not changed much. A *National Geographic* story from October 24, 2016, about the same region is entitled, "This Remote Pakistani Village Is Nothing Like You'd Expect." These formulations—referring to the natural beauty as displayed by the photographs—enroll the reader into seeing beauty as an anomaly in this part of the world; it is unexpected.

38. Moon Charania, *Will the Real Pakistani Woman Please Stand Up? Empire, Visual Culture, and the Brown Female Body* (New York: McFarland, 2015), 29.

39. *Ismat* 81, no. 1 (1948).

40. *Tehzib* 52, no. 2 (1949): 34.

41. Satish Deshpande, *Contemporary India: A Sociological View* (New York: Viking Press, 2003).

42. *Ismat* 82, no. 5 (1949).

43. *Ismat* 92, no. 6 (1954).

44. Asaf Hussain, *The Educated Pakistani Girl* (Karachi: Ima Printers, 1963), 6.

45. Ibid., 23. "Teddy girls" refers to a British subculture signified by women wearing men's clothing, especially suits. According to Hussain, the term was used in Pakistan to mark ultramodern girls.

46. Ibid., 21.

47. Ibid., 22.

48. Ibid., 25–31.

49. Ibid., 33.

50. Ibid., 13.

51. Ibid., 13–14.

52. Ibid., 14.

53. Ibid.

54. Ibid., 15.

55. Ibid.

56. Ibid.

57. Ibid., 16.

58. Margaret Bourke-White, "Pakistan Struggles for Survival," *Life Magazine*, January 1948, 20.

59. Ibid., 26.

60. Second meeting of the ABEP, 1949, 7, as cited in Noreen, "Dynamics of Secondary Curriculum," 144.

61. Ibid.

62. As cited in ibid., 141.

63. Ibid.

64. *Ismat* 97, no. 2 (1956).

65. Geraldine Forbes, "Education for Women," in *Women and Social Reform in Modern India: A Reader,* ed. Sumit Sarkar and Tanika Sarkar (Bloomington: Indiana University Press, 2008), 61.

66. *Ismat* 97, no. 4 (1956).

67. *Ismat* 99, no. 6 (1957): 327.

68. As cited in Rafiqul Islam, "The Bengali Language Movement and the Emergence of Bangladesh," in *Language and Civilization in South Asia,* ed. Clarence Maloney (Leiden: Brill), 144.

69. Toor, *State of Islam,* 24.

70. *Ismat* 97, no. 2 (1956): 102–3.

71. *Tehzib* 51, nos. 18–19 (1948).

72. Noreen, "Dynamics of Secondary Curriculum."

73. *Tehzib* 51, no. 26 (1948).

74. *Ismat* 98, no. 1 (1957): 32.

75. See "Women and the Future of Pakistan," in *Tehzib* 51, no. 48 (1948); "Women's Education and Nurturance," in *Ismat* 92, no. 2 (1954); "Ignorant Bibiyan and Progressive Women," in *Ismat* 95, no. 1 (1955); "Quran Hakim and the Muslim Woman," in *Ismat* 95, no. 1 (1955); "Today's Girl by Sughra Abdul Khan," in *Ismat* 99, no. 5 (1958); "Teaching in English Medium by *Iffat ilahi ulumi saheba,*" in *Ismat* 101, no. 3 (1958).

76. *Ismat* 81, no. 1 (1948).

77. Ibid., 15.

78. Sajid Ali, "Education Policy Borrowing in Pakistan: Public-Private Partnerships," in *Education in the Broader Middle East: Borrowing a Baroque Arsenal,* ed. G. Donn and Y. A. Manthri (Oxford: Symposium Books, 2012), 23–40.

79. Ibid.

80. Government of Pakistan, *National Policy* (Karachi: Ministry of Education, Government of Pakistan, 2009), 10.

81. Unicef.org, data from 2008–12; www.unicef.org/infobycountry/pakistan_pakistan_statistics.html (accessed February 26, 2018).

82. Tahir Andrabi et al., "The Madrasa Myth," *Foreign Policy* (June 2009), http://foreignpolicy.com/2009/06/01/the-m-myth (accessed February 26, 2018).

83. Tahir Andrabi, Jishnu Das, and Asim Khwaja, *Students Today, Teachers Tomorrow: Identifying Constraints on the Provision of Education* (Washington, DC: World Bank, 2011).

84. Laura Bier, *Revolutionary Womanhood: Feminisms, Modernity, and the State in Nasser's Egypt* (Stanford, CA: Stanford University Press, 2011).

85. John Esposito and Natana DeLong-Bas, *Women in Muslim Family Law* (Syracuse, NY: Syracuse University Press, 2001).

86. For more see Saadia Toor, "The State, Fundamentalism, and Civil Society," *Interventions* 9, no. 2 (2007): 255–75; Tariq Ali, *The Clash of Fundamentalisms: Crusades, Jihads, and Modernity* (London: Verso, 2002).

87. Rubina Saigol, *Feminism and the Women's Movement in Pakistan Actors, Debates, and Strategies* (Karachi: Friedrich-Ebert-Stiftung, 2016.), 14. For more see, Shahnaz Rouse, "Zina, Transnational Feminism, and the Moral Regulation of Pakistani Women," *Journal of Middle East Women's Studies* 6, no. 3 (2010): 195–97.

88. Amina Jamal, "Gender, Citizenship, and the Nation-State in Pakistan: Willful Daughters of Free Citizens," *Signs* 31, no. 2 (2006): 283–304, observes that during Zia's time women from middle and lower classes entered urban-based universities in sizable numbers.

CHAPTER 4. THE EMPOWERED GIRL

1. Ban Ki-moon, "Female Energy, Talent, Strength Represent Humankind's Most Valuable Untapped Resource, Secretary-General Says in Message for International Women's Day," United Nations, March 2, 2012, www.un.org/press/en/2012/sgsm14140.doc.htm (accessed January 24, 2018).

2. As cited in Grace Toohey, "First Lady, Pakistan's First Daughter Champion Educating Girls," McClarchy DC, October 22, 2015. www.mcclatchydc.com/news/politics-government/white-house/article41013888.html (accessed January 24, 2018).

3. Jim Yong Kim, "World Bank Group President Jim Yong Kim's Remarks at 'Let Girls Learn' Spring Meetings Event," World Bank, April 13, 2016, www.worldbank.org/en/news/speech/2016/04/13/world-bank-group-president-jim-yong-kims-remarks-at-let-girls-learn-spring-meetings-event (accessed January 24, 2018).

4. Umer Farooq, "Attack on Malala Was Staged, Claims PTI MNA," *Express Tribune,* May 20, 2017, https://tribune.com.pk/story/1414861/pti-mna-musarrat-ahmad-zeb-claims-attack-malala-staged (accessed January 24, 2018).

5. Associated Press, "Pakistani Private Schools Ban Malala's Book." *Dawn,* November 10, 2013, www.dawn.com/news/1055440 (accessed January 24, 2018).

6. Willy Oppenheim and Amy Stambach, "Global Norm Making as Lens and Mirror: Comparative Education and Gender Mainstreaming in Northern Pakistan," *Comparative Education Review* 58, no. 3 (2014): 377–400.

7. In September 2017, the Sindh High Court called on the federal government to file details of the monies acquired by Maryam Nawaz for Let Girls Learn. Civil rights campaigner Bisma Naureen filed a petition alleging misuse of aid money and embezzlement, since no new education projects had been set up for girls. For more see Tahir Siddiqui, "Federal Govt Asked to Provide Details of Let Girls Learn Project," *Dawn Newspaper,* September 27, 2017, www.dawn.com/news/1360248 (accessed February 26, 2018).

8. Reuters, "Madonna Sells Abstract Painting to Fund Girls' Education," April 3, 2013, www.reuters.com/article/entertainment-us-madonna/madonna-sells-abstract-painting-to-fund-girls-education-idUSBRE9320RO20130403 (accessed January 24, 2018).

9. Lyndsay Hayhurst, "Corporatising Sport, Gender, and Development: Postcolonial IR Feminisms, Transnational Private Governance and Global Corporate Social Engagement," *Third World Quarterly* 32, no. 3 (2011): 532.

10. See Ofra Koffman and Rosalind Gill, "'The Revolution Will Be Led by a 12-Year-Old Girl': Girl Power and Global Biopolitics," *Feminist Review* 105, no. 1 (2013): 82–102; Jessica Taft, "The Political Lives of Girls," *Sociology Compass* 8, no. 3 (2014): 259–67; Heather Switzer, "(Post)Feminist Development Fables: The Girl Effect and the Production of Sexual Subjects," *Feminist Theory* 14, no. 3 (2013): 345–60; Michelle Murphy, "The Girl: Mergers of Feminism and Finance in Neoliberal Times," *Scholar and Feminist Online* 11, nos. 1–2 (2012–13), http://sfonline.barnard.edu/gender-justice-and-neoliberal-transformations/the-girl-mergersof-feminism-and-finance-in-neoliberal-times (accessed January 24, 2018);

Jessica Ringrose and Valerie Walkerdine, "Regulating the Abject: The TV Make-Over as Site of Neoliberal Reinvention toward Bourgeois Femininity," *Feminist Media Studies* 8, no. 3 (2008): 227–46; Maria Hengeveld, *Girl Branded: Nike, the UN, and the Construction of the Entrepreneurial Adolescent Girl Subject* (Austin: Rapoport Center for Human Rights and Justice, 2016).

11. See Mary Cobbett, "Beyond 'Victims' and 'Heroines': Constructing 'Girlhood' in International Development," *Progress in Development Studies* 14, no. 4 (2014): 309–20; Nandita Dogra, "The Mixed Metaphor of 'Third World Woman': Gendered Representations by International Development NGOs," *Third World Quarterly* 32, no. 2 (2011): 333–48.

12. Anita Harris, *Future Girl: Young Women in the 21st Century* (New York: Routledge, 2004).

13. Ibid.

14. For more on this, see James Ferguson, "The Uses of Neoliberalism," *Antipode* 41, no. 1 (2009): 166–84.

15. Shenila Khoja-Moolji, "Pedagogical (Re)Encounters: Enacting a Decolonial Praxis in Teacher Development in the Global South," *Comparative Education Review* 61, no. S1 (2017): 146–70.

16. Thomas Lemke, "Foucault, Governmentality, and Critique," *Rethinking Marxism* 14, no. 3 (2002): 49–64.

17. For more, see David Harvey, "Neoliberalism as Creative Destruction," *Annals of the American Academy of Political and Social Science* 610 (2007): 22–44; Peter Penz, Jay Drydyk, and Pablo Bose, *Displacement by Development: Ethics, Rights, and Responsibilities* (Cambridge: Cambridge University Press, 2011).

18. Amartya Sen, "Development as Capability Expansion," *Journal of Development Planning* 19, no. 1 (1989): 41–58; Martha Nussbaum, *Women and Human Development: The Capabilities Approach* (Cambridge: Cambridge University Press, 2001).

19. See Bina Agarwal, Jane Humphries, and Ingrid Robeyns, *Amartya Sen's Work and Ideas: A Gender Perspective* (London: Routledge, 2005), for more about the similarities and differences in Sen and Nussbaum's approaches.

20. See Elizabeth Anderson, "Justifying the Capabilities Approach to Justice," in *Measuring Justice: Primary Goods and Capabilities,* ed. H. Brighouse and I. Robeyns (Cambridge: Cambridge University Press, 2010), 81–100; and Janet Raynor, "Schooling Girls: An Inter-Generational Study of Women's Burdens in Rural Bangladesh," in *Gender Education and Equality in a Global Context,* ed. Shailaja Fennell and Madeleine Arnot (London: Routledge, 2008), 117–30.

21. Elaine Unterhalter, "The Capability Approach and Gendered Education: An Examination of South African Complexities," *Theory and Research in Education* 1, no. 1 (2003): 7–22; Elaine Unterhalter, "Inequality, Capabilities, and Poverty in Four African Countries: Girls' Voice, Schooling, and Strategies for Institutional Change," *Cambridge Journal of Education* 42, no. 3 (2012): 307–25.

22. See Abu-Lughod, *Do Muslim Women Need Saving?* (Cambridge, MA: Harvard University Press, 2013); and Talal Asad, *Formations of the Secular: Christianity, Islam, Modernity* (Stanford, CA: Stanford University Press, 2003).

23. Shenila Khoja-Moolji, "Producing Neoliberal Citizens: Critical Reflections on Human Rights Education in Pakistan," *Gender and Education* 26, no. 2 (2015): 103–18.

24. Jason Hickel, "The 'Girl Effect': Liberalism, Empowerment and the Contradictions of Development," *Third World Quarterly* 35, no. 8 (2014): 1355–73.

25. Katharyne Mitchell and Matthew Sparke, "The New Washington Consensus: Millennial Philanthropy and the Making of Global Market Subjects," *Antipode* 43, no. 3 (2015): 724–49.

26. Ibid., 725.

27. See SPRING website, www.springaccelerator.org.

28. All quotes from SPRING website: www.springaccelerator.org and USAID website: ww.usaid.gov/what-we-do/gender-equality-and-womens-empowerment/spring-initiative (accessed: September 5, 2015).

29. Mitchell and Sparke, "New Washington Consensus," 726.

30. Shaun French, Andrew Leyshon, and Thomas Wainwright, "Financializing Space, Spacing Financialization," *Progress in Human Geography* 35, no. 6 (2011): 813.

31. Karen Mundy and Antoni Verger, "The World Bank and the Global Governance of Education in a Changing World Order," *International Journal of Educational Development* 40 (2015): 13.

32. Ibid., 9.

33. Willy Oppenheim, "Imagining 'Demand' for Girls' Schooling in Rural Pakistan," Ph:D. diss. (Department of Education, Oxford University, 2016).

34. Arlie Hochschild and Anne Machung, *The Second Shift* (New York: Penguin Books, 2003).

35. Nerine Guin'ee, "Empowering Women through Education: Experiences from Dalit Women in Nepal," *International Journal of Educational Development* 39 (2014): 183–90; and Craig Jeffery, Patricia Jeffery, and Roger Jeffery, *Degrees without Freedom? Education, Masculinities, and Unemployment in North India* (Stanford, CA: Stanford University Press, 2008).

36. Ayesha Khurshid, "From Gender Parity to Gender (In)Equity: Women's Education among Rural Communities in Pakistan," *International Journal of Educational Development* 51 (2016): 43–50.

37. Ibid., 44.

38. Oppenheim, "Imagining 'Demand' for Girls' Schooling," 90.

39. Government of Pakistan, *National Education Policy* (Karachi: Ministry of Education, Government of Pakistan, 2009), 19.

40. Iffat Farah and Sadaf Rizvi, "Public-Private Partnerships: Implications for Primary Schooling in Pakistan," *Social Policy and Administration* 41, no. 4 (2007): 339–54; Sajid Ali, "Education Policy Borrowing in Pakistan: Public-Private Partnerships," in *Education in the Broader Middle East: Borrowing a Baroque Arsenal,* ed. G. Donn and Y. A. Manthri (Oxford: Symposium Books, 2012), 23–40.

41. Government of Pakistan, *National Education Policy,* 66–67.

42. Oppenheim, "Imagining 'Demand' for Girls' Schooling," 25.

43. See Khoja-Moolji, "Producing Neoliberal Citizens"; and Shenila Khoja-Moolji, "Doing the 'Work of Hearing': Girls' Voices in Transnational Educational Development Campaigns," *Compare: A Journal of Comparative and International Education* (2015): 1–19.

44. The organization I partnered with has sister agencies that run after-school religious education centers.

45. Hartley Dean, "Underclassed or Undermined? Young People and Social Citizenship," in *Youth, the "Underclass," and Social Exclusion,* ed. Robert MacDonald (London: Routledge, 1997), 59.

46. This is a tradition followed by some families in Pakistan, where one child takes time off from school to spend a few years at a madrasa to memorize the Quran and become a *hafiz.* After completing the exercise, the child returns to school. While not prevalent in the particular community where I was working, this tradition is well known and my participants were likely familiar with other children who had decided to pursue this path.

47. Paul Bylsma, "The Teleological Effect of Neoliberalism on American Higher Education," *College Student Affairs Leadership* 2, no. 2 (2015): 2.

48. Ibid.

49. Fida Adely, *Gendered Paradoxes: Educating Jordanian Women in Nation, Faith, and Progress* (Chicago: University of Chicago Press, 2012).

50. Ibid., 134.

51. Willy Oppenheim, "Why Should Girls Stay in School? Qualitative Aspects of Demand for Girls' Schooling in Rural Pakistan," *St. Antony's International Review* 8, no. 2 (2013): 107.

52. Ibid., 111.

53. Krishna Kumar, *Political Agenda of Education: A Study of Colonialist and Nationalist Ideas* (New Delhi: Sage Publications, 2005), 200–201.

54. In an earlier study conducted in the same community (Khoja-Moolji, "Producing Neoliberal Citizens"), I learned about the difficulties that young men with bachelor's and master's degrees were having in obtaining employment.

55. Khoja-Moolji, "Doing the 'Work of Hearing.'"

56. Government of Pakistan, "Labor Force Participation Rates, 2013–2014," Pakistan Bureau of Statistics, www.pbs.gov.pk/content/labour-force-survey-2013-14-annual-report (accessed February 27, 2018)

57. Government of Pakistan, "Pakistan Economic Survey, 2015–2016," Ministry of Finance, www.finance.gov.pk/survey/chapters_16/Annexure_III_Poverty.pdf, p. 285, table 1. (accessed February 27, 2018)

58. Haroon Jamal, "Poverty and Vulnerability Estimates: Pakistan, 2016," Social Policy and Development Centre, 2017, http://spdc.org.pk/Data/Publication/PDF/RR-99.pdf (accessed January 24, 2018), p. 10, table 5.

59. Anita Weiss, "Within the Walls: Home-Based Work in Lahore," in *Pakistani Women: Multiple Locations and Competing Narratives,* ed. Sadaf Ahmad (Oxford: Oxford University Press, 2010), 12–24.

60. Ibid., 20.

61. Nicholas Kristof, "Two Cheers for Sweatshops," *New York Times,* September 24, 2000.

62. Cynthia Enloe, *The Curious Feminist: Searching for Women in a New Age of Empire* (Berkeley: University of California Press, 2004), 48.

63. International Labour Organization Research Department, "World of Work Report, 2014: Developing with Jobs," International Labor Organization, May 27, 2014, www.ilo.org/global/research/global-reports/world-of-work/2014/lang--en/index.htm (accessed February 27, 2018).

64. Government of Pakistan, *National Education Policy,* 9.

65. Asma Ghani, "IIUI Students Told to Wear Appropriate Clothing," *Express Tribune,* October 18, 2017, https://tribune.com.pk/story/1533926/iiui-students-told-wear-appropriate-clothing (accessed January 24, 2018).

66. News Desk, "Faculty Member at Top Educational Institute in Karachi Gets Schooled on 'Improper Attire,'" *Express Tribune.* October 5, 2017, https://tribune.com.pk/story/1523647/faculty-member-top-educational-institute-karachi-gets-schooled-improper-attire (accessed January 24, 2018).

67. Jamaat-e-Islami is a political party established in 1941 in Lahore by Abul ala Mawdudi. After 1947 the party moved to West Pakistan and its affiliates in India decided to call themselves Jamaat-e-Islami Hind.

68. *Express Tribune,* "Academic Modification: JI Wants Secular Material Removed from Textbooks," September 5, 2014, http://tribune.com.pk/story/757919/academic-modification-ji-wants-secular-material-removed-from-textbooks (accessed January 24, 2018).

69. Asad Zia, "Revised Curriculum: JI Pushes Through Its Agenda on Textbooks in K-P," *Express Tribune,* October 17, 2014, http://tribune.com.pk/story/781717/revised-curriculum-ji-pushes-through-its-agenda-on-textbooks-in-k-p (accessed January 24, 2018).

70. Nosheen Ali, "Books vs. Bombs? Humanitarian Development and the Narrative of Terror in Northern Pakistan," *Third World Quarterly* 31, no. 4 (2010): 541–59.

71. Pew Survey. "Pakistani Public Opinion," Pewglobal.org, August 13, 2009, www.pewglobal.org/2009/08/13/pakistani-public-opinion (accessed January 24, 2018).

72. Shenila Khoja-Moolji, "Reading Malala: (De)(Re)Territorialization of Muslim Collectivities," *Journal of Comparative Studies of South Asia, Africa, and the Middle East* 35, no. 3 (2015): 539–56.

73. Chelsea Clinton, "Malala Yousafzai," *Time,* April 18, 2013.

74. This analysis and more details appear in Khoja-Moolji, "Reading Malala."

75. Malala Yousafzai and Christina Lamb, *I Am Malala: The Girl Who Stood Up for Education and Was Shot by the Taliban* (New York: Little, Brown, 2013), 14.

76. Ibid., 23.

77. Ibid., 38, 41.

78. Ibid., 73.

79. Ibid., 63.

80. Ibid., 106.

81. Ibid., 14.

82. Ibid., 22.

83. Ibid., 44.

84. Ibid., 13.

85. Ibid., 43.

86. Ibid., 43.

87. Ibid., 44.

88. Ibid., 245.

89. Ibid., 266.

90. Ibid., 138.

91. Ibid., 149.

92. Ibid., 139.

CHAPTER 5. AKBARI AND ASGHARI REAPPEAR

1. Michael O'Malley, Jake Sandlin, and Jennifer Burdick, "Public Pedagogy," in *Encyclopedia of Curriculum Studies,* ed. Craig Kridel (Thousand Oaks, CA: Sage Publications, 2010), 697–701.

2. Saher Abbas, "Seeing Each Other in Black and White," *Express Tribune,* August 8, 2013, http://tribune.com.pk/story/587863/seeing-each-other-in-black-and-white (accessed January 24, 2018).

3. It first appeared in an Urdu digest, *Shua,* and was later produced as a drama for HUM TV. In 2015, the same drama aired in India under the new title of *Aaja sajna miliye juliye.* In 2016, it was aired on HUM Europe. The HUM TV production is directed by Haissam Hussain and produced by Samina Humayun Saeed.

4. This show, too, was later in 2014 aired in India under the new title *Aaina dulhan ka* (The Bride's Mirror).

5. English-medium in the context of Pakistan means schools that use English as the primary language of instruction as opposed to Urdu or provincial languages. English-medium schools often tend to be private and more expensive, when compared to their public and/or Urdu-medium counterparts.

6. *Mirat-ul-uroos* (Geo TV, 2012), episode 1. The show is directed by Anjum Shehzad, written by Umera Ahmed, and produced by 7th Sky Entertainment.

7. Ibid., episode 13.

8. Ibid., episode 16.

9. Ibid., episode 18.

10. Purnima Mankekar, *Screening Culture, Viewing Politics: An Ethnography of Television, Womanhood, and Nation in Postcolonial India* (Durham, NC: Duke University Press, 1999), 114.

11. As cited in Sadaf Siddique and Sadaf Haider, "What's It Like Being a Sought-After TV Writer in Pakistan? Faiza Iftikhar Tells All," Images, April 29, 2016, http://images.dawn.com/news/1175082 (accessed January 24, 2018).

12. Ibid.

13. *Mirat-ul-uroos,* episode 6.

14. Deniz Kandiyoti, "Bargaining with Patriarchy," *Gender and Society* 2, no. 3 (1988): 274.

15. Mahmood Mamdani, *Good Muslim, Bad Muslim: America, the Cold War, and the Roots of Terror* (New York: Pantheon Books, 2004).

CHAPTER 6. TRACING STORYLINES

1. Michel Foucault, *Language, Counter-Memory, Practice,* trans. Donald Bouchard and Sherry Simon (Ithaca, NY: Cornell University Press, 1977), 140.

2. Gilles Deleuze, *Difference and Repetition,* trans. Paul Patton (New York: Columbia University Press, 1994), 1.

3. Sara Struckman, "The Veiled Women and Masked Men of Chechnya: Documentaries, Violent Conflict, and Gender," *Journal of Communication Inquiry* 30 (2006): 337–53.

4. Edward McAllister, "Female Attacker Stands Out in California Mass Shooting," Reuters, December 3, 2015, www.reuters.com/article/us-california-shooting-women-idUSKBN0TM2Y420151203 (accessed January 24, 2018).

5. Yasmeen Abutaleb and Rory Carroll, "From 'Happy' Bride to Shooter: Mosque Members Confounded by California Massacre," *Reuters*, December 5, 2015, www.reuters.com/article/california-shooting-mosque-idUSKBN0TO03320151205 (accessed January 24, 2018)

6. Salman Masood and Declan Walsh, "Tashfeen Malik, San Bernardino Suspect, Attended Conservative Religious School in Pakistan," *New York Times*, December 7, 2015.

7. Ibid.

8. Shakira Hussein, *From Victims to Suspects: Muslim Women since 9/11* (Sydney: University of New South Wales Press, 2016).

9. Oliver Franklin-Wallis, "Extremely Together Is playing ISIS at Its Own Game to Tackle Extremism," *Wired*, October 2, 2016.

10. Kofi Anan Foundation, "Empowering Young People to Prevent Violent Extremism," news release, December 3, 2015, www.kofiannanfoundation.org/news-releases/empowering-young-people-to-prevent-violent-extremism (accessed January 24, 2018).

11. Bina Shah, "Naureen Laghari, Pakistan's Very Own IS Bride," Express Tribune Blogs, April 18, 2017, https://blogs.tribune.com.pk/story/48864/naureen-laghari-pakistans-very-own-is-bride (accessed January 24, 2018).

12. DG ISPR, "Media Briefing about Noreen Laghari Case," Power TV Talk Shows, April 17, 2017, www.youtube.com/watch?v=OSkWF2-T32w (accessed March 2, 2018).

13. DG ISPR, "Full Press Conference," SAMAA TV, May 10, 2017, www.youtube.com/watch?v=WHiyEm9njxE (accessed March 2, 2018).

14. PTI, "Lahore Raid: Arrested Woman Terror Suspect Linked to ISIS," *The Hindu*, April 16, 2017, www.thehindu.com/news/international/lahore-raid-arrested-woman-terror-suspect-linked-to-isis/article18071417.ece (accessed January 24, 2018).

15. Leigh Gilmore and Elizabeth Marshall, "Girl in Crisis: Rescue and Transnational Feminist Autobiographical Resistance," *Feminist Studies* 36, no. 3 (2010): 668.

16. Ibid.

17. While I have focused on Muslim women who wrote primarily in Urdu, Elora Shehabuddin ("Gender and the Figure of the 'Moderate Muslim,'" in *The Question of Gender: Joan W. Scott's Critical Feminism*, ed. Judith Butler and Elizabeth Weed [Bloomington: Indiana University Press, 2011], 102–42), highlights the life and work of Rokeya Hossein, who wrote in Bengali and English, to show how she, too, disrupts stereotypical certainties about Muslim women.

18. *Tehzib* 10 (January 5, 1907): 13, as cited in Gail Minault, "Women's Magazines in Urdu as Sources for Muslim Social History," *Indian Journal for Gender Studies* 5, no. 2 (1998): 201–14.

19. *Khatun* 1, no. 2 (1907): 41–44.

20. As cited in Minault, "Women's Magazines," 205–6.

21. As cited in Akbar Ahmed, *Jinnah, Pakistan, and Islamic Identity: The Search for Saladin* (London: Routledge, 1997), 60.

22. Sarah Ansari, "Polygamy, Purdah, and Political Representation: Engendering Citizenship in 1950s Pakistan," *Modern Asian Studies* 43, no. 6 (2009): 1421–61.

23. Xari Jalil, "Fatima Sughra No More," *Dawn News*, September 26, 2017, www.dawn.com/news/1360098 (accessed March 2, 2018).

24. Rubina Saigol, *Feminism and the Women's Movement in Pakistan Actors, Debates, and Strategies* (Islamabad: Friedrich-Ebert-Stiftung, 2016).

BIBLIOGRAPHY

Abbas, Saher. "Seeing Each Other in Black and White." *Express Tribune,* August 8, 2013, http://tribune.com.pk/story/587863/seeing-each-other-in-black-and-white (accessed January 24, 2018).

Abu-Lughod, Lila. *Do Muslim Women Need Saving?* Cambridge, MA: Harvard University Press, 2013.

———, ed. *Remaking Women: Feminism and Modernity in the Middle East.* Princeton, NJ: Princeton University Press, 1998.

Abubakar, Aminu. "Boko Haram Kidnaps 30 in Northeast Nigeria." CNN, October 28, 2014, www.cnn.com/2014/10/27/world/africa/boko-haram-abductions (accessed January 24, 2018).

Abutaleb, Yasmeen, and Rory Carroll. "From 'Happy' Bride to Shooter: Mosque Members Confounded by California Massacre." Reuters, December 5, 2015, www.reuters.com/article/california-shooting-mosque-idUSKBN0TO03320151205 (accessed January 24, 2018).

Adatia, A. K., and N. Q. King. "Some East African Firmans of H. H. Aga Khan III." *Journal of Religion in Africa* 2, no. 2 (1969): 179–91.

Adely, Fida. *Gendered Paradoxes: Educating Jordanian Women in Nation, Faith, and Progress.* Chicago: University of Chicago Press, 2012.

Aftab, Tahera. *Inscribing South Asian Muslim Women: An Annotated Bibliography and Research Guide.* Leiden, Netherlands: Brill, 2008.

———. "Women's Education, Zenana Instruction, and the American Missions in Northern India, Later 19th C." *Pakistan Journal of American Studies* 5, no 1 (1987): 104–30.

Agarwal, Bina, Jane Humphries, and Ingrid Robeyns. *Amartya Sen's Work and Ideas: A Gender Perspective.* London: Routledge, 2005.

Ahmad, Imtiaz. "The Ashraf-Ajlaf Dichotomy in Muslim Social Structure in India." *The Indian Economic and Social History* 3, no. 3 (1966): 268–78.

Ahmad, Sadaf. "The Multiple Locations and Competing Narratives of Pakistani Women." In *Pakistani Women: Multiple Locations and Competing Narratives,* ed. Sadaf Ahmad, 1–11. Karachi: Oxford University Press, 2010.

Ahmed, Akbar. *Jinnah, Pakistan, and Islamic Identity: The Search for Saladin.* London: Routledge, 1997.

Ahmed, Leila. *Women and Gender in Islam: Historical Roots of a Modern Debate.* New Haven, CT: Yale University Press, 1992.

Ali, Mumtaz. *Huqooq-e-niswaan.* Lahore: Punjab Publishers, 1898.

Ali, Nosheen. "Books vs. Bombs? Humanitarian Development and the Narrative of Terror in Northern Pakistan." *Third World Quarterly* 31, no. 4 (2010): 541–59.

Ali, Sajid. "Education Policy Borrowing in Pakistan: Public-Private Partnerships." In *Education in the Broader Middle East: Borrowing a Baroque Arsenal,* ed. G. Donn and Y. A. Manthri, 23–40. Oxford: Symposium Books, 2012.

Ali, Tariq. *The Clash of Fundamentalisms: Crusades, Jihads, and Modernity.* London: Verso, 2002.

Allender, Tim. *Learning Femininity in Colonial India, 1820–1932.* Manchester: Manchester University Press, 2016.

Anagol, Padma. "Agency, Periodisation, and Change in the Gender and Women's History of Colonial India." *Gender and History* 20, no. 3 (2008): 603–27.

———. "Feminist Inheritances and Foremothers: The Beginnings of Feminism in Modern India." *Women's History Review* 19, no. 4 (2010): 523–46.

Anderson, Elizabeth. "Justifying the Capabilities Approach to Justice." In *Measuring Justice: Primary Goods and Capabilities,* ed. H. Brighouse and I. Robeyns, 81–100. Cambridge: Cambridge University Press, 2010.

Andrabi, Tahir, et al. "The Madrasa Myth." *Foreign Policy* (June 2009), http://foreignpolicy.com/2009/06/01/the-madrasa-myth/ (accessed February 26, 2018).

Andrabi, Tahir, Jishnu Das, Asim Khwaja. *Students Today, Teachers Tomorrow: Identifying Constraints on the Provision of Education.* Washington, DC: World Bank, 2011.

Ansari, Sarah. "Polygamy, Purdah, and Political Representation: Engendering Citizenship in 1950s Pakistan." *Modern Asian Studies* 43, no. 6 (2009): 1421–61.

Arbab, Afridi. "A Comparative Study of the Disparity between Urban-Rural Education at Elementary Level in NWFP and Development of an Action Plan (2010–2015)." Doctoral thesis, Allama Iqbal Open University, Islamabad, 2007.

Asad, Talal. *Formations of the Secular: Christianity, Islam, Modernity.* Stanford, CA: Stanford University Press, 2003.

Asghar Ali, Azra. *The Emergence of Feminism among Indian Muslim Women, 1920–1947.* Karachi: Oxford University Press, 2000.

Ashcroft, Bill, Gareth Griffiths, and Helen Tiffin, eds. *The Post-Colonial Studies Reader.* New York: Routledge, 1995.

Associated Press. "Pakistani Private Schools Ban Malala's Book." *Dawn,* November 10, 2013, www.dawn.com/news/1055440 (accessed January 24, 2018).

Aziz, K. K, ed. *Aga Khan III: Selected Speeches and Writings of Sir Sultan Muhammad Shah.* 2 vols. London: Kegan Paul International, 1997.

Baron, Beth. *The Women's Awakening in Egypt: Culture, Society, and the Press.* New Haven, CT: Yale University Press, 1994.

Batsha, Nishant. "The Uneducated: Education and the Mediation of Muslim Identity in the British Raj, 1858–1882." Unpublished undergraduate thesis, Department of History, Columbia University, 2010.

Begum, Muhammadi. *Hayat-e-Ashraf.* Lahore: Imambara Sayyida Mubarak Begum, 1899.

———. *Sharif beti.* Lahore: Dar-ul-isha, 1908.

———. *Sughar beti.* Lahore: Dar-ul-isha, 1905.

Bengali, Kaiser. *History of Educational Policy Making and Planning in Pakistan.* Working Paper Series 40. Islamabad: Sustainable Development Policy Institute, 1999.

Bier, Laura. *Revolutionary Womanhood: Feminisms, Modernity, and the State in Nasser's Egypt.* Stanford, CA: Stanford University Press, 2011.

Booth, Marilyn. *May Her Likes Be Multiplied: Biography and Gender Politics in Egypt.* Berkeley: University of California Press, 2001.

Bourdieu, Pierre. *Distinction: A Social Critique of the Judgment of Taste.* Trans. Richard Nice. Cambridge, MA: Harvard University Press, 1984.

Bourke-White, Margaret. "Pakistan Struggles for Survival." *Life Magazine,* January 1948.

Brown, Gordon. "Girl Power." Project Syndicate, June 15, 2014, www.project-syndicate.org/commentary/gordon-brown-highlights-girls--emerging-leadership-in-the-struggle-to-secure-their-rights?barrier=accessreg. (accessed February 20, 2018).

———. "Malala: Everyone's Daughter in the Flight for Girls' Education." *New Perspectives Quarterly* 30, no. 1 (2013): 59–60.

Burton, Antoinette. *Burdens of History: British Feminists, Indian Women, and Imperial Culture, 1865–1915.* Chapel Hill: University of North Carolina, 1994.

Bush, Laura. "A Nation Challenged: The First Lady; Mrs. Bush Cites Women's Plight under Taliban." *New York Times,* November 18, 2001.

Butler, Judith. *Bodies That Matter: On the Discursive Limits of "Sex."* New York: Routledge, 1993.

———. *Gender Trouble.* New York: Routledge, 1990.

Bylsma, Paul. "The Teleological Effect of Neoliberalism on American Higher Education." *College Student Affairs Leadership* 2, no. 2 (2015): 1–14.

Canal, Emily. "How Shiza Shahid and the Malala Fund Are Championing for Girls' Rights." *Forbes,* September 18, 2014.

Chacko, Mary Ann. "Schooling as Counter-Socialization: Krishna Kumar's Contributions to Curriculum." In *Curriculum Studies in India,* ed. William Pinar, 65–81. New York: Palgrave Macmillan, 2015.

Chandra Mohanty, "Under Western Eyes: Feminist Scholarship and Colonial Discourses." *Feminist Review* 30 (1988): 61–88.

Charania, Moon. *Will the Real Pakistani Woman Please Stand Up? Empire, Visual Culture, and the Brown Female Body.* New York: McFarland, 2015.

Chatterjee, Partha. "Beyond the Nation? Or Within?" *Social Text* 16, no. 3 (1998): 57–69.

———. *The Black Hole of Empire: History of a Global Practice of Power.* Princeton, NJ: Princeton University Press, 2012.

———. "Empire as a Practice of Power: Introduction." *Humanity Journal,* June 10, 2014, http://humanityjournal.org/blog/empire-as-a-practice-of-power-introduction (accessed January 24, 2018).

Cherryholmes, Cleo H. "Reading Research." *Journal of Curriculum Studies* 25, no. 1 (1993): 1–31.

Clinton, Chelsea. "Malala Yousafzai." *Time,* April 18, 2013.

Cobbett, Mary. "Beyond 'Victims' and 'Heroines': Constructing 'Girlhood' in International Development." *Progress in Development Studies* 14, no. 4 (2014): 309–20.

Connell, R. W. *Gender and Power.* Stanford, CA: Stanford University Press, 1987.

Daechsel, Markus. *Islamabad and the Politics of International Development in Pakistan.* Cambridge, MA: Cambridge University Press, 2015.

Dean, Hartley. "Underclassed or Undermined? Young People and Social Citizenship." In *Youth, the "Underclass," and Social Exclusion,* ed. Robert MacDonald, 55–69. London: Routledge, 1997.

Deeb, Lara. *An Enchanted Modern: Gender and Public Piety in Shi'i Lebanon.* Princeton, NJ: Princeton University Press, 2006.

Deleuze, Gilles. *Difference and Repetition.* Trans. Paul Patton. New York: Columbia University Press, 1994.

Deleuze, Gilles, and Felix Guattari. *A Thousand Plateaus: Capitalism and Schizophrenia.* Trans. Brian Massumi. Minneapolis: University of Minnesota Press, 1987.

Deshpande, Satish. *Contemporary India: A Sociological View.* New York: Viking Press, 2003.

Devji, Faisal. "Gender and the Politics of Space: The Movement for Women's Reform in Muslim India, 1857–1900." *South Asia: Journal of South Asian Studies* 14, no. 1 (1991): 141–53.

———. "India in the Muslim Imagination: Cartography and Landscape in 19th Century Urdu Literature." *South Asia Multidisciplinary Academic Journal* 10 (2014): 1–17.

DG ISPR. "Full Press Conference." SAMAA TV, May 10, 2017, www.youtube.com/watch?v=WHiyEm9njxE (accessed March 2, 2018).

———. "Media Briefing about Noreen Laghari Case." Power TV Talk Shows, April 17, 2017, www.youtube.com/watch?v=OSkWF2-T32w (accessed March 2, 2018).

Dockterman, Eliana. "After Boko Haram: Hillary Clinton Promises Education for 14 Million Girls." *Time,* September 24, 2014.

Dogra, Nandita. "The Mixed Metaphor of 'Third World Woman': Gendered Representations by International Development NGOs." *Third World Quarterly* 32, no. 2 (2011): 333–48.

Eichhorn, Kate. *The Archival Turn in Feminism.* Philadelphia: Temple University Press, 2014.

Enloe, Cynthia. *The Curious Feminist: Searching for Women in a New Age of Empire.* Berkeley: University of California Press, 2004.

Esposito, John, and Natana DeLong-Bas. *Women in Muslim Family Law.* Syracuse, NY: Syracuse University Press, 2001.

The Express Tribune. "Academic Modification: JI Wants Secular Material Removed from Textbooks." *Express Tribune,* September 5, 2014, http://tribune.com.pk/story/757919/academic-modification-ji-wants-secular-material-removed-from-textbooks (accessed January 24, 2018).

Farah, Iffat, and Sadaf Rizvi. "Public-Private Partnerships: Implications for Primary Schooling in Pakistan." *Social Policy and Administration* 41, no. 4 (2007): 339–54.

Farooq, Umer. "Attack on Malala Was Staged, Claims PTI MNA." *Express Tribune,* May 20, 2017, https://tribune.com.pk/story/1414861/pti-mna-musarrat-ahmad-zeb-claims-attack-malala-staged (accessed January 24, 2018).

Ferguson, James. "The Uses of Neoliberalism." *Antipode* 41, no. 1 (2009): 166–84.

Forbes, Geraldine. "Education for Women." In *Women and Social Reform in Modern India: A Reader,* ed. Sumit Sarkar and Tanika Sarkar, 58–77. Bloomington: Indiana University Press, 2008.

Foucault, Michel. *Discipline and Punish: The Birth of the Prison.* Trans. Alan Sheridan. New York: Vintage Books, 1977.

———. "The Ethics of the Concern of the Self as a Practice of Freedom." In *Ethics: Subjectivity and Truth,* ed. Paul Rainbow, 281–301. New York: Penguin Books, 1984.

———. "Foucault." In *Dictionnaire des philosophes* (1984), https://foucault.info/doc/foucault/biography-html, 942–44.

———. "Governmentality." In *Michel Foucault: Power,* ed. J. D. Faubion, 201–22. New York: New Press, 2000.

———. *History of Sexuality, Vol. I: An Introduction.* Trans. Robert Hurley. New York: Vintage Books, 1978.

———. *Language, Counter-Memory, Practice.* Trans. Donald Bouchard and Sherry Simon. Ithaca, NY: Cornell University Press, 1977.

Franklin-Wallis, Oliver. "Extremely Together Is playing ISIS at Its Own Game to Tackle Extremism." *Wired,* October 2, 2016.

French, Shaun, Andrew Leyshon, and Thomas Wainwright. "Financializing Space, Spacing Financialization." *Progress in Human Geography* 35, no. 6 (2011): 798–819.

Ghani, Asma. "IIUI Students Told to Wear Appropriate Clothing." *Express Tribune,* October 18, 2017, https://tribune.com.pk/story/1533926/iiui-students-told-wear-appropriate-clothing (accessed January 24, 2018).

Ghosh, Suresh. "English in Taste, in Opinions, in Words and Intellect: Indoctrinating the Indian through Textbook, Curriculum, and Education." In *The Imperial Curriculum: Racial Images and Education in the British Colonial Experience,* ed. J. A. Mangan, 175–94. London: Routledge, 1993.

Gilmore, Leigh, and Elizabeth Marshall. "Girl in Crisis: Rescue and Transnational Feminist Autobiographical Resistance." *Feminist Studies* 36, no. 3 (2010): 667–90.

Gonick, Marnina. *Between Femininities: Ambivalence, Identity and the Education of Girls.* Albany: State University of New York Press, 2003.

Government of Pakistan. *Commission on National Education.* Karachi: Government of Pakistan, 1959.

———. *The Constituent Assembly of Pakistan Debates: Official Report of the Fifth Session of the Constituent Assembly of Pakistan.* Karachi: Government of Pakistan, 1949.

———. *Country Report of Pakistan Regarding: Accelerating Millennium Development Goals, 2013–15.* Karachi: Ministry of Education and Training, Government of Pakistan, 2013.

———. "Labor Force Participation Rates, 2013–2014." Pakistan Bureau of Statistics, www.pbs.gov.pk/sites/default/files//Labour%20Force/publications/lfs2013–14/t18-pak-fin.pdf (accessed February 27, 2018)

———. *National Education Policy.* Karachi: Ministry of Education, Government of Pakistan, 2009.

———. "Pakistan Economic Survey, 2015–2016." Ministry of Finance, www.finance.gov.pk/survey/chapters_16/Annexure_III_Poverty.pdf (accessed February 27, 2018)

Grant, George. "The Ford Foundation Program in Pakistan." *Annals of the American Academy of Political and Social Science* 323 (1959): 150–59.

Guin'ee, Nerine. "Empowering Women through Education: Experiences from Dalit Women in Nepal." *International Journal of Educational Development* 39 (2014): 183–90.

Gupta, Akhil. "Blurred Boundaries: The Discourse of Corruption, the Culture of Politics, and the Imagined State." *American Ethnologist* 22, no. 2 (1995): 375–402.

Haggis, Jane. "White Women and Colonialism: Towards a Non-Recuperative History." In *Gender and Imperialism*, ed. Clare Midgley, 45–75. Oxford: St. Martin's Press, 1998.

Hali, Altaf Hussain. *Majalis-un-nissa*. Lahore: Matba-yi Muagmmadi, 1874.

Hall, Stuart. *Policing the Crisis: Mugging, the State, and Law and Order*. London: Macmillan, 1978.

Harding, Sandra. "The Instability of the Analytical Categories of Feminist Theory." *Signs* 11, no. 4 (Summer 1986): 645–64.

Harvey, David. "Neoliberalism as Creative Destruction." *Annals of the American Academy of Political and Social Science* 610 (2007): 22–44.

Harris, Anita. *All about the Girl: Culture, Power, and Identity*. New York: Routledge, 2004.

———. *Future Girl: Young Women in the 21st Century*. New York: Routledge, 2004.

Hayhurst, Lyndsay. "Corporatising Sport, Gender, and Development: Postcolonial IR Feminisms, Transnational Private Governance and Global Corporate Social Engagement." *Third World Quarterly* 32, no. 3 (2011): 531–49.

Hemba, Joe. "Nigerian Islamists Kill 59 Pupils in Boarding School Attack." Reuters, February 26, 2014, www.reuters.com/article/2014/02/26/us-nigeria-violence-id USBREA1P10M20140226 (accessed January 24, 2018).

Hengeveld, Maria. *Girl Branded: Nike, the UN, and the Construction of the Entrepreneurial Adolescent Girl Subject*. Austin: Rapoport Center for Human Rights and Justice, 2016.

Hesford, Wendy. *Spectacular Rhetorics: Human Rights Visions, Recognitions, Feminisms*. Durham, NC: Duke University Press, 2011.

Hickel, Jason. "The 'Girl Effect': Liberalism, Empowerment and the Contradictions of Development." *Third World Quarterly* 35, no. 8 (2014): 1355–73.

Hochschild, Arlie, and Anne Machung. *The Second Shift*. New York: Penguin Books, 2003.

Hunter, Ian. *Rethinking the School: Subjectivity, Bureaucracy, Criticism*. New York: St. Martin's Press, 1994.

Hussain, Asaf. *The Educated Pakistani Girl*. Karachi: Ima Printers, 1963.

Husain, Israt. "The Role of Politics in Pakistan's Economy." *Journal of International Affairs* 63, no. 1 (2009): 1–18.

Hussein, Shakira. *From Victims to Suspects: Muslim Women since 9/11*. Sydney: University of New South Wales Press, 2016.

International Labour Organization Research Department. "World of Work Report, 2014: Developing with Jobs." International Labor Organization, May 27, 2014, www.ilo.org/global/research/global-reports/world-of-work/2014/lang--en/index.htm (accessed February 27, 2018).

Islam, Rafiqul. "The Bengali Language Movement and the Emergence of Bangladesh." In *Language and Civilization in South Asia*, ed. Clarence Maloney, 142–54. Leiden: Brill.

Jalal, Ayesha. *Self and Sovereignty: Individual and Community in South Asian Islam since 1850*. New York: Routledge, 2002.

Jalil, Xari. "Fatima Sughra no more." *Dawn News*, September 26, 2017. www.dawn.com/news/1360098 (accessed March 2, 2018).

Jamal, Amina. "Gender, Citizenship, and the Nation-State in Pakistan: Willful Daughters of Free Citizens." *Signs* 31, no. 2 (2006): 283–304.

Jamal, Haroon. "Poverty and Vulnerability Estimates: Pakistan, 2016." Social Policy and Development Centre, 2017, http://spdc.org.pk/Data/Publication/PDF/RR-99.pdf (accessed January 24, 2018).

Jeffery, Craig, Patricia Jeffery, and Roger Jeffery. *Degrees without Freedom? Education, Masculinities, and Unemployment in North India.* Stanford, CA: Stanford University Press, 2008.

Jhala, Angma Dey. *Courtly Indian Women in Late Imperial India.* London: Pickering & Chatto, 2008.

Kabeer, Naila. "Is Microfinance a 'Magic Bullet' for Women's Empowerment? Analysis of Findings from South Asia." *Economic and Political Weekly* 40, nos. 44–45 (2005): 4709–18.

Kandiyoti, Deniz. "Bargaining with Patriarchy." *Gender and Society* 2, no. 3 (1988): 274–90.

Keating, Christine, Claire Rasmussen, and Pooja Rishi. "The Rationality of Empowerment: Microcredit, Accumulation by Dispossession, and the Gendered Economy." *Signs* 36, no. 1 (2010): 153–76.

Kenway, Jane, et al. *Class Choreographies: Elite Schools and Globalization.* London: Palgrave, 2017.

Khan, Aga. *India in Transition: A Study in Political Evolution.* New York: G. Putnam, 1918.

———. *The Memoirs of Aga Khan: World Enough and Time.* New York: Simon and Schuster, 1954.

———. *Message to the World of Islam.* Karachi: Ismailia Association of Pakistan, 1977.

Kharas, Homi. "Pakistan's Emerging Middle Class: Lessons from a Country in Transition." Urban Institute, October 31, 2017, www.urban.org/events/pakistans-emerging-middle-class-lessons-country-transition (accessed January 24, 2018).

Khoja-Moolji, Shenila. "Doing the 'Work of Hearing': Girls' Voices in Transnational Educational Development Campaigns." *Compare: A Journal of Comparative and International Education* (2015): 1–19.

———. "Pedagogical (Re)Encounters: Enacting a Decolonial Praxis in Teacher Development in the Global South." *Comparative Education Review* 61, no. S1 (2017): 146–70.

———. "Producing Neoliberal Citizens: Critical Reflections on Human Rights Education in Pakistan." *Gender and Education* 26, no. 2 (2014): 103–18.

———. "Reading Malala: (De)(Re)Territorialization of Muslim Collectivities." *Journal of Comparative Studies of South Asia, Africa, and the Middle East* 35, no. 3 (2015): 539–56.

———. "Redefining Muslim Women: Aga Khan III's Reforms for Women's Education." *South Asia Graduate Research Journal* 20, no. 1 (2011): 69–95.

———. "Suturing Together Girls and Education: An Investigation into the Social (Re)Production of Girls' Education as a Hegemonic Ideology." *Journal of Diaspora, Indigenous, and Minority Education* 9, no. 2 (2015): 87–107.

Khurshid, Ayesha. "From Gender Parity to Gender (In)Equity: Women's Education among Rural Communities in Pakistan." *International Journal of Educational Development* 51 (2016): 43–50.

Kim, Jim Yong. "World Bank Group President Jim Yong Kim's Remarks at 'Let Girls Learn' Spring Meetings Event." World Bank, April 13, 2016, www.worldbank.org/en/news/speech/2016/04/13/world-bank-group-president-jim-yong-kims-remarks-at-let-girls-learn-spring-meetings-event (accessed January 24, 2018).

Ki-moon, Ban. "Female Energy, Talent, Strength Represent Humankind's Most Valuable Untapped Resource, Secretary-General Says in Message for International Women's Day." United Nations, March 2, 2012, www.un.org/press/en/2012/sgsm14140.doc.htm (accessed January 24, 2018).

Koffman, Ofra, and Rosalind Gill. "'The Revolution Will Be Led by a 12-Year-Old Girl': Girl Power and Global Biopolitics." *Feminist Review* 105, no. 1 (2013): 82–102.

Kofi Anan Foundation. "Empowering Young People to Prevent Violent Extremism." News release, December 3, 2015, www.kofiannanfoundation.org/news-releases/empowering-young-people-to-prevent-violent-extremism (accessed January 24, 2018).

Kristof, Nicholas. "Meet Sultana, the Taliban's Worst Fear." *New York Times*, June 4, 2016.

———. "Two Cheers for Sweatshops," *New York Times*, September 24, 2000.

———. "What's So Scary about Smart Girls?" *New York Times*, May 10, 2014.

Kumar, Krishna. *Political Agenda of Education: A Study of Colonialist and Nationalist Ideas.* New Delhi: Sage Publications, 2005.

———. *Politics of Education in Colonial India.* London: Routledge, 2014.

Lal, Ruby. *Coming of Age in Nineteenth-Century India: The Girl-Child and the Art of Playfulness.* New York: Cambridge University Press, 2013.

Lambert-Hurley, Siobhan. "Life/History/Archive Identifying Autobiographical Writing by Muslim Women in South Asia." *Journal of Women's History* 25, no. 2 (2013): 61–84.

Lemke, Thomas. "Foucault, Governmentality, and Critique." *Rethinking Marxism* 14, no. 3 (2002): 49–64.

Lesko, Nancy. *Act Your Age! A Cultural Construction of Adolescence.* New York: Routledge, 2012.

Lindsey, Benjamin. *The Companionate Marriage.* New York: Boni & Liveright, 1927.

Lutz, Catherine, and Jane Collins. "The Photograph as an Intersection of Gazes: The Example of *National Geographic.*" *Visual Anthropology Review* 7, no. 1 (1993): 134–49.

Lyon, Stephen M. "Power and Patronage in Pakistan." Ph.D. diss., University of Kent, 2002.

Mahmood, Saba. *Politics of Piety: Islamic Revival and the Feminist Subject.* Princeton, NJ: Princeton University Press, 2005.

Malick, Qayyum. *His Royal Highness Prince Aga Khan: Guide, Philosopher, and Friend of the Islamic world.* Karachi: Ismailia Association for Pakistan, 1969.

Mamdani, Mahmood. *Good Muslim, Bad Muslim: America, the Cold War, and the Roots of Terror.* New York: Pantheon Books, 2004.

Mankekar, Purnima. *Screening Culture, Viewing Politics: An Ethnography of Television, Womanhood, and Nation in Postcolonial India.* Durham, NC: Duke University Press, 1999.

Martin, Jane Roland. *Reclaiming a Conversation: The Ideal of the Educated Woman.* New York: Palgrave Macmillan, 1985.

Masood, Salman, and Declan Walsh. "Tashfeen Malik, San Bernardino Suspect, Attended Conservative Religious School in Pakistan." *New York Times*, December 7, 2015.

McAllister, Edward. "Female Attacker Stands Out in California Mass Shooting." Reuters, December 3, 2015, www.reuters.com/article/us-california-shooting-women-idUSKBN0TM2Y420151203 (accessed January 24, 2018).

McMahon, Robert. *The Cold War on the Periphery: The United States, India, and Pakistan.* New York: Columbia University Press, 1994.

McRobbie, Angela. "Top Girls? Young Women and the Post-Feminist Sexual Contract." *Cultural Studies* 21, nos. 4–5 (2007): 718–37.

Mernissi, Fatima. *The Veil and the Male Elite: A Feminist Interpretation of Women's Rights in Islam.* Reading, MA: Addison-Wesley Publishing, 1991.

Metcalf, Barbara. *Perfecting Women: Maulana Ashraf 'Ali Thanawi's Bihishti Zewar.* Berkeley: University of California Press, 1992.

Midgley, Clare. *Feminism and Empire.* London: Routledge, 2007.

Minault, Gail. *Secluded Scholars: Women's Education and Muslim Social Reform in Colonial India.* New York: Oxford University Press, 1998.

———. "Women's Magazines in Urdu as Sources for Muslim Social History." *Indian Journal for Gender Studies* 5, no. 2 (1998): 201–14.

Mitchell, Katharyne, and Matthew Sparke. "The New Washington Consensus: Millennial Philanthropy and the Making of Global Market Subjects." *Antipode* 43, no. 3 (2015): 724–49.

Moghissi, Haideh. *Feminism and Islamic Fundamentalism: The Limits of Postmodern Analysis.* London: Zed Books, 1999.

Mundy, Karen, and Antoni Verger. "The World Bank and the Global Governance of Education in a Changing World Order." *International Journal of Educational Development* 40 (2015): 9–18.

Murphy, Dan. "'Boko Haram' Doesn't Really Mean 'Western Education Is a Sin.'" *Christian Science Monitor,* May 6, 2014.

Murphy, Michelle. "The Girl: Mergers of Feminism and Finance in Neoliberal Times." *Scholar and Feminist Online* 11, nos. 1–2 (2012–13), http://sfonline.barnard.edu/gender-justice-and-neoliberal-transformations/the-girl-mergersof-feminism-and-finance-in-neoliberal-times (accessed January 24, 2018).

Naim, C.M. *The Repentance of Nussooh (Taubatal-Nasûh): The Tale of a Muslim Family a Hundred Years Ago.* Trans. M. Kempson. Delhi: Permanent Black, 2004.

Najmabadi, Afsaneh. "Crafting an Educated Housewife in Iran." In *Remaking Women,* ed. Lila Abu-Lughod, 91–125. Princeton, NJ: Princeton University Press, 1998.

———. "Veiled Discourse-Unveiled Bodies." *Feminist Studies* 19, no. 3 (1993): 487–518.

Naseem, Ayaz. *Education and Gendered Citizenship in Pakistan.* New York: Palgrave Macmillan, 2010.

News Desk. "Academic Modification: JI Wants Secular Material Removed from Textbooks." *Express Tribute.* September 5, 2014, http://tribune.com.pk/story/757919/academic-modification-ji-wants-secular-material-removed-from-textbooks (accessed January 24, 2018).

———. "Faculty Member at Top Educational Institute in Karachi Gets Schooled on 'Improper Attire.'" *Express Tribune.* October 5, 2017, https://tribune.com.pk/story/1523647/faculty-member-top-educational-institute-karachi-gets-schooled-improper-attire (accessed January 24, 2018).

Noreen, Sumaira. "Dynamics of Secondary Curriculum Organisation in Pakistan: An Historical Perspective from 1947 to 1970." Ph:D. diss., Department of History, University of London, 2014.

Nussbaum, Martha. *Women and Human Development: The Capabilities Approach*. Cambridge: Cambridge University Press, 2001.

Oesterheld, Christina. "Islam in Contemporary South Asia: Urdu and Muslim Women." *Oriente Moderno*, n.s., 23, no. 84 (2004): 217–43.

Ola, Lanre. "Boko Haram Abduct Dozens of Boys in Northeast Nigeria—Witnesses." Reuters, August 15, 2014, http://uk.reuters.com/article/2014/08/15/uk-nigeria-violence-idUKKBN0GF0U720140815 (accessed January 24, 2018).

O'Malley, Michael, Jake Sandlin, and Jennifer Burdick. "Public Pedagogy." In *Encyclopedia of Curriculum Studies*, ed. Craig Kridel, 697–701. Thousand Oaks, CA: Sage Publications, 2010.

Oppenheim, Willy. "Imagining 'Demand' for Girls' Schooling in Rural Pakistan." Ph:D. diss. Department of Education, Oxford University, 2016.

———. "Why Should Girls Stay in School? Qualitative Aspects of Demand for Girls' Schooling in Rural Pakistan." *St. Antony's International Review* 8, no. 2 (2013): 106–26.

Oppenheim, Willy, and Stambach, Amy. "Global Norm Making as Lens and Mirror: Comparative Education and Gender Mainstreaming in Northern Pakistan." *Comparative Education Review* 58, no. 3 (2014): 377–400.

Penz, Peter, Jay Drydyk, and Pablo Bose. *Displacement by Development: Ethics, Rights, and Responsibilities*. Cambridge: Cambridge University Press, 2011.

Pernau, Margrit. *Ashraf into Middle Classes: Muslims in Nineteenth-Century Delhi*. Oxford: Oxford University Press, 2013.

Peshkin, Alan. "Education, the Muslim Elite, and the Creation of Pakistan." *Comparative Education Review* 6, no. 2 (1962): 152–59.

Pew Survey. "Pakistani Public Opinion." Pewglobal.org, August 13, 2009, www.pewglobal.org/2009/08/13/pakistani-public-opinion (accessed January 24, 2018).

Pirbhai, Reza. "Pakistan and the Political Awakening of the Muslim 'New Woman,' 1937–1947." *HAWWA: Journal of the Women of the Middle East and the Islamic World* 12 (2014): 1–35.

Popkewitz, Thomas. *Struggling for the Soul: The Politics of Schooling and the Construction of the Teacher*. New York: Teachers College Press, Columbia University, 1998.

Porter, Maureen. "Making Gender Matter: Paradigms for Equality, Equity, and Excellence." In *Policy Debates in Comparative, International, and Development Education*, ed. John N. Hawkins and W. James Jacob, 131–54. New York: Palgrave Macmillan, 2011.

PTI. "Lahore Raid: Arrested Woman Terror Suspect Linked to ISIS." *The Hindu*, April 16, 2017, www.thehindu.com/news/international/lahore-raid-arrested-woman-terror-suspect-linked-to-isis/article18071417.ece (accessed January 24, 2018).

Qadri, Syed Shamsuddin ibn Miansaheb. *Risala talim-niswan*. Mumbai: University of Bombay, 1895.

Quinby, Lee. *Genealogy and Literature*. Minneapolis: University of Minnesota Press, 1995.

Ramusack, Barbara. *The Indian Princes and Their States*. Cambridge: Cambridge University Press, 2004.

Ray-Chaudhuri, Tapan, and Geraldine Forbes. *The Memoirs of Dr. Haimabati Sen: From Child Widow to Lady Doctor*. New Delhi: Roli Books, 2000.

Raynor, Janet. "Schooling Girls: An Inter-Generational Study of Women's Burdens in Rural Bangladesh." In *Gender Education and Equality in a Global Context*, ed. Shailaja Fennell and Madeleine Arnot, 117–30. London: Routledge, 2008.

Reuters. "Madonna Sells Abstract Painting to Fund Girls' Education." April 3, 2013, www. reuters.com/article/entertainment-us-madonna/madonna-sells-abstract-painting-to-fund-girls-education-idUSBRE9320RO20130403 (accessed January 24, 2018).

Ringrose, Jessica. *Postfeminist Education? Girls and the Sexual Politics of Schooling.* London: Routledge, 2013.

Ringrose, Jessica, and Valerie Walkerdine. "Regulating the Abject: The TV Make-Over as Site of Neoliberal Reinvention toward Bourgeois Femininity." *Feminist Media Studies* 8, no. 3 (2008): 227–46.

Rose, Nicholas. *Powers of Freedom: Reframing Political Thought.* Cambridge: Cambridge University Press, 1999.

Rouse, Shahnaz. "Zina, Transnational Feminism, and the Moral Regulation of Pakistani Women." *Journal of Middle East Women's Studies* 6, no. 3 (2010): 195–97.

Said, Edward. *Orientalism.* New York: Vintage Books, 1978.

——. *Reflections on Exile.* Cambridge, MA: Harvard University Press, 2000.

Saigol, Rubina. *Becoming a Modern Nation: Educational Discourse in the Early Years of Ayub Khan (1958–64).* Islamabad: Council of Social Sciences, 2003.

——. *Feminism and the Women's Movement in Pakistan Actors, Debates, and Strategies.* Islamabad: Friedrich-Ebert-Stiftung, 2016.

Sarkar, Mahua. "Muslim Women and the Politics of (In)Visibility in Late Colonial Bengal." *Journal of Historical Sociology* 14, no. 2 (2001): 226–50.

——. *Visible Histories, Disappearing Women: Producing Muslim Womanhood in Late Colonial Bengal.* Durham, NC: Duke University Press, 2008.

Sarkar, Tanika. *Words to Win: The Making of Amar Jiban; A Modern Autobiography.* Delhi: Kali for Women, 1999.

Scott, Joan. "Gender: A Useful Category of Historical Analysis." *American Historical Review* 91, no. 5 (1986): 1053–75.

Sen, Amartya. "Development as Capability Expansion." *Journal of Development Planning* 19, no. 1 (1989): 41–58.

Seth, Sanjay. *Subject Lessons: The Western Education of Colonial India.* Durham, NC: Duke University Press, 2007.

Siddiqui, Habibullah. *Education in Sind Past and Present.* Sindh, Pakistan: University of Sindh Press, 1987.

Siddique, Sadaf, and Sadaf Haider. "What's It Like Being a Sought-After TV Writer in Pakistan? Faiza Iftikhar Tells All." Images, April 29, 2016, http://images.dawn.com/news/1175082 (accessed January 24, 2018).

Siddiqui, Shahid. *Education Policies in Pakistan: Politics, Projections, and Practices.* Karachi: Oxford University Press, 2016.

Shah, Bina. "Naureen Laghari, Pakistan's Very Own IS Bride." Express Tribune Blogs, April 18, 2017, https://blogs.tribune.com.pk/story/48864/naureen-laghari-pakistans-very-own-is-bride (accessed January 24, 2018).

Shaheen, Anwar. "Patriarchal Education and Print Journalism: Their Emancipating Impact on Muslim Women of India during 1869–1908." *Pakistan Journal of History and Culture* 30, no. 2 (2009): 1–42.

Shakry, Omina. "Schooled Mothers and Structured Play: Child Rearing in Turn-of-the-Century Egypt." In *Remaking Women: Feminism and modernity in the Middle East,* ed. Lila Abu-Lughod, 3–27. Princeton, NJ: Princeton University Press, 1998.

Shehabuddin, Elora. "Gender and the Figure of the 'Moderate Muslim.'" In *The Question of Gender: Joan W. Scott's Critical Feminism,* ed. Judith Butler and Elizabeth Weed, 102–42. Bloomington: Indiana University Press, 2011.

Shiner, Larry. "Reading Foucault: Anti-Method and the Genealogy of Power-Knowledge." *History and Theory* 21, no. 3 (1982): 382–98.

Shor, Franc, and Jean Shor. "At World's End in Hunza: This Strange Shangri-La near the Himalayas Has Few Laws or Taxes and No Army; Bridegrooms Take Mother on the Honeymoon." *National Geographic Magazine,* October 1953.

Smeyers, Paul, and Marc Depaepe. *Educational Research: The Educationalization of Social Problems.* New York: Springer, 2008.

St. Pierre, Elizabeth Adams. "Deleuzian Concepts for Education: The Subject Undone." *Educational Philosophy and Theory* 36, no. 3 (2004): 283–96.

Struckman, Sara. "The Veiled Women and Masked Men of Chechnya: Documentaries, Violent Conflict, and Gender." *Journal of Communication Inquiry* 30 (2006): 337–53.

Suhrawardy, Shaista. *A Critical Survey of the Development of the Urdu Novel and Short Story.* London: Longmans Green, 1945.

Sunawar, Lubna, and Coutto, Tatiana. "U.S. Pakistan Relations during the Cold War." *Journal of International Relations, Peace Studies, and Development* 1, no. 1 (2015): 1–11.

Switzer, Heather. "(Post)Feminist Development Fables: The Girl Effect and the Production of Sexual Subjects." *Feminist Theory* 14, no. 3 (2013): 345–60.

Tadiar, Neferti. "Empire." *Social Text* 27, no. 3 (2009): 112–17.

Taft, Jessica. "The Political Lives of Girls." *Sociology Compass* 8, no. 3 (2014): 259–67.

Thanawi, Ashraf. *Bahishti zewar.* New Delhi: Islamic Book Service, 1905.

Thomas, Henry Harington. *The Late Rebellion in India and Our Future Policy.* London: W. Kent, 1858.

Toohey, Grace. "First Lady, Pakistan's First Daughter Champion Educating Girls." McClarchy DC, October 22, 2015. www.mcclatchydc.com/news/politics-government/white-house/article41013888.html (accessed January 24, 2018).

Toor, Saadia. "The State, Fundamentalism, and Civil Society." *Interventions* 9, no. 2 (2007): 255–75.

———. *The State of Islam: Culture and Cold War Politics in Pakistan.* New York: Pluto Press, 2011.

Turnham, Steve. "Donald Trump to Father of Fallen Soldier: 'I've Made a Lot of Sacrifices.'" ABC News, June 30, 2016, http://abcnews.go.com/Politics/donald-trump-father-fallen-soldier-ive-made-lot/story?id=41015051 (accessed February 20, 2018).

UNICEF. Pakistan Statistics, 2013, www.unicef.org/infobycountry/pakistan_pakistan_statistics.html#117 (accessed January 24, 2018).

United Nations. "Press Release: Female Energy, Talent, Strength Represent Humankind's Most Valuable Untapped Resource, Secretary-General Says in a Message for International Women's Day." United Nations Department of Public Information, March 2, 2012, www.un.org/News/Press/docs/2012/sgsm14140.doc.htm (accessed January 24, 2018).

Unterhalter, Elaine. "The Capability Approach and Gendered Education: An Examination of South African Complexities." *Theory and Research in Education* 1, no. 1 (2003): 7–22.

———. "Inequality, Capabilities, and Poverty in Four African Countries: Girls' Voice, Schooling, and Strategies for Institutional Change." *Cambridge Journal of Education* 42, no. 3 (2012): 307–25.

Vatuk, Sylvia. "*Hamara Daur-I Hayat*: An Indian Muslim Women Writes Her Life." In *Telling Lives in India: Biography, Autobiography, and Life History*, ed. David Arnold and Stuart H. Blackburn, 144–74. Bloomington: Indiana University Press, 2004.

Vavrus, Fran. *Desire and Decline: Schooling amid Crisis in Tanzania*. New York: Peter Lang, 2003.

Viswanathan, Gauri. "The Beginnings of English Literary Study in British India." *Oxford Literary Review* 9, nos. 1–2 (1987): 2–26.

Weedon, Chris. *Feminist Practice and Poststructuralist Theory*. 2nd ed. Boston: Blackwell, 1997.

Weinbaum, Eve, and Modern Girl around the World Research Group. *The Modern Girl around the World: Consumption, Modernity, and Globalization*. Durham, NC: Duke University Press, 2008.

Weiss, Anita. "Within the Walls: Home-Based Work in Lahore." In *Pakistani Women: Multiple Locations and Competing Narratives*, ed. Sadaf Ahmad, 12–24. Oxford: Oxford University Press, 2010.

Willinsky, John. *Learning to Divide the World: Education at Empire's End*. Minneapolis: University of Minnesota Press, 1998.

Wirsing, Robert. "Precarious Partnership: Pakistan's Response to U.S. Security Policies." *Asian Affairs: An American Review* 30, no. 2 (2003): 70–78.

The White House. "Executive Order Protecting the Nation from Foreign Terrorist Entry into the United States." Official of the Press Secretary, March 6, 2017, www.whitehouse. gov/the-press-office/2017/03/06/executive-order-protecting-nation-foreign-terrorist-entry-united-states (accessed January 24, 2018).

Yousafzai, Malala, with Christina Lamb. *I Am Malala: The Girl Who Stood Up for Education and Was Shot by the Taliban*. New York: Little, Brown, 2013.

Zaman, Muhammad Qasim. *Ashraf Ali Thanawi: Islam in Modern South Asia*. Oxford: Oneworld Publications, 2008.

———. "Religious Education and the Rhetoric of Reform: The Madrasa in British India and Pakistan." *Comparative Study of Society and History* 41, no. 2 (1999): 294–323.

Zia, Asad. "Revised Curriculum: JI Pushes Through Its Agenda on Textbooks in K-P." *Express Tribune*, October 17, 2014, http://tribune.com.pk/story/781717/revised-curriculum-ji-pushes-through-its-agenda-on-textbooks-in-k-p (accessed January 24, 2018).

INDEX

Aaina dulhan ka (The Bride's Mirror) (TV drama), 178n4
Aaja sajna miliye juliye (TV drama), 178n3
Abu-Lughod, Lila, 52, 151
activism, Muslim women's, 53–54, 153, 154–57
Adely, Fida, 112, 151
Adolescent Girls Initiative, 10
advertisements: Dalda oil advertisement, 73 *fig.*12; Dettol advertisements, 74 *fig.*13; Ostermilk advertisements, 76 *fig.*14; Pakistan International Airlines, 61 *fig.*7, 70 *fig.*10; Pakistan Savings Certificate scheme, 79 *fig.*16, 80 *fig.*17; tourism promotion, 71 *fig.*11; United Bank Limited, 77 *fig.*15
Afghanistan, 2, 5, 95, 99
Aga Khan, Sultan Mahomed Shah, 31–32, 33, 34, 165n33, 165n34, 166n38, 166n40, 166n41
Age of Consent Act 1891, 11
Ahmed, Nazir, 19, 20, 26, 27, 33, 57, 125. *See also Mirat-ul-uroos* (The Bride's Mirror) (Ahmed)
Ahmed, Umera, 178n6
Aima (literary character), 126–35, 149
Aiza (literary character), 126–35, 149
ajlaf (lower status) social class: in colonial British Indian, 23, 24; education and, 31, 32, 57; interactions with, 26, 133; mobility of, 23, 52, 57, 134
Akbari (literary character), 26, 58, 125–35

Akbari Asghari (2011 TV show) (Hussain), 126, 135–44, 178n3
Al-Huda Center, 152
Ali, Azra Asghar, 22
Ali, Mumtaz, 30–31, 32, 33, 34. *See also Tehzib-e-Niswan*
Aligarh Institute Gazette (periodical), 12
Aligarh Movement, 28
Aligarh Muslim University, 29, 31. *See also* Muhammadan Anglo-Oriental College
Allah, Raza, 155
Allendar, Tim, 12
All India Muhammadan Education Congress/Conference, 38, 52, 53, 155, 167n66
All India Muslim League, 31, 62
All India Progressive Writers Association, 169n3
All Pakistan Progressive Writers Association, 169n3
All Pakistan Women's Association, 157
Ansari, Sarah, 156
archives: analysis of, 19–20, 145; assembly of, 18–19. *See also* genealogies
Asghari (literary character), 26, 51, 52, 125–37
ashraf (respectable) families, 48, 149
ashraf (respectable) men, 37, 38, 39
ashraf (respectable) Muslims, 145, 147
ashraf (respectable) social class, 147–48; in colonial British Indian, 24–28; economic decline and, 24, 147; privilege of, 23, 149

195

CPSIA information can be obtained
at www.ICGtesting.com
Printed in the USA
LVHW04s0440120618
580383LV00001B/3/P